Curating Culture

Curating Culture

How Twentieth-Century Magazines Influenced America

Edited by
Sharon Bloyd-Peshkin
Columbia College Chicago

Charles Whitaker
Northwestern University

ROWMAN & LITTLEFIELD
Lanham • Boulder • New York • London

Credits and acknowledgments for material borrowed from other sources, and reproduced with permission, appear on the appropriate pages within the text.

Published by Rowman & Littlefield
An imprint of The Rowman & Littlefield Publishing Group, Inc.
4501 Forbes Boulevard, Suite 200, Lanham, Maryland 20706
www.rowman.com

86-90 Paul Street, London EC2A 4NE, United Kingdom

Copyright © 2021 by The Rowman & Littlefield Publishing Group, Inc.

All rights reserved. No part of this book may be reproduced in any form or by any electronic or mechanical means, including information storage and retrieval systems, without written permission from the publisher, except by a reviewer who may quote passages in a review.

British Library Cataloguing in Publication Information Available

Library of Congress Cataloging-in-Publication Data

Names: Bloyd-Peshkin, Sharon, 1961- editor. | Whitaker, Charles, 1958- editor.
Title: Curating culture : how twentieth-century magazines influenced America / edited by Sharon Bloyd-Peshkin, Charles Whitaker.
Description: Lanham : Rowman & Littlefield, [2021] | Includes bibliographical references and index. | Summary: "Curated case studies illuminate how twentieth-century magazines created, cultivated, and served specific communities, laying the groundwork for contemporary media forms to continue that role today. Chapters examine how cultural niches were cultivated, how they changed over time, and how they influenced broader cultural conversations"—Provided by publisher.
Identifiers: LCCN 2021014387 (print) | LCCN 2021014388 (ebook) | ISBN 9781538138106 (cloth) | ISBN 9781538138113 (paperback) | ISBN 9781538138120 (epub)
Subjects: LCSH: American periodicals—History—20th century. | Literature and society—United States—History—20th century.
Classification: LCC PN4877 .C87 2021 (print) | LCC PN4877 (ebook) | DDC 051—dc23
LC record available at https://lccn.loc.gov/2021014387
LC ebook record available at https://lccn.loc.gov/2021014388

Contents

Acknowledgments   vii

Introduction   1
Sharon Bloyd-Peshkin and Charles Whitaker

SECTION 1: IDEAS AND IDEOLOGIES   7

1. Ideas *in* America and Ideas *of* America: Thought Leader Magazines and the Life of the Mind in the Twentieth Century   9
Kevin M. Lerner

2. Speaking Out: Leftist Magazines and Political Advocacy   25
Erika J. Pribanic-Smith

3. "Things You Want to Keep": *McSweeney's* and the Periodical as a Perennial Object   37
Pablo Calvi

4. 1960s American Folk Music Magazines: Counter-Hegemonic Voices of Social Transformation   53
Krystyna Henke

SECTION 2: THE PRACTICAL AND THE PERSONAL   71

5. Reaffirming the Pastoral Life: Reiman Publications 1970–2007   73
Sheila Webb

6. Tilling Fertile Ground: The Trailblazing Role of Farming Magazines   83
Catherine M. Staub

7	Magazine as Gay Lifeline: AIDS and the Emergence of *POZ* *Gary R. Hicks*	105
8	From Marginal to Mainstream: Vegetarian Magazines vs. the Standard American Diet *Sharon Bloyd-Peshkin*	121
9	Read Them for the Articles: Masculinity, U.S. Men's Magazines, and the Tension between Niche and Mainstream Audiences *Kevin M. Lerner*	135

SECTION 3: THE FAMILIAR AND THE FUTURE — 149

10	Getting the Last Laugh: Domestic Chaos Writers Outlasted Their Critics *Betsy Edgerton*	151
11	Craving to Connect: Zines and the Celebration of Creativity and Control *Peggy Dillon*	167
12	Branding the Local Lifestyle: City, State, and Regional Magazines *Norma Green*	179
13	A Style Guide for the Digital World *Aileen Gallagher*	191

Notes	203
Index	205
About the Editors and Contributors	211

Acknowledgments

We are extremely indebted to the village of friends, family, and colleagues who made this book possible. First and foremost among them are our spouses, Alec Bloyd-Peshkin and Stephanie Whitaker, who showed unfailing patience and support through the long slog to the publishing finish line.

Then there are our "work spouses," Columbia College Chicago associate professor Betsy Edgerton and Medill executive assistant Parth Joshi, who provided critical eyes for the manuscript in the final push to completion.

We are also grateful for the support of our institutions, Columbia College Chicago and Northwestern University, for giving us the time and, in some instances, the resources for this project.

Finally, we must thank our colleagues in the Association for Education in Journalism and Mass Communication (AEJMC) Magazine Media Division, many of whom are represented in these pages, who were a tremendous source of inspiration and scholarly advice.

Introduction
Sharon Bloyd-Peshkin and Charles Whitaker

Print magazines were the original niche medium. Long before the internet allowed audiences to find specialized content and coalesce into communities, consumer magazines provided information, inspiration, empathy, and advocacy for readers with specific interests, identities, goals, and concerns.

In so doing, twentieth-century consumer magazines created "communities" long before the internet allowed audiences to assemble virtually in digital space. The cultural niches they created and covered were powerful social influences on a wide variety of readers, from farmers to feminists, and covered everything from big ideas to personal passions. With missions to serve specific readers, and led by editors who were champions of their interests, even the most practical of magazines were cultural arbiters that wielded influence well beyond their pages. Often, the smaller the niche, the more profound the power.

During the twentieth century, these magazines thrived. David E. Sumner (2010), professor emeritus of journalism at Ball State University, deemed the 1900s "The Magazine Century" in his book of the same name, noting that from 1900 to 2000, the number of American magazines increased from about 3,500 to about 17,815. "It was . . . a *magazine century* and an *American magazine century* without a doubt," he wrote.

But twentieth-century magazines thrived on the very business model that hurt them in the long run. Unable to compete with television for delivery of a mass audience, print magazine publishers doubled down on the niching of their product, selling advertisers on the appeal of highly targeted audiences—a practice that presaged the contemporary algorithms and metrics that now threaten the continued existence of legacy media of all stripes. Reliance on a transactional financial model—selling advertisers on reader eyeballs and providing magazines at a negligible cost to readers—was ultimately unsustainable when advertisers could find much more segmented niche audiences elsewhere through search engines and social media. Search and social media not only delivered a mass audience that was in the mood to buy; their invisible, though invasive, algorithms provided advertisers more information about those consumers' habits and digital traffic patterns than legacy media ever could. Thus, the niching that had been the very strength of twentieth-century magazines became a twenty-first-century liability.

Many magazines survived the seismic shift, though they made considerable sacrifices to stay in business. Gone were the profligate spending, lavish parties, and padded mastheads of the go-go 1990s. In the wake of the digital revolution, editorial staffs and budgets were slashed at the same time as editors' work increased and sped up to compete in the 24/7 virtual information marketplace (Ember and Grynbaum 2017). Some magazines shuttered their print publications and shifted online, putting their editorial muscle into the competition for online audiences. Some reduced their frequency or even folded, unable to provide a value proposition to support the cost of staying in business. And yet, despite the financial challenges, print consumer magazines reached a peak in 2012, with 7,390 in the American market, and remained at 7,357 in 2019 (MPA 2020).

Despite the belt tightening and the masthead trimming, magazines maintain a hold on American culture, as the chapters in this book attest. Many of the communities and the conversations forged by and with twentieth-century magazines are still present today well beyond the pages they were once largely confined to. And a look back at their roots helps make sense of what those communities, and the media that connected and shaped them, have become.

INSPIRED BY NICHE MEDIA

We became interested in exploring the enduring influence of twentieth-century magazines after working together on a case study of *Ebony* magazine, "On Johnson's Shoulders: The Lessons and Legacy of *Ebony* Magazine," which was published as a chapter in another book (Sternadori and Holmes 2020). While collaborating on that article, our conversations frequently turned to the ways that looking at twentieth-century magazines helped us better understand what drives and what ails contemporary media.

Today, the media landscape is splintered and distrusted. Unlike a generation or two ago, when most media consumers turned to a relatively small number of media properties for news, information, advice, and entertainment, we are in a time of proliferating, unmediated communication—a time in which the information disseminated on many of these channels is lightly sourced and difficult to verify.

This has caused many critics and consumers of contemporary media to call for some type of quality control. Again, twentieth-century magazines got there first. *The New Yorker* virtually invented[1] the thorough fact-checking processes that top-tier magazines of the twentieth century practiced, ensuring verification prior to publication. This practice was gradually modified during times of diminished resources and tight turnarounds, and almost abandoned as more and more digital outlets (and the digital extensions of legacy publications) raced to be the first to publish in the twenty-four-hour news cycle.

The growth and development of twentieth-century niche magazines, we realized, foretold the balkanization of contemporary media and the breakdown of fact checking.

But the niches of the twentieth century still exist in the twenty-first century, and a look back at their consolidation can inform a look forward at their continuation. Print magazines and the brands they represent are still evolving. Print isn't dead, but it is costly. Nonetheless, many magazines—including tech-centric ones like *WIRED*, thought leaders like *The Atlantic*, fashion powerhouses like *Vogue*, and enthusiast magazines like *Golf Digest*, not to mention a raft of cooking, gardening, business, and lifestyle magazines—still recognize the power and revenue-generating potential of print and maintain their print publications, mostly out of financial necessity. For even as contemporary magazines furiously create digital brand extensions to capitalize on the migration away from print media, digital advertising revenue has not yet supplanted print revenue for many legacy publishing houses. As the late *New York Times* columnist David Carr (2008) noted when asked about publishers' stubborn resistance to abandoning their print products: "For readers, the drastic diminishment of print raises an obvious question: if more people are reading newspapers and magazines, why should we care whether they are printed on paper? The answer is that paper is not just how news is delivered; it is how it is paid for."

Moreover, we are in a period of resurgent consumer interest in physical books, with provocative research supporting the human need for tactile experiences with reading material.[2] During this "print is dead; long live print" moment, it's worth recalling the longstanding tradition of loyal subscribers keeping years' worth of back issues of "evergreen" twentieth-century magazines like *National Geographic* and service magazines like Rodale's *Organic Gardening*, which long provided not only information but also a sense of belonging; readers could define themselves as adventurers or eco-conscious gardeners even if they never purchased a plane ticket or a garden hoe. Many estate sales feature piles of magazines, carefully collected and protected by readers who valued the communities they represented.

Finally, a look back at the power of magazines to unite cultural communities offers the promise of helping us better understand contemporary community-building media, from blogs to podcasts, that continue many of the forms and functions of twentieth-century magazines.

THE PAST AS PROLOGUE

This book is a curated collection of case studies that collectively shed light on the cultural niches that American consumer magazines of the twentieth century covered and created. Written by media and cultural scholars, these chapters examine how these niches were cultivated, how they changed over time, and how they influenced broader cultural conversations. It also looks at the enduring social influence of twentieth-century American print magazines, and the contemporary magazines and other media forms whose shape and voice derive from these twentieth-century antecedents.

We deliberately took a media-and-society perspective, rather than a strictly historical and media-studies perspective, in order to connect the emergence and evolution of individual magazines and their niches to the communities they reflected and affected. We mostly avoided examinations of the largest categories of magazines (e.g., women's magazines, shelter magazines, music magazines) in favor of those that more tightly reflect and create communities around interests, ideologies, life stages, and life situations (e.g., farming magazines, folk magazines, fanzines). And we sidestepped conventional examinations of the economic forces that shaped magazines in favor of a look at how magazines shaped and were shaped by the cultural forces of their times.

In these regards, the case studies contained in this book attempt to illuminate how the development of these niche publications anticipated the proliferation of the virtual communities (and the information outlets that serve them) that currently exist in cyberspace. This book addresses both what twentieth-century niche magazines provided for readers in these communities and what magazines derived from those readers—a mutuality that endeared these publications to their audiences.

At a time when the term "the media" is little more than a meaningless generalization for a wide range of cultural influences, this book seeks to make sense of something very specific: the enduring legacy of twentieth-century print magazines as places where people found community, and as influences on the larger society.

Students, scholars, media consumers, and media practitioners should find in these pages reasons to hope that contemporary media forms might emulate the ways in which twentieth-century magazines, as carefully constructed communities, brought and in many cases continue to bring people together, instead of splitting them apart.

REFERENCES

Carr, David. 2008. "Mourning Old Media's Decline." *New York Times*, October 28. https://www.nytimes.com/2008/10/29/business/media/29carr.html.

Ember, Sydney, and Michael M. Grynbaum. 2017. "The Not-So-Glossy Future of Magazines." *New York Times*, September 23. https://www.nytimes.com/2017/09/23/business/media/the-not-so-glossy-future-of-magazines.html.

MPA. "Number of print consumer magazines in the United States from 2002 to 2019." Chart. August 31, 2020. Statista. Accessed May 19, 2021. https://www.statista.com/statistics/238589/number-of-magazines-in-the-united-states/.

Sternadori, Miglena, and Tim Holmes. 2020. *The Handbook of Magazine Studies*. New York: Wiley-Blackwell.

Sumner, David E. 2010. *The Magazine Century: American Magazines Since 1900*. Bern, Switzerland: Peter Lang US.

Section 1

IDEAS AND IDEOLOGIES

Chapter 1

Ideas *in* America and Ideas *of* America

Thought Leader Magazines and the Life of the Mind in the Twentieth Century

Kevin M. Lerner

When intellectual historians write the history of ideas, they often focus on scholars, philosophers, peer-reviewed academic journals, and books. But in the day-to-day life of the mind, and the transmission of ideas to the culture more broadly, magazines have played a vital role in shaping American attitudes about politics, race, and gender, as well as about literature and the arts.

The importance of magazines in shaping the life of the mind in the United States reached its apex in the twentieth century, largely through a category of magazines that can be called "thought leaders." These are largely a group of elite—and sometimes elitist—highbrow magazines that combine in-depth reporting, belletristic essays, thoughtful criticism of literature and the arts, and sometimes fiction. Many of them are niche political magazines representing particular points of view. Others appeal to a more general interest. And still others do much of the same work, but exist at the fringes of a definable category or cross over from different categories entirely.

While some of these magazines have tiny circulations (none of them would really be seen as true general-interest publications), the ideas they debate and develop nevertheless have had an outsized influence on American culture, partially because thought leader magazines tend to reach influential readers in positions of power in government and industry, and partially because they are read by journalists for other media. Consequently, the ideas they promulgate filter down through more general-interest media and help set the cultural and political agenda.

Magazines in this category include *The Atlantic*, *Harper's*, and, for much of its history, *The New Yorker*. Political magazines such as *The New Republic*, *National Review*, and *The Nation* attempt to achieve a similar kind of influence on the world of ideas, including advocacy journalism and the arts. The magazines that can be called thought leaders all share a similar aim: to spark conversation among the country's political and intellectual elite.

Using that as a definition, several titles from New York City join the ranks of the national thought leader publications despite their regional titles. *New York*, a city magazine, tries to become a part of the national conversation by taking advantage of New York City's status as a capital of media and industry, by supplementing its coverage of local issues with national and international political stories. *The New York Times Magazine* plays a similar role as the weekly magazine of a national newspaper. And while *New York*, *The New Yorker*, and *The New York Times Magazine* all have sizable circulations when compared to the elite intellectual magazines, they still aim to reach an elite, educated, and affluent audience.

Contemporary readers of thought leader magazines know that they will find in their pages examples of scrupulous, longform, in-depth reporting. But they also know that these magazines will offer incisive, authoritative works of criticism—not just a book review, but also a book review essay, one that uses a recently published work as the basis for an explication of cultural mores or weaves together several volumes to tell a historical story from more than one point of view. Readers won't just find a movie review as a piece of service, but rather one that treats the movie as literature and explores how cinema works to evoke emotion. Or maybe a work of cultural criticism that blends reporting on the deterioration of a beloved work of art with an essay on the ephemerality of aesthetic perfection.

Over most of the course of the twentieth century, the ideas propagated by thought leader magazines made their way to the general public through general-interest titles such as *The Saturday Evening Post* and *Time*, which, while not really thought leaders themselves, played an important role in the dissemination of ideas that were filtered through their editors and writers—who themselves were reading the thought leader magazines. Later, of course, this role was taken over by television and, in the twenty-first century, by the internet.

THE NATION AND THE RISE OF LITERARY CRITICISM

The Nation, the oldest continuously published weekly magazine in the United States, began its run as an abolitionist journal; it was founded in 1865 as the Civil War was coming to an end (Foner 2015). Long a journal of opinion—mostly the opinion of founding editor E. L. Godkin—the magazine largely focused on policy. For example, at the end of the nineteenth century and into the twentieth, the magazine's editorials and reported stories staunchly opposed the United States' growing imperialist tendencies (Guttenplan 2015, 61–74). But around that same time, just before the turn of the twentieth century, *The Nation* began publishing a regular section on books and culture, in emulation of European literary journals, though here confined to a distinct section—the part of a magazine editors often refer to by the shorthand "the back of the book" (75–76). This literary and arts section was led by editor Wendell Phillips Garrison, a son of abolitionist printer William Lloyd Garrison.

The Nation may have been the first publication to combine a general interest or political opinion magazine with critical essays—or, as the section's introductory note put it, "competent criticism of art exhibitions and works of art, the drama, etc." "So far as I know," publisher Henry Holt wrote, "doing this as a matter of course was something new in American journalism" (qtd. in Guttenplan, 76). D. D. Guttenplan, who wrote an authorized history of *The Nation* (and went on to serve as its editor), cautions that Holt may have overstated the case, but either way, the practice was not commonplace at the turn of the twentieth century, and *Nation* competitors such as *Harper's* did not include a back-of-the-book reviews section.

While the idea of bringing a dedicated literature, arts, and culture section to a magazine devoted to other matters may have been unprecedented, the style of writing was hardly unheard of. There had been several theatrical reviews in American history, as early as the first half of the nineteenth century (Tebbel and Zuckerman 1991, 10). Prior to the U.S. Civil War, magazine writing styles had been mostly literary, florid, and first-person, of a piece with the earliest newspapers, the editing of which, in the first half of the nineteenth century, had been "an intensely personal matter (Schudson 1981, 16). But magazines, including *The Nation* itself, had been attempting to emulate a change in newspaper writing that developed after the rise of the Penny Papers in the 1830s. E. L. Godkin, *The Nation*'s first editor, found that his writers were reluctant to forgo the long-windedness of the European intellectual journal. "[I]t is very difficult to get men of education in America to handle any subject with a light touch," Godkin wrote. "They all want to write ponderous essays if they write at all" (qtd. in Tebbel and Zuckerman 1991, 61). So it is perhaps not coincidental that Godkin's own magazine would be among the first to append a cultural essays department to the magazine, offering its writers—and its readers—a more introspective, intellectual approach to journalism that existed before the United States' cultural shift toward "objective" reporting.

By the turn of the twentieth century, *The Nation* had established its bona fides as an authoritative influence on American culture, having championed the poet Emily Dickinson and the philosopher Charles Sanders Peirce. The magazine's circulation remained small—it peaked at 187,000 in 2006—owing in large part to its politics, which range from liberal to radical. Nonetheless, it managed to establish itself as a thought leader, a magazine read by powerful people and by other journalists. It is in this role that *The Nation*'s back-of-the-book proved most influential because, whether or not it invented the model, it established a pattern for smart magazines of the twentieth century to follow.

NINETEENTH-CENTURY HOLDOVERS

The Nation was not alone in surviving the turn of the twentieth century as a thought leader among American magazines. *Harper's* and *The Atlantic* were also self-consciously intellectual magazines, written for elite audiences. There was, of course, a class element to these magazines' circulation, too. Their audiences had money and time to devote to leisure activities such as theater and novels (Tebbel and Zuckerman 1991). While *The Saturday Evening Post* sought a mass, middle-class audience with its wholesome, upbeat vision of America, a vision forged by its editor George Horace Lorimer (Cohn 1990), the thought leader magazines cultivated an audience of people with university educations (still fairly rare in the early twentieth century) and knowledge of literature.

The Atlantic began publishing in the 1850s, and like *The Nation*, it was conceived of as an anti-slavery journal, but one that would "bring the literary influence of New England" to that cause, in the words of Francis Underwood, who came up with the idea for the magazine (qtd. in Tebbel and Zuckerman, 24). Like *The Saturday Evening Post*, *The Atlantic* also saw itself as representing something uniquely American, though it was a different vision of America, one of high culture, trying to match the literati of Europe in a fledgling nation. *The Atlantic*'s "American idea," as they called it, was a kind of conscience for the country, an aspirational best self (Goodman 2011, ix).

By the turn of the twentieth century, *The Atlantic* was a thought leader for American intellectuals. It published the poem "Battle Hymn of the Republic" in its first issue, and became the sort of magazine every writer aspired to be in or be mentioned in as a sign of achieving legitimacy. Scholar Susan Goodman, who wrote a book about the magazine's circle of contributors, asserts that the magazine wielded "influence far beyond its immediate readership" and "successfully cast itself as the conscience of the American public" (2011, x). In the first decades of the twentieth century, those contributors included Booker T. Washington and W. E. B. Du Bois, who brought discussions of "the Negro Problem" to the pages of *The Atlantic* in long, learned essays (Goodman 2011, 183–92). Former president Theodore Roosevelt and future president Woodrow Wilson contributed to the discourse on progressive politics (Goodman 2011, 193–205). Environmentalists, including John Muir,

John Burroughs, Mary Austin, and the Native American writer Zitkala-Sa, brought conservation issues to *The Atlantic*'s readership just as Theodore Roosevelt (with help from Muir) established Yosemite National Park. Muir's essays for *The Atlantic* were an essential piece of building the case for the National Park System, both in reaching the people who had the power to make change happen, such as Roosevelt, and in persuading the public that these changes were in the public interest.

The second of the nineteenth-century holdovers to steadily build its influence in the twentieth century, *Harper's* emerged as one of the great intellectual magazines in the United States. But unlike the abolitionist *Nation* and *Atlantic*, *Harper's* sought to stay above the fray of politics in the 1850s, as the country was on the verge of collapsing into a civil war. *Harper's*, along with some of the other large general-circulation magazines, "appeared to be operating on another planet" (Tebbel and Zuckerman 1991, 15). Partly, this was because *Harper's* was founded as an outlet for promoting the books of Harper Brothers publisher, a sort of mid-nineteenth-century branded content publication. So the magazine began almost entirely as a business proposition, meant to keep the company's presses rolling when they were not printing books and also to direct readers to those books.

Originally edited by Henry J. Raymond, who would go on to found *The New York Times* in 1851, *Harper's* was aimed at an educated, upper-class audience. "This was the audience that had the money to buy Harper books and the leisure time to read them" (Tebbel and Zuckerman 1991, 21). And without any direct intention from the publishers, *Harper's* became, like *The Atlantic* and *The Nation*, a journal of "serious people" who were in a position to influence public discourse. "It was, in short, a forum for the governing class—professionals, industrialists, those in public service—people who influenced decisions on issues and set standards" (Tebbel and Zuckerman 1991, 21).

THE RISE OF REPORTING

When it comes to magazines and the intellectual life of the United States, the nineteenth-century prehistory is essential to understanding the twentieth-century history, because these magazines existed primarily as magazines of ideas at a time when that was the expected rhetorical mode. Arguments and essays dominated the serious magazines of the nineteenth century, as they had dominated most serious discourse before magazines even existed. The belletristic form existed long before the rise of reporting and was actually the dominant form of journalism until around the turn of the twentieth century.

This is a tradition as old as writing and an outgrowth of the human desire to understand the world. But as the norm of objectivity, the interview, and the piling on of fact became the standard for journalism in the United States, and superseded the essay and the review in the popular conception of what journalism is and should be, American magazines managed to maintain the tradition of intellectual inquiry aimed at a general audience. This happened both in political opinion journals and the back-of-the-book sections of general-interest magazines (which are not always in the back) as well as in specialized magazines such as the *New York Review of Books*. This tradition of wrestling with ideas shaped American intellectual life over the entire course of the twentieth century.

But by the end of the nineteenth century, a new epistemology of journalism began to take hold, both in newspapers and in magazines: the idea of the factual report. In the past, an argument against slavery would have been made on moral grounds, appealing to religion or humanism, with facts secondary to the argument. One notable exception to this was Thomas Paine's *Common Sense*, which perched the argument to secede from Britain on top of a pile of facts, which is why many historians include Paine in a history of American journalism (see, for example, Daly 2018). But by the beginning of the twentieth century, even magazines were beginning to focus on the idea of reporting as a mode of argumentation (Schudson 1981). The muckraking magazines of the early twentieth century were the most important instance of this new way of seeing the world. Titles such as *Munsey's* and the first incarnation of *Cosmopolitan* picked up on this epistemology, which was not only a new idea in the history of ideas, but also had the benefit of being popular. The publisher William Randolph Hearst, in fact, turned *Cosmopolitan* into a muckraking magazine precisely to capitalize on the new thirst for factual reporting. (Decades later, the magazine was reinvented again as a lifestyle magazine for women.)

The recognized pioneer in muckraking was the magazine *McClure's*, the namesake of publisher S. S. McClure. The landmark January 1903 issue included an installment of Ida Tarbell's history of the Standard Oil Company; Lincoln Steffens's report on municipal corruption in Minneapolis; and a dispatch from a labor dispute, written by Ray Stannard Baker (Fitzpatrick 1994). There is no question that these three articles had ideas behind them, and that their authors had points of view from which they wrote. The thesis that American institutions had become corrupt and were not serving common people united the three, and the muckrakers fit squarely in the Progressive movement of the early twentieth century (Hofstadter 2011). But their arguments were not made on purely rhetorical grounds. Instead, they were built on a foundation of the diligent collection of facts. As this style became the dominant rhetorical mode for American journalism, a rise that became noticeable throughout the twentieth century, essays and literature became merely one part of the landscape of magazines, rather than the whole of it, and it was in this atmosphere that the idea of reviews, essays, and criticism living in the back of the book also took hold, displaced from its primacy, but maintaining an important foothold in the general-interest magazine. Where the reported magazine story aimed to increase *knowledge*, essays and works of criticism continued to struggle with *understanding*.

THE NEW REPUBLIC

In 1914, not long after the fad of the muckraking magazines began to fade, and with it their subscription numbers, a group of thinkers led by Herbert Croly founded a magazine called *The New Republic*. It was a journal of political liberalism, but one that tempered its politics with a strong literary section. In some ways, the structure of the magazine was not very different from that of *The Nation*, though its politics were less radical. Also, like *The Nation*, and unlike *McClure's* or *Collier's*, *The New Republic* was intended, from the start, to be a journal not just of fact but of ideas. *The New Republic* was going to be an intellectual magazine (Foer 2014, xv).

Croly had a conception of how his magazine would effect change in the world. Croly was not attempting to reach a popular audience like that of *The Saturday Evening Post*. Nor was he attempting to limit himself to conducting an airy colloquy among disconnected elites, as he saw in publications such as *The Atlantic* or *The Nation*. Croly did want to reach those elites, but without making *The New Republic* "a clubby conversation among the hyperliterate" (Foer, xv). Instead, the elites "were meant to be a vanguard that would very self-consciously shape the political culture of the country and set its artistic standards. Croly wanted his publication to serve as a transmission belt of ideas, carrying the thoughts of intellectuals to a much broader and, therefore, much more meaningful audience" (Foer, xv).

The "big idea" of *The New Republic*, writ large, was American liberalism, the idea that the country should build a welfare state and protect civil liberties as its core values. Among that founding group of writers was Walter Lippmann, who eventually drifted away from liberalism, but whose ideas were so influential in the twentieth century that his biographer made the claim that "Lippmann had left his fingerprints on, and had even helped mold, almost every major issue in American life over six decades" (Steel 2017). Of course, not all of that work was done in *The New Republic*. Much of Lippmann's career took him directly into contact with powerful people. He also wrote a newspaper column for many years. But his sensibility and that of *The New Republic* were similar, and he was a part of its orbit and emblematic of the type of writer the editors of the magazine brought on board: bright, well-educated, and idealistic young people who were willing to work for little money in order to influence the ideas of the powerful.

Over the course of the eighty-five or so years of the twentieth century that *The New Republic* published, it gathered an impressive list of contributors, some of whom were already famous, and some of whom launched their careers as intellectual journalists in the magazine's pages: John Maynard Keynes wrote on Soviet Russia, and Margaret Sanger on birth control. Edmund Wilson and John Dos Passos wrote about the Great Depression. Virginia Woolf contributed an essay about an air raid during World War II. Vladimir Nabokov, the bilingual novelist, wrote an essay about the art of translation. Poet W. H. Auden on Sigmund Freud. Philip Roth. Film critic Pauline Kael. H. L. Mencken, who would co-found *The American Mercury*, itself a short-lived but influential intellectual magazine. Nicholas Lemann, who would go on to write for *The New Yorker*. Michael Kinsley, who would edit *The New Republic*, *Harper's*, and *Slate*, the online magazine he helped start in the 1990s. All of these writers passed through *The New Republic*'s stable at various times, helping to define the intellectual life of the country.

The New Republic had several editors over the course of the twentieth century, but perhaps none was as influential as Leon Wieseltier, the literary editor from 1983 until 2014, when he was part of a mass resignation from the magazine's masthead (Lizza 2014). Though Wieseltier's legacy is now tainted by accusations of sexual misconduct, his back-of-the-book section at *The New Republic* helped guide three decades of intellectual life in the United States (Schuessler 2017).

THE 1920s

The years after World War I saw the founding of several new magazines that would influence American culture, both highbrow and middlebrow, including the launch of the publishing empire that would supplant *The Saturday Evening Post* as the chronicle of middlebrow America's mindset: Time/Life.

Whereas *Time* and *Life* were magazines that became institutions, another one of these magazines, *The American Mercury*, falls into the class of magazines that burn hot and bright, but quickly fade. Originally the idea of cantankerous journalist and social critic H. L. Mencken, *The American Mercury* was, for the decade of its run, a collaboration between the journalist Mencken, theater critic George Jean Nathan, and publisher Alfred Knopf. Mencken "was an apostle of realism, a fanatic for libertarianism. He detested the rural rube and shunned the avant-garde intellectual." Nathan's theater reviews were "dripping with vitriol at the boorishness of his fellow citizens. As Mencken was a critic of American life, Nathan was a critic of

American culture." And Knopf, as the publisher both of the magazine and of literary fiction and nonfiction, was most responsible for getting authors, including Kahlil Gibran, Thomas Mann, and André Gide, into the magazine's pages (Russell 1984, v). This is in addition to the authors that Mencken and Nathan published in *The Smart Set*, a predecessor magazine to *The American Mercury*, a stable that included F. Scott Fitzgerald, Theodore Dreiser, James Joyce, and Aldous Huxley, many of whom saw publication for the first time—or at least U.S. publication for the first time—in the pages of *The Smart Set*.

The New Yorker, today perhaps the gold standard of upper-middlebrow intellectual life in the United States, actually began its life as a humor magazine in the 1920s. This was a period during which New York City became the center of America's intellectual life as well. Publishing had been decentralized up until the turn of the twentieth century, with significant outposts in Boston—the original home of *The Atlantic*—and Philadelphia, where Curtis Publishing and *The Saturday Evening Post* were based (Yagoda 2000). The launch of a magazine with "New York" in its name marked, coincidentally, the beginning of something new: a cosmopolitan sensibility that would mark New York as the cultural capital of the country, to be rivaled only by the rise of Los Angeles and the entertainment industry. The early *New Yorker* was a magazine of light satire and wit, more in line with a Dorothy Parker sketch than with a 40,000-word reported investigation. William Shawn, the founding editor, was a regular part of the Round Table meetings of wits at the Algonquin Hotel in midtown Manhattan, where the magazine had its offices.

Over the next eight decades, *The New Yorker* incorporated the objective style of the muckrakers into its journalism (which the magazine, in its own twee argot calls "fact" pieces), and developed a legendary fact-checking department. Even though some of its supposed "fact" pieces were later questioned, particularly those of novelist Truman Capote, whose *In Cold Blood* the magazine serialized (Helliker 2013) and the stories of Joseph Mitchell (Kunkel 2015), the magazine published some of the most monumental reporting of the twentieth century. John Hersey's *Hiroshima* and Rachel Carson's environmental epic *Silent Spring* forced the country to reckon with the destructive power of nuclear energy and the fragility of the natural world, respectively. But theirs were works of positivist objectivity, even if they use emotional storytelling to grip readers. Through the years, *The New Yorker* has also brought cosmopolitan American readers pastoral essays by E. B. White, the political commentary of Hendrik Hertzberg, and the cultural criticism of Louis Menand, as well as the sly, humanist reporting of Susan Orlean and the historically informed public intellectualism of Jill Lepore.

LIBERALS, CONSERVATIVES, AND THE LITERATI AFTER WORLD WAR II

After World War II, American intellectual discourse continued at both the rarified level of *The Nation, The New Republic, The Atlantic, The New Yorker*, and *Harper's*, and at the more mass-market level of *Time, Life*, and *The Saturday Evening Post*. The conformist stereotype of the 1950s was not exactly a fiction, but it was also not the complete story. At the same time as *Life* and *The Post* perpetuated a vision of a peaceful, consumerist American Dream, intellectual life continued in the thought leader magazines, which debated the role of nuclear weapons; the validity of pro- and anti-communist political stances; and the cultural value of new artists, filmmakers, and the new medium of television.

The smaller intellectual magazines, particularly the political journals, always subsisted on a tight budget determined less by advertising and more by subscriptions and donations from wealthy supporters and foundations (Navasky 2006; Tebbel and Zuckerman 1991). Counterintuitively, though, that reliance on donors and readers allowed them to survive during fallow periods for other magazines, since their readers and funders cared so deeply about them. Victor Navasky, a former editor and publisher of *The Nation*, joked that the only time the magazine ever made a profit was in years when wartime paper rationing forced them to print shorter issues. The larger, general-interest magazines were more susceptible to competition from outlets such as television. *The Saturday Evening Post* switched from weekly to biweekly publication in 1963 and later quarterly. *Life* ceased regular publication in 1972, but appeared intermittently after that as special issues. Other large-circulation, general-interest magazines like *Time, Newsweek*, and the new *U.S. News and World Report* soldiered on during this period, with *Time* broadly representing Republicans; *Newsweek*, which was purchased by the Graham family, owners of the *Washington Post*, reflecting liberal points of view; and *U.S. News* providing for those who could stomach neither of its rivals (Tebbel and Zuckerman 1991, 304–5).

By contrast, the intellectual magazines not only survived in the postwar decades—they were joined by a new batch of titles that broadened the range of voices in their conversation. Chief among these was *The National Review*, started in 1955 by William F. Buckley, Jr., a young conservative intellectual who had risen to national prominence with the publication of his book *God and Man at Yale*. In that book, Buckley argued that Yale University, his alma mater, was indoctrinating students with a secular and collectivist ideology. In founding *The National Review*, Buckley hoped to give a unified voice to disparate conservative voices in the United States, which he felt had never been able to speak out against the liberal consensus (Daly 2018, 416; Tebbel and Zuckerman 1991, 328; Buckley 2010). Press historian Chris Daly credits *The National Review* with beginning the entire conservative movement in the United States, first with the magazine itself and later through the patrician, erudite Buckley's appearances on the television show *Firing Line* (Daly 2018, 416). This inspired subsequent conservative voices in radio and television at the end of the twentieth century and into the twenty-first, influencing American politics in seismic ways (Hemmer 2016). *The National Review* remained the intellectual conscience of the movement, growing throughout the second half of the twentieth century as other media outlets (including the magazine *The Weekly Standard*, started in 1995) joined it and helped to popularize its ideas.

The more liberal journals of ideas continued, too, and published some of the most influential work of the second half of the century, notably in pushing the Civil Rights movement forward. *The Atlantic*, for example, published the Martin Luther King, Jr. essay that would later become known as "Letter from Birmingham Jail" (Vare 2008). *The Atlantic*, in particular, had a consistent mission of attempting to define American intellectual life by working to define what it means to be American. *The New Yorker*, *New York*, and *The New York Times Magazine* defined what it meant to be cosmopolitan, including reading the "right" books and watching the "right" movies.

The post–World War II period also saw the launch or rise to prominence of several "little" magazines, some of which were explicitly journals of political ideas and others that focused on literature. *Partisan Review* began publication in 1934 as a magazine of the Communist Party of the United States, though it quickly adopted an anti-communist stance after some of the abuses of the Soviet Union came to light. Cultural critic Dwight Macdonald became an editor at *Partisan Review* and continued the magazine's tradition of publishing essays of cultural commentary. In an indication of the perceived influence of *Partisan Review* and other literary-cultural journals like it, the Central Intelligence Agency secretly funneled money to the magazine to help keep it afloat as a part of the "cultural Cold War" of the 1950s (Wilford 2009, 103). *Commentary*, which debuted in 1945, also began as a magazine of liberal intellectuals, but drifted rightward. Originally funded by the American Jewish Committee, the magazine was one of the first to publish important American authors such as Philip Roth, Cynthia Ozick, and Saul Bellow, and criticism by writers including Lionel Trilling and Alfred Kazin. The magazine was also the first to publish parts of *The Diary of Anne Frank* (Balint 2010).

The Paris Review, a literary journal, launched in 1953 with an issue containing an interview with the British novelist E. M. Forster—the first in what would become a series of interviews about the writing process that would continue into the twenty-first century. George Plimpton, the patrician editor, led the magazine for more than fifty years out of his New York City townhouse, and culled the more than 2,000 manuscripts sent to the magazine each year to find fiction and essays from authors such as Susan Sontag, Joyce Carol Oates, John Updike, and James Baldwin (Plimpton 2004). For such a small magazine, it maintained an outsized influence on the intellectual life of the United States.

During the New York City newspaper strike of 1962–1963, a group of intellectual writers lamented the temporary loss of book reviews in the dormant newspapers of their city. As a reaction to this, two editors, Barbara Epstein and Robert Silvers, published an experimental issue of a new magazine, slightly bigger than a tabloid and printed on matte paper, which they called *The New York Review of Books*. David Remnick, who became the editor of *The New Yorker* at the turn of the twenty-first century, called that first issue "surely the best first issue of any magazine ever" (Tucker 2013). Stories in the *Review* were unapologetically long, unfailingly learned, and often only tangentially related to a recently published book—and sometimes not at all. Epstein and Silvers edited the *Review* for the remainder of the twentieth century, adding not only literature, but also art, politics, history, science, and American culture—all with a progressive bent—to its editorial mix.

DUSTY LIBRARY STACKS AND THE MOVE ONLINE

As the twentieth century moved into its last decade, venerable titles such as *The Nation*, *Harper's*, and *The Atlantic* as well as younger publications including *The New York Review of Books* were all publishing regularly and bringing the writing of public intellectuals to American life. In *The Nation*, for example, the 1990s brought a new wave of political and literary thought from authors such as Christopher Hitchens, Salman Rushdie, Barbara Ehrenreich, and Molly Ivins (Wiener 2016). But public intellectuals were, of course, not the only thinkers working in the realm of big ideas. Scholars also were trafficking in groundbreaking intellectual concepts; they simply had no place, beyond academic journals, to transmit their ideas.

In 1990, a former Yale University professor named Jeffrey Kittay had an idea for a new magazine that would chronicle academic life for a popular audience. The resulting magazine, *Lingua Franca*, lasted just over a decade, but gathered a stable of young writers who would go on to bring the "*Lingua Franca*-style story" to other publications and diffuse that style across the American magazine landscape. That story type was one that took the dusty academic seriously and wrestled with ideas that previously had been limited to the ivory tower. In one archetypal *Lingua Franca* story, the writer Jack Hitt chronicled the scholars who were at work annotating Benjamin Franklin's papers. Hitt joked to one of the scholars that they must be reading every laundry list Franklin ever wrote, and the scholars took him seriously. It was a moment of gentle humor and humanity in the writing (Star 2002). By couching scholarly ideas in engaging narrative writing, *Lingua Franca* broadened the minds of the American public.

The last years of the twentieth century brought new experiments in online magazines of ideas. A trio of publications—*Slate*, *Salon*, and *Suck*—often get grouped together because of their similar early approaches, as well as for alliterative purposes. *Suck* and *Salon* both went live in 1995; *Slate* debuted the following summer. *Slate* was, by far, the most successful of these publications. Originally a partnership with the software company Microsoft, *Slate* was intended to be printed out and read as an issue of a magazine, but the first editor, Michael Kinsley, and the rest of the team quickly figured out that the internet was a completely different medium, with different rules about publication.

Kinsley had been an editor at *The New Republic* and briefly at *Harper's* (he was also considered for the top job at *The New Yorker*). He knew the world of intellectual magazines, and developed a style of counter-intuitive essays and reporting that became known as the "Slate pitch." Eventually, the magazine was sold to the owners of the *Washington Post* (Weisberg and Kinsley 2006). *Salon* continued to publish, but its influence waned after its early years. *Suck* flamed out quickly, only just barely making it into the 2000s, but its influence on the culture of internet writing was unmistakable.

Among digital-media pundits and amateur web historians, *Suck* is regularly credited as the progenitor of a certain style of internet writing: fast-paced, snarky, and merrily irreverent; simultaneously condescending and self-deprecating. In its first few months, *Suck* offered commentary and criticism on popular culture, mainstream media, and technology: from the browser wars to TED conferences ("attendees sitting at the feet of would-be uberati, soaking up tips regarding the get-rich opportunities of the digital future"). The tone was something like the library-steps chatter of critical-theory students with Adderall scripts and twenty-four-hour access to the microfiche room (Wiener 2016). *Suck* was also one of the first magazines to try to understand the culture of the internet itself, treating it not only as a medium, but also a *place*, and one with a particular culture.

The rise of the internet also promised to solve the biggest ongoing problem for the intellectual magazines: how to afford the cost of printing. Of course, the internet also posed challenges to the subscription and advertising model that sustained these magazines for so long. Although their donor and membership models insulated them somewhat from the loss of ad revenue, it took these magazines some time to realize that loyalty was their real strength. In a report for the Shorenstein Center at Harvard University, Heidi Legg (2020) argued:

The promise of the future is that subscription revenue, aggregator revenue, events revenue, and brand-adjacent products will provide enough revenue to fund newsrooms where editorial, reporting, and directorial talent can be encouraged, thought leadership valued, and the national conversation fostered. Membership around brand loyalty, for both nonprofit and for-profit magazines, is the key now. Our intellectual rigor and the spreading of innovative ideas, cultural security, a sense of belonging, and democracy depend on a thriving magazine sector.

Legg cites the success of the progressive thought leader magazine *Mother Jones* in fostering this brand loyalty, describing a mix of subscription revenue, donations, and newsletter subscriptions that keeps the small-circulation muckraking magazine in business.

However they continue to be funded, the longevity of *Harper's*, *The Atlantic*, *The Nation*, and other thought leader powerhouses from the twentieth century stands as a testament to the desire in American life for intellectual voices to stand above and apart from popular passions and give the United States a life of the mind.

REFERENCES

Balint, Benjamin. 2010. *Running Commentary: The Contentious Magazine That Transformed the Jewish Left into the Neoconservative Right*. Public Affairs.

Buckley, William F., Jr. 2010. *Cancel Your Own Goddam Subscription: Notes and Asides from National Review*. ReadHowYouWant.com.

Cohn, Jan. 1990. *Creating America: George Horace Lorimer and The Saturday Evening Post*. University of Pittsburgh Press.

Daly, Christopher B. 2018. *Covering America: A Narrative History of a Nation's Journalism*. University of Massachusetts Press.

Fitzpatrick, Ellen F. 1994. *Muckraking: Three Landmark Articles*. Bedford/St. Martin's.

Foer, Franklin. 2014. *Insurrections of the Mind: 100 Years of Politics and Culture in America*. HarperCollins.

Foner, Eric. 2015. "Introduction." In *The Nation: A Biography*, by D. D. Guttenplan. The Nation Co. LLC.

Goodman, Susan. 2011. *Republic of Words: The Atlantic Monthly and Its Writers, 1857–1925*. UPNE.

Guttenplan, D. D. 2015. *The Nation: A Biography*. The Nation Co. LLC.

Helliker, Kevin. 2013. "Capote Classic 'In Cold Blood' Tainted by Long-Lost Files." *Wall Street Journal*, February 9, sec. Life and Style. https://www.wsj.com/articles/SB10001424127887323951904578290341604113984.

Hemmer, Nicole. 2016. *Messengers of the Right: Conservative Media and the Transformation of American Politics*. University of Pennsylvania Press.

"History of The Saturday Evening Post | The Saturday Evening Post." n.d. Accessed January 31, 2020. https://www.saturdayeveningpost.com/history-saturday-evening-post/.

Hofstadter, Richard. 2011. *The Age of Reform*. Knopf Doubleday Publishing Group.

Kunkel, Thomas. 2015. *Man in Profile: Joseph Mitchell of the New Yorker*. Random House.

Legg, Heidi. 2020. "Preserving America's Thought Leader Magazines." Shorenstein Center on Media, Politics and Public Policy. https://shorensteincenter.org/preserving-americas-thought-leader-magazines/.

Lizza, Ryan. 2014. "Inside the Collapse of The New Republic." *The New Yorker*. December 12, 2014. https://www.newyorker.com/news/news-desk/inside-collapse-new-republic.

Luce, Henry Robinson, and John K. Jessup. 1969. *The Ideas of Henry Luce*. Atheneum.

Navasky, Victor S. 2006. *A Matter of Opinion*. Picador.

Plimpton, George. 2004. *The Paris Review Book: Of Heartbreak, Madness, Sex, Love, Betrayal, Outsiders, Intoxication, War, Whimsy, Horrors, God, Death, Dinner, Baseball, Travels, The Art of Writing, and Everything Else in the World Since 1953*. Macmillan.

Russell, Richard K. 1984. "Foreword to the Reprint Edition." In *American Mercury: Facsimile Edition of Volume I*, 1st edition, by H. L. Mencken and George Jean Nathan. Garber Communications.

Schudson, Michael. 1981. *Discovering the News: A Social History of American Newspapers*. Basic Books.

Schuessler, Jennifer. 2017. "Leon Wieseltier Admits 'Offenses' Against Female Colleagues as New Magazine Is Killed." *The New York Times*, October 24, sec. Arts. https://www.nytimes.com/2017/10/24/arts/leon-wieseltier-magazine-harassment.html.

Star, Alexander, ed. 2002. *Quick Studies: The Best of Lingua Franca*. 1st edition. Farrar, Straus and Giroux.

Steel, Ronald. 2017. *Walter Lippmann and the American Century*. Routledge.

Tebbel, John William, and Mary Ellen Zuckerman. 1991. *The Magazine in America, 1741–1990*. Oxford University Press.

Tucker, Neely. 2013. "The New York Review of Books Turns 50." *Washington Post*, November 6, sec. Style. https://www.washingtonpost.com/lifestyle/style/the-new-york-review-of-books-turns-50/2013/11/06/5e031f64-4703-11e3-a196-3544a03c2351_story.html.

Vare, Robert. 2008. *The American Idea: The Best of the Atlantic Monthly*. Crown/Archetype.

Vidal, Gore. 2000. *The Best of The Nation: Selections from the Independent Magazine of Politics and Culture*. 1st edition. Edited by Victor Navasky and Katrina vanden Heuvel. Nation Books.

Weisberg, Jacob, and Michael Kinsley. 2006. *The Best of Slate: A 10th Anniversary Anthology*. 10th anniversary edition. Edited by David Plotz. Atlas Books.

Wiener, Anna. 2016. "The Best Magazine on the Early Web." *The Atlantic*. March 18. https://www.theatlantic.com/technology/archive/2016/03/suck-webzine/473853/.

Wilford, Hugh. 2009. *The Mighty Wurlitzer: How the CIA Played America*. Harvard University Press.

Yagoda, Ben. 2000. *About Town: The New Yorker and the World It Made*. Simon & Schuster.

Chapter 2

Speaking Out

Leftist Magazines and Political Advocacy

Erika J. Pribanic-Smith

Societal and political events of the twentieth century created significant highs and lows for leftist movements. The magazines intertwined with those movements chronicled the shifts. Some struggled to maintain or extend their influence with a changing audience; others emerged to meet the needs of left-leaning readers.

Liberal intellectual journals such as *The Nation* and *The New Republic* were mainstays throughout the century. Targeted at an elite audience, these publications were known as the great influencers of influencers, affecting thought among an existing intellectual community. Other leftist magazines appeared as changing times called for new voices. Some of these perished within a few years, while others, like *Mother Jones* and *In These Times*, lasted for decades and are still published. These periodicals not only affected thought but also shaped culture and nurtured community among their readers.

Leftist magazines were born into a period of social activism and reform at the turn of the century. As big businesses "exploited people and corrupted politics with no apparent accountability" (Adams 2001, 33), a massive chasm emerged between those who profited from industrialism's spoils and those who toiled in unsafe conditions and lived in poverty. "Of necessity," McGerr (2003) argued, "working men, women, and children lived by a different set of cultural rules that . . . aroused both fear and sympathy in the middle class" (13)—a white-collar segment of society afforded more luxuries than manual laborers but fewer than the truly wealthy.

The overwhelmingly middle-class, intellectual progressive movement viewed the state as a positive instrument for social justice (Adams 2001, 34; McGerr 2003). During this period of reform, influential editors—most prominently those of *The Nation* and *The New Republic*—not only brought the era's social ills to the attention of their well-educated, affluent, and socially active readers but also shaped perceptions by their framing of the issues. These liberal intellectual journals had "an extremely important role in the diffusion of attitudes on social problems" (Shermis and Barth 1981, 52).

The Nation already had a liberal tone upon its founding in 1865; its prospectus called for attention to labor and education issues and promised to bring an independent, critical discussion to political questions (vanden Heuvel 1990, 1). First under founding editor Edwin Lawrence Godkin and then under Oswald Garrison Villard—who took the helm in 1918—*The Nation* exhibited a passion for social justice (Neale 1941, 8). The editors aimed to inspire action by telling the truth and allowing readers "to reason from it with regard to their own duty" (quoted in Christman 1965, 14). Similarly, *The New Republic* founding editor Herbert Croly insisted that his magazine was created "less to inform or entertain its readers than to start little insurrections in the realm of their convictions" (quoted in Seideman 1986, ix).

Founded in 1914, *The New Republic* frequently spoke out against the evils brought about by industrialism. Its editors lamented that although industrialism created unprecedented wealth, it was unequally distributed. The magazine sought elevation of the poor so that they could participate fully in the economy (Seideman 1986, 7). The editors also advocated on behalf of labor to the extent that the magazine "sometimes read like a union newsletter" (Seideman 1986, 32). Instituting a minimum wage, or requiring that employers pay a "living wage," was among *The New Republic*'s key issues. One editorial contested arguments that had been raised against a minimum wage for women, such as that women had someone providing for their needs and they just wanted a little spending money for luxuries. The article countered that most women worked because their families needed their income to survive, and it argued that the entire family's income combined—or the women's sole income, if she was on her own—often was barely adequate for basic needs. The editorial called the refusal to pay a living wage "immoral" and "stupid," and asked, "How long will society continue to pay the cost of these absurd pin-money wages in the lessened health and lowered morale of the workers, in prostitution, pauperism and degradation?" ("Objects of Charity" 1915, 10).

Neither *The Nation* nor *The New Republic* could claim a large audience. In 1920, *The Nation* reported just over 38,000 readers annually and *The New Republic* 37,000; in comparison, *Cosmopolitan* and *Collier's* boasted circulations of more than a million each, and *The Saturday Evening Post* reached more than 2 million (Ayer 1920, 1193). The content of *The Nation* and *The New Republic* was intended for niche audiences, but the small circulations belied their reach. Both publications counted powerful people among their most faithful readers; thus, they extended their influence by targeting a community of influencers (Shermis and Barth 1981, 66). Because the publications' editors were considered liberal authorities, their ideas reverberated through both intellectual and political circles; both were quoted in the halls of Congress as representatives debated policy (Neale 1941, 9, 11, 87–88). The magazines' function was to analyze and interpret events while fostering a social philosophy that served to "educate, stimulate, and finally awake to action the men and women of the nation" (Neale 1941, 88).

RADICAL MAGAZINES SEEK REVOLUTION

The issues that filled these liberal magazines' pages did not directly affect the affluent editors (Seideman 1986, 28). Perhaps for that reason, those editors were content with slow, incremental reforms to existing social structures. On the other hand, radical magazines—such as *Challenge, Mother Earth, The Masses*, and *Wilshire's*—sought revolution to initiate fundamental change (Seideman 1986, 3, 18; Shermis and Barth 1981, 62). Lumsden (2014) identified the Progressive era as the heyday for the radical press. The issues in anarchist, socialist, and International Workers of the World periodicals were no different from those that liberal magazines discussed. They, too, were concerned with unfair income distribution and inhumane working conditions, but they believed the reforms liberal journals advocated merely treated symptoms rather than correcting the root causes. While preaching revolution, radical magazines amplified voices that were absent from magazines like *The Nation* and *The New Republic* (Lumsden 2014, 2). During the Progressive era, two of the most influential radical voices were the anarchist *Mother Earth* and socialist *Masses*.

Founded in 1906 and edited by Emma Goldman, a Russian immigrant, *Mother Earth* spoke out on working conditions and poverty. The language Goldman used in *Mother Earth* and other venues led to her notoriety. Though she preached nonviolent means to achieve revolutionary aims, she was arrested multiple times because of her influence on others—including claims that she inspired the assassination of President William McKinley and instigated laborers to insurrection by encouraging them to take direct action to improve their condition (Pribanic-Smith and Schroeder 2019).

Advocating for birth control led to one of Goldman's arrests. She had witnessed firsthand the plight of impoverished women and children, who carried "the heaviest burden of our ruthless economic system" (Goldman 1934, 185–87). She vowed she would never "acquiesce or submit to authority, nor will I make peace with a system which degrades women to a mere incubator and which fattens on her innocent victims." She proclaimed, "I now and here declare war upon this system and shall not rest until the path has been cleared for a free motherhood and a healthy, joyous and happy childhood" (Goldman 1916, 475). Not only did *Mother Earth* help Goldman galvanize her audience on important issues, it also fostered a sense of community among anarchists. The magazine sponsored social gatherings, and its office provided a communal space for kindred spirits to gather (Lumsden 2014, 170).

A frequent contributor to *Mother Earth*, Max Eastman became editor of *The Masses* in 1912, a year after its founding. A product of its bohemian Greenwich Village surroundings, the socialist journal balanced revolutionary advocacy with artistic expression (Lumsden 2014, 198–99; O'Neill 1966, 18–19, 21). *The Masses*' editors and contributors "helped to create a radical culture that rejected all conventions and questioned all faiths" (Lumsden 2014, 198), offering readers new ways to organize society and express themselves.

Although Eastman and other writers for *The Masses* identified similar evils of industrialism to those exposed in *The Nation* and *The New Republic*, the liberal and radical magazines took great pains to point out their ideological differences. "We intend a social revolution, to be accomplished by a class-conscious struggle against capital and privilege," Eastman wrote of the difference between socialists and the progressives. "They intend a social amelioration to be accomplished by the enlightened self-interest of the privileged, combined with a little altruism and a great deal of altruistic oratory" (quoted in O'Neill 1966, 133).

Jabs at Eastman and *The Masses* were equally common in *The New Republic*, which found socialist tactics too extreme, but Croly was nonetheless incensed when *The Masses* faced censorship during World War I, calling the suppression of periodicals for criticizing the war an "extreme case of arbitrary administrative discretion" (Seideman 1986, 55–56). Advocacy of free speech and a free press was a hallmark of the liberal agenda, and the Espionage Act of 1917 brought that issue to the forefront. Intended to silence voices of dissent so that President Woodrow Wilson could lead a united nation into war, the Espionage Act criminalized communication that interfered with military operations, supported enemy activities, encouraged disloyalty among military personnel or obstructed the draft. *The Masses* was among 100 periodicals Postmaster General Albert Burleson declared unmailable (Blanchard 1992, 72, 75–76). At issue were four cartoons and four written passages that the government believed were intended to interfere with the war effort. Among the offensive passages were editorials by Eastman praising the courage of draft resisters and advocating respect for Goldman and her comrade Alexander Berkman, editor of the anarchist *Blast* magazine (Sayer 1988, 47–48). *The Masses* successfully fought the censorship in federal court.

Goldman and Berkman were arrested in 1917 for writings and speeches against the draft; they were sentenced to two years in prison and then deported. The government also deemed *Mother Earth* unmailable under the Espionage Act. Pleas to lift the mailing ban were futile, leaving *Mother Earth*'s publishers with no choice but to cease publication (Pribanic-Smith and Schroeder 2019, 113–16). An excerpted letter to the Postmaster in the *Mother Earth Bulletin*—a newsletter issued to serve faithful readers after the magazine's demise—stated that a growing number of Americans "are anxious, desirous and determined to read radical literature" such as that contained in *Mother Earth, The Masses*, and other suppressed publications. The letter called those magazines "the Bible for millions of people," insisting that readers were "determined to have them" and radical publishers would find a way to meet the need. "The more a government suppresses a paper that the readers really want," the letter warned, "the more it is read with reverence, and the more powerful the paper becomes in its influence on the community" (Reitman 1917).

WAR LAUNCHES A NEW ERA

World War I effectively ended the Progressive era, ushering in a conservative age during which liberal magazines struggled. As the "politics of purpose gave way to the politics of lassitude" in the 1920s (Schlesinger 1962, 85), the word "reform" went from buzzword to bad word. Nonetheless, the idea of social justice remained woven into the fabric of liberal magazines. Because most readers no longer wanted to hear about reform, their audiences shrank to those who remained interested in the magazines' missions, and the publications "faced a constant battle to keep their financial footing" (Bennion 1971, 713). Forced to file for bankruptcy and restructure in the 1920s, *The New Republic* coped, in part, by launching a publishing company to help raise revenue by producing works on social and economic problems (Seideman 1986, 81–83). *The New Republic* continued its focus on labor issues along with public ownership of industry, congressional and judicial reform, and education (Bennion 1971, 659). Croly continued calling liberal readers to action, asking them "to re-examine the social environment, to correct weaknesses, and to support any movements which seemed likely to help rebuild civilization on a more humane basis" (Wallace 1986, 26).

Meanwhile, *The Nation* tackled issues including immigration policy and racial discrimination. Villard had a long history of involvement in race issues. Grandson of abolitionist William Lloyd Garrison and heir to his ideals, Villard was among the founders of the National Association for the Advancement of Colored People in 1909 (Kellogg 2009). Fellow NAACP co-founder W. E. B. Du Bois and African American author Langston Hughes were on *The Nation*'s roll of contributors in the 1920s. Du Bois argued in one article that "occasions of revolt against the present political and industrial situation have thus far ignored the Negro as an active factor in the revolution. But he cannot be ignored. In truth there can be no successful economic change in Georgia without the black man's cooperation" (in vanden Heuvel 1990, 65).

Both *The Nation* and *The New Republic* attempted, during the 1920s, to connect more with the people whose interests they defended, a practice that intensified during the Great Depression. While the editors proposed theories on how to reverse the crisis, they sent writers across the country to document the conditions Americans were facing (Seideman 1986, 97–100). For instance, Margaret Bourke-White's 1935 article in *The Nation*, "Dust Changes America," artfully detailed the conditions in Midwestern and Southwestern states affected by dust storms—while taking jabs at the New Deal's Agricultural Adjustment Act (in vanden Heuvel 1990, 121–23). New readers found truth in the intellectual journal's pages, and people "from universities and from mining camps" wrote in, "eager to tell a story that the newspapers were missing" (Christman 1965, 38).

President Franklin D. Roosevelt's series of New Deal regulations, programs, and public works projects aimed to provide relief and recovery for Depression-stricken Americans while reforming the financial system to prevent similar crises in the future. Though considered a liberal program, it was not the same type of liberalism to which the intellectual magazines were accustomed because it elevated economic concerns over progressive morality and civil rights (Brinkley 1995; Gerstle 1994, 1044–45). The New Deal moved traditional liberal intellectuals to the center, between the laissez-faire capitalists on the right and the radicals on the left (Alterman and Mattson 2012, 13). The complicated politics of the Cold War era drove leftists and liberals further apart (Rossinow 2008, 8–9), and new magazines emerged to serve readers that no longer felt served by the old liberal periodicals.

COLD WAR PRESENTS NEW CHALLENGES

Dissent was among the new magazines that arose to challenge the prevalent ideas of American leftism. An intellectually disparate group helmed by Irving Howe and Lewis Coser began *Dissent* in 1954 "to provide, in a quarterly of limited circulation, a forum for the discussion of ideas and problems" (Howe 1969, 11). The magazine's editorial team merged socialists and other radicals seeking a fresh perspective into a fraternity dedicated to the tenets of democratic socialism. Because adherents of democratic socialism were few, *Dissent*'s circulation consistently hovered around 5,000 (Schuessler 2013). Nonetheless, the magazine's editors and contributors aimed for a broader influence. Their goal was to make radicalism more relevant to an intellectual community that had lapsed into political complacence due to a wave of postwar prosperity that suggested society's ills had been solved (Howe 1969, 11–12). Though the magazine targeted an elite audience, its criticisms of politics and culture were grounded in the everyday American experience. Therefore, in its infancy, *Dissent* asserted itself as both anticommunist and anti-McCarthyist, because its editors saw both as distractions from the concerns that were important to ordinary Americans (Reiner 2013, 757–58).

Another product of this period was a new kind of liberal magazine that emerged far from the New York intellectual center where *Dissent*, *The Nation*, and *The New Republic* resided. Published by the nonprofit Texas Democracy Foundation, the *Texas Observer* was founded in 1954 to discuss issues ignored or underreported in other media, expose injustice, and produce impactful journalism that changes lives for the better (*Texas Observer* n.d.). As former *Observer* editor and writer Molly Ivins noted on the magazine's fiftieth anniversary, Texas "is a peculiar place: it both deserves and needs an independent magazine devoted solely to its politics and other oddities" (Ivins 2004, xii). She hailed the *Observer*'s struggles for economic and political justice dating "back to the days when it was the only publication read by white people that addressed the problems and concerns of black and brown Texans" (Ivins 2004, xii). But the magazine was not just concerned with Texas. Early on, editor Ronnie Duggar made a plea for liberals to remember their commitment to personal liberty, averring, "We must test our system, not by whether we get to the moon, but by whether a man can freely and fully express himself here on Earth; not by whether we are ahead in weapons, but by whether we are ahead in real room to be free and alive . . . to be ourselves" (quoted in Moyers 2005).

Dissent and the *Texas Observer* ushered in a new era for leftist and left-leaning magazines, as new ideas flooded the landscape. Inspired by the British New Left movement, native Texan sociologist C. Wright Mills stirred an American New Left movement with an open letter originally published in the British journal *New Left Review* in 1960. Arguing that an international "young intelligentsia" had become the new engine of left-wing social change, Mills called for a shift away from the Old Left's labor focus toward other avenues of radical change (Geary 2008, 713). New Left activists—many of them collegians associated with Students for a Democratic Society (SDS)—took on civil rights, women's rights (including reproductive rights), gay rights, and drug policy reforms. They also protested against the Vietnam War. In the United States, new and existing magazines sought to engage adherents to the New Left movement with varying success. These potential readers' differing responses to *Dissent* and more radical periodicals exemplified the ideological split that plagued leftism at the time.

Dissent co-founder and eventual editor Michael Walzer drew influence from the British New Left movement, having associated with some of its adherents while studying at Oxford in the mid-1950s (Geary 2008, 716). However, *Dissent* failed to connect with New Left readers, in part because Howe supported the Vietnam War and argued that the SDS's views on democracy were Stalinist. Although many liberals opposed the Vietnam War, some—including Howe—believed the war was necessary to combat communism. Radicals like those in the New Left viewed opposition to the war as "a reactionary effort to stop the global forces of progress" (Rossinow 2008, 233). In labeling the New Left as too radical, Howe aligned himself with the Old Left. Eventually, the brand of socialism *Dissent* advocated became practically indistinguishable from traditional liberalism, leading some critics to call it by the epithet *Consent* (Reiner 2013, 757, 759–60). SDS leadership considered traditional liberals to be part of the "establishment" and called them "the most dangerous enemy we confront" (Rossinow 2008, 242).

The SDS had its own magazine: *Radical America*. Founded in 1967 by historians Paul and Mari Jo Buhle, the bimonthly journal at first was supported by the University of Wisconsin SDS chapter and distributed nationally through SDS groups. As the SDS crumbled in 1969, the magazine split from the organization and marketed itself strictly as an "American Left" magazine until its demise in 1999 (Brown University Library n.d.). Front matter in one of the earliest issues stated that the goals of the magazine were to educate SDS members about the country's radical traditions, provide a forum for students of American radicalism to exchange views, and shatter "the walls between 'activist' and 'intellectual' members of the New Left." It also promised to bridge the gap between the Old Left and New Left by publishing memoirs of and interviews with the former (*Radical America* 1967).

Radical America did not heed Wright's call to move away from labor as a focus; International Workers of the World board member Fred Thompson was an early contributor, and working-class issues were frequent topics. However, issues of race, gender, and sexuality were prominent as well. The Buhles dedicated the entire February 1970 issue to articles on women's liberation, under the direction of special editor Edith Hoshino Altbach. One essay focused on the plight of the middle-class woman who, though liberated on many other fronts, was the victim of archaic ideas about traditional family roles at home. These ideas were pervasive and reinforced by societal forces, leading the author to conclude, "It is clear that we are dealing with fundamental problems, which are not to be solved by slogans, by Congress, or under the leadership of Communist or Socialist parties." The problems only could be solved by a complete overhaul of societal practices (James 1970, 3–4).

READER-SUPPORTED JOURNALS
SURVIVE POLITICAL SHIFTS

Another magazine of the New Left, *In These Times* began publishing in 1976 as a national weekly newspaper out of Chicago. At that time, progressivism seemed to be on the rise again. The Vietnam era birthed protest movements that had "put hundreds of thousands of Americans into the streets" and "shaken the country to its core" (Hochschild 2001). At the same time, a sharp right turn in American politics threatened the success of leftist publications like *In These Times*. Founder James Weinstein noted on the magazine's twenty-fifth anniversary that the left "foundered and shriveled, leaving us to paddle furiously against the tide just to keep from being swept into oblivion." *In These Times* survived and continued its mission, which—similar to *Radical America*—was to inform New Left readers and give their movement direction (Weinstein 2002, xiv). As a nonprofit like the *Texas Observer*, the magazine thrived largely due to financial support from individual readers who found its contents valuable, as well as from sponsoring organizations and foundations. Craig Aaron's (2002) twenty-fifth-anniversary anthology of the magazine's articles demonstrates an emphasis on issues important to readers in the last quarter of the twentieth century: gender, race, ethnicity, sexuality, environmentalism, and nuclear dangers.

The same year that *In These Times* began, a new magazine named for Progressive-era writer Mary Harris "Mother" Jones was born. Like the *Texas Observer* and *In These Times*, *Mother Jones* was a nonprofit publication unbeholden to any political or business interests. Inspired equally by the protest atmosphere of the Vietnam era and the resurgence in investigative reporting brought about by the *Washington Post*'s Watergate coverage, a handful of journalists met in Paul Jacobs's San Francisco living room to plan the magazine. They sought to unleash their investigative prowess on the "great unelected power wielders" of their time: multinational corporations. Co-founder Adam Hochschild noted that investigative reporting on politicians was fashionable at the time, but no one had taken on corporations (Hochschild 2001). *Mother Jones*'s investigations had immediate results; a 1977 exposé on the explosive Pinto demonstrated that Ford knew the car was dangerous but sold it anyway. Mainstream media picked up the story, and although Ford initially dismissed it as untrue and attempted to undermine *Mother Jones*'s credibility, the company ultimately recalled 1.5 million Pintos for repairs (Hochschild 2001).

In addition to taking on corporate America, *Mother Jones* also was (and remains) a strong voice for social justice, including racial discrimination, women's rights, environmental justice, and the plight of immigrants. As the twentieth century drew to a close, *Mother Jones* boasted a global community of readers. In 1993, it became the first general-interest magazine to publish on the internet, not only taking dissenting points of view all over the world but also allowing people to communicate with each other (Hochschild 2001), much as readers of *Mother Earth* did in Emma Goldman's office.

Leftist magazines in the twentieth century were far from homogeneous. They varied in their degree of leftism as well as in their contents: from critical editorials, essays, and art to investigative journalism. They varied in the class of their intended audience, from an intellectual elite to the masses. And they varied in their appearance, from mimeographed sheets to glossy pages.

But they shared similar struggles, including bewildering ideological shifts, attacks from other ideological groups, financial burdens, and, in some cases, censorship. Most important, they shared an interest in correcting society's ills and creating a better life for their fellow men and women. Their impact can still be directly felt, as many still operate and have adapted to the digital landscape; even the tightly focused *Dissent* carries on, now as a nonprofit supported by readers who find its work important. These publications continue to reach audiences not only via the written word but also in podcasts and other multimedia productions, and they offer a forum for like-minded individuals to express themselves.

The legacy of fearless, independent journalism also lives in other publications that have adopted the nonprofit model. Finally, the spirit of leftism has carried on in new magazines of the twenty-first century such as *Jacobin*, whose founder aimed to combine the resolutely socialist politics of *Dissent* with the accessibility of *The Nation*—to be for socialists what *The New Republic* had been for liberals (Sunkara 2014).

REFERENCES

Adams, Ian. 2001. *Political Ideology Today*, 2nd ed. Manchester, UK: Manchester University Press.

Ayer, N. W. 1920. *N. W. Ayer & Son's American Newspaper Annual and Directory*. Philadelphia: N. W. Ayer & Son.

Alterman, Eric, and Kevin Mattson. 2012. *The Cause: The Fight for American Liberalism from Franklin Roosevelt to Barack Obama*. New York: Viking.

Aaron, Craig, ed. 2002. *Appeal to Reason: 25 Years In These Times*. New York: Seven Stories Press.

Bennion, Sherilyn Cox. 1971. "Reform Agitation in the American Periodical Press, 1920–1929." *Journalism Quarterly* 48 (4): 652–59, 713.

Blanchard, Margaret. 1992. *Revolutionary Sparks: Freedom of Expression in Modern America*. New York: Oxford University Press.

Brinkley, Alan. 1995. *The End of Reform: New Deal Liberalism in Recession and War*. New York: Knopf.

Brown University Library. n.d. "Radical America." Accessed July 30, 2019. https://library.brown.edu/cds/radicalamerica/about.html.

Christman, Henry M., ed. 1965. *One Hundred Years of The Nation: A Centennial Anthology*. New York: MacMillan Press.

Geary, Daniel. 2008. "'Becoming International Again': C. Wright Mills and the Emergence of a Global New Left, 1956–1962." *Journal of American History* 95 (3): 710–36.

Gerstle, Gary. 1994. "The Protean Character of American Liberalism." *American Historical Review* 99 (October): 1043–73.

Goldman, Emma. 1916. "The Social Aspects of Birth Control." *Mother Earth*, April.

———. 1934. *Living My Life*. Garden City, NY: Garden City Publishing.

Hochschild, Adam. 2001. "Mother Jones: The Magazine." *Mother Jones*, May/June. https://www.motherjones.com/about/history/.

Howe, Irving. 1969. "A Few Words About Dissent." In *Voices of Dissent: A Collection of Articles from Dissent Magazine*, 11–14. Freeport, NY: Books for Libraries Press.

Ivins, Molly. 2004. "Foreword." In *Fifty Years of the Texas Observer*, edited by Char Miller, xi–xv. San Antonio: Trinity University Press.

James, Selma. 1970. "The American Family: Decay and Rebirth." *Radical America*, February. Brown University Library Center for Digital Scholarship.

Kellogg, Flint. 2009. "Oswald Villard, the NAACP and The Nation." *The Nation*, July 2. https://www.thenation.com/article/oswald-villard-naacp-and-nation/.

Lumsden, Linda. 2014. *Black, White, and Red All Over: A Cultural History of the Radical Press in Its Heyday, 1900–1917*. Kent, OH: Kent State University Press.

McGerr, Michael. 2003. *A Fierce Discontent: The Rise and Fall of the Progressive Movement in America*. New York: Oxford University Press.

Moyers, Bill. 2005. "The Texas Observer at 50." *HuffPost*, November 21. https://www.huffpost.com/entry/the-texas-observer-at-50_b_10990.

Neale, Sylvia. 1941. "The Attitude and Possible Effect on Legislation of Four Liberal Magazines from 1914 to 1924 (*Outlook, Independent, Nation, New Republic*)." Master's thesis, University of Oregon.

"Objects of Charity." 1915. *The New Republic*, January 23.

O'Neill, William L. 1966. *Echoes of Revolt: The Masses, 1911–1917*. Chicago: Quadrangle Books.

Pribanic-Smith, Erika J., and Jared Schroeder. 2019. *Emma Goldman's No-Conscription League and the First Amendment*. New York: Routledge.

Radical America. 1967. Front matter, *Radical America*, September–October. Brown University Library Center for Digital Scholarship.

Reiner, J. Toby. 2013. "Toward an Overlapping Dissensus: The Search for Inclusivity in the Political Thought of Dissent Magazine." *Political Research Quarterly* 66 (4): 756–67.

Reitman, Ben L. 1917. "To the Postmaster: Excerpts from a Letter." *Mother Earth Bulletin*, October.

Rossinow, Doug. 2008. *Visions of Progress: The Left-Liberal Tradition in America*. Philadelphia: University of Pennsylvania Press.

Sayer, John. 1988. "Art and Politics, Dissent and Repression: The Masses Magazine versus the Government, 1917–1918." *American Journal of Legal History* 32 (1): 42–78.

Schlesinger Jr., Arthur. 1962. *The Politics of Hope*. Boston: Riverside Press.

Schuessler, Jennifer. 2013. "A Lion of the Left Wing Celebrates Six Decades." *New York Times*, October 27. https://www.nytimes.com/2013/10/28/arts/dissent-magazine-connects-with-younger-readers.html.

Seideman, David. 1986. *The New Republic: A Voice of Modern Liberalism*. New York: Praeger.

Shermis, S. Samuel, and James L. Barth. 1981. "Liberal Intellectual Journals and Their Functions in Shaping the Definition of Social Problems." *Indiana Social Studies Quarterly* 34 (1): 52–69.

Sunkara, Bhaskar. 2014. "Interview: Project Jacobin." *New Left Review*, November/December.

Texas Observer. n.d. "About the Texas Observer." Accessed August 14, 2019. https://www.texasobserver.org/about/.

Vanden Heuvel, Katrina, ed. 1990. *The Nation, 1865–1990: Selections from the Independent Magazine of Politics and Culture*. New York: Thunder's Mouth Press.

Wallace, James M. 1986. "A New Means for Liberals: Liberal Responses to Adult and Worker Education in the 1920s." *Labor Studies Journal* 11 (Spring): 26–41.

Weinstein, James. 2002. "Foreword." In *Appeal to Reason: 25 Years In These Times*, edited by Craig Aaron, xiii–xiv. New York: Seven Stories Press.

Chapter 3

"Things You Want to Keep"[1]

McSweeney's *and the Periodical as a Perennial Object*

Pablo Calvi

On March 8, 2018, at 11 a.m., inside a sun-drenched, one-story Renaissance Revival copper-roofed building in San Francisco, the rare book gallery PBA put on auction some 360 items as part of an eclectic catalog. Among the pieces were an 1882 author's edition of *Leaves of Grass*, signed by Walt Whitman; six 1930s volumes in French of the complete letters of Marcel Proust; a 1900 first edition of Jack London's debut novel, *The Son of the Wolf*; a signed limited edition of John Fante's *Ask the Dust*; and "Lot 172," which included the first thirteen issues of *Timothy McSweeney's Quarterly Concern*, the literary magazine started by writer Dave Eggers in 1998.

Although PBA (Pacific Book Auction), heir to Maurice Power's California Book Auction Galleries, is one of the most prestigious rare-book sellers and antiquarians in the Bay Area, Lot 172 was hardly an antique. Thirty to 140 years younger than some of the other items in the pool and, generally speaking, substantially more recent than items usually auctioned by PBA, Lot 172 sold for $960, matching and even beating the prices of some of its companions in the auction, while revealing the interest that *McSweeney's* already carries for collectors and archivists.

Eggers wasn't aware of that specific auction but, as an amateur collector himself, he conceded that the idea of creating a perennial object was one of the early forces behind *McSweeney's Quarterly Concern* and, later, *The Believer* (Eggers, 2020).

"I love antiquarian book fairs and whenever I've seen *Issue One* [of *McSweeney's*] at an antiquarian book fair behind glass, it's very gratifying . . . but that was the idea," Eggers said. "If you put enough into the design and craft of the book, maybe it will last and persist. And then if it persists, maybe the work inside will continue to be read. That was all in our philosophy."

The first four issues of *McSweeney's Quarterly Concern* were printed in Reykjavik, Iceland, and assembled in Eggers's Brooklyn kitchen—the same place he cooked breakfasts and dinners until he moved back to California. He wrote at length about his first experience as a magazine founder and editor in his multi-award-winning memoir *A Heartbreaking Work of Staggering Genius* (2000). *McSweeney's* predecessor, *Might Magazine*, had a sixteen-issue run between 1994 and 1997 and, for about three and a half years, Eggers and *Might* co-founders Marny Requa and David Moodie tried to break into the commercial magazine market.

> We thought with *Might* we had the chance to create a real, widely read, mass market magazine. [. . .] We thought we would grow to be like *Rolling Stone* had been in the '70s, so we sought advertising, and tried to play the distribution game. And we sat in countless meetings with media planners, trying to sell the magazine to liquor advertisers, beer advertisers, and I think it dawned on us rather quickly that we were not equipped to play that game that would require millions. (Eggers, 2020)

After *Might*, and partially as a reaction to the disappointment, Eggers took a different path with *McSweeney's*, which he launched as a quarterly journal in 1998 with only $2,500.

ORIGINS, CIRCULATION, AND THE SEARCH FOR A NEW READERSHIP

Unlike most legacy periodicals at the time, *McSweeney's* didn't circulate on newsstands. Its circulation was primarily based on subscriptions, along with some single-copy sales through its website, McSweeney's Internet Tendency (www.mcsweeneys.net), which offered daily and weekly content to solidify the quarterly's presence and attract new, younger readers. The other legs of the circulation strategy were a word-of-mouth promotional approach based on events (parties and happenings in New York or San Francisco) and bookstore sales.

> When we began, I carried boxes of the journal around New York myself, on the subway. I would hand-deliver to the first stores that took it—Community Bookstore on 7th Avenue in Brooklyn, St. Mark's Bookstore in the East Village,

and a handful of other stores. Eventually we began to work with distributors, who made the magazine available at small stores around the country. (Dave Eggers, interview follow-up email, August 2020)

The quarterly was designed to seem as close to a book—or a book-like object—as possible. "The quarterlies, magazines, and books are notably well-crafted," Daniel Worden (2006) writes in his essay about the journal.

Number One had the look of a nineteenth-century pamphlet, text heavy, in black and white, with a center-justified cover. It was, however, written colloquially, in a playful appeal to the readers. It quickly sold out, as did the subsequent ones with print runs of 5,000 and up to 7,500.

This playfulness soon contaminated the formatting and design and, after Number Four, the quarterly's print appearance started shifting and mutating with every new issue.

McSweeney's Quarterly Concern Number Four is a series of small novellas in a box, Number Six contains a soundtrack by They Might Be Giants to be listened to while reading, Number Sixteen contains a Robert Coover story printed on a deck of playing cards that can be shuffled and read in any order. *McSweeney's* interest in experimental form is evident in the *Quarterly Concern's* experimental designs as well as the variety of materials published. (Worden, 2006, p. 892)

"We had every writer you can think of sending us their work, from David Foster Wallace to George Saunders to Lydia Davis," Amanda Uhle, executive director of the magazine since 2018, notes (Uhle, 2020).

By choosing not to focus on advertising revenue or national distribution, Eggers and his team were able to cater to the aesthetic and editorial interests of a narrower audience that would treasure, collect, and consume *McSweeney's* slowly—digest it over time and then pass it along to others as a cultural object.

"It was a reaction against the design, the economics and the advertising model of mainstream magazines," Eggers said. Not only were the issues black-and-white, with "one font, no ads, no possibility of a profit" (Eggers, 2020), they also initially published only pieces that were rejected by other magazines. Eggers regarded his publication as the literary equivalent of the *Salon des Refusés*, the "exhibition rejects." The term refers specifically to the Paris Salon of 1863, whose "rejects" included work by Johan Jongkind, Gustave Courbet, Camille Pissarro, and, notably, Édouard Manet's *Déjeuner sur l'herbe*.

McSweeney's was not simply intended as a commodity or consumable product to be read and discarded; just like a book, both in presentation and distribution, the quarterly was meant to be received by its readers as a present and a gift (Hamilton, 2010). By focusing on making *McSweeney's* something to be read, reread, kept, and passed along, Eggers leveraged the journal into a different sphere of circulation making it a collectible. In this way, *McSweeney's* distanced itself from magazines with related content and ideas, like *Harper's* or *The New Yorker*. Rather, according to Amy Hungerford "McSweeney's is in the business of human connection" (2012, p. 665).

THE LATTICE

Traditional "Letters to the Editor" sections in magazines print readers' correspondence, including complaints, concerns, or clarifications relative to an article or a topic published in a prior issue of that same publication. *McSweeney's* repurposed and reimagined the section as both a humoristic space and a connections forum, running a combination of letters from readers and commissioned letters from writers.

One letter reprinted in the first *Better of McSweeney's* collection requested that "the magazine facilitate Lynne Tillman's reconnection with a former lover" (Hungerford, 2012, p. 654). In Number 38 (2011), Peter Orner addresses a letter in this section to his then-fifteen-month-old daughter, Phoebe, from a convent in Peosta, Iowa, where he sequestered himself to finish a book "I know I will never finish" (McSweeney's 38, 2011, p. 12). In the same issue, the editor published four short letters from humorist Jen Statsky (McSweeney's 38, 2011, pp. 6, 8, 11, 13) asking someone on the editorial team to check whether the magazine had ever published an interview with Helen Hunt in which she revealed her grandmother's coconut macaroon recipe (or perhaps the interview was published in *Redbook*, she wonders).

That same approach to human and physical interconnectedness—aesthetic as well as physical—resonates in the metaphor that *McSweeney's* (and *Might* before it) utilized to define relations that allow not only for the magazine to exist but especially for its contributors and readers to become a social unit: the *lattice*.

In his memoir, Eggers explains the use of this figure as part of a generational image:

> The lattice is the connective tissue. The lattice is everyone else, the lattice is my people, collective youth, people like me, hearts ripe, brains aglow. . . . I see us as one, as a vast matrix, an army, a whole, each one of us responsible to one another, because no one else is. . . . all these people, the people who come to us or we come to, the subscribers, our friends, their friends, their friends, who knows who knows who . . . So people, the connections between people, the

people you know, become sort of lattice, and the more people, good people . . . the wider and stronger the lattice. (Eggers, 2000, p. 211–12)

Eggers made a first attempt to structure his lattice at *Might*, but he was only able to perfect it with *McSweeney's*, by connecting writers in different moments of their careers with artists and readers.

"Most of the writers in the first few issues were people I'd met in San Francisco and New York," Eggers noted. "Some of them we'd published in *Might* magazine back in the mid-90s (David Foster Wallace, for instance). As you know, the world of writers in a given city is very small. Within a few months, it's hard not to bump into a slew of writers—especially those around your own age."

For the first issue of *McSweeney's*, Eggers also had some help from Sean Wilsey and Lawrence Weschler, who connected him with the work of more established writers. "After the first issue, though, it wasn't too hard finding good work to publish—it was coming through the mail every day. The lesson is that good writing always needs a good home," Eggers said.

This mishmash of up-and-coming and well-established names representing that original idea of a lattice came vividly to fruition in *McSweeney's* Number Four. Added to the work of well-established authors such as Jonathan Lethem, Haruki Murakami, and George Saunders, the magazine published stories by up-and-coming Rachel Cohen and Sheila Heti. Many of these authors, famous and not, shared what Judith Shulevitz (2001) calls a "minor key" satirical voice.

The connections and associations created at *McSweeney's*, the magazine, were also fostered by the pedagogical work stemming from other areas of *McSweeney's* as a company, which grew to include a series of parallel and somewhat related projects, including 826, a network of innovative and engaging writing tutor centers, and "Voice of Witness," a book and education series promoting human rights by amplifying stories of people affected by injustice.

As a graphic, ornamental pattern, and as a physical reference to the world of architecture and construction, the lattice (symmetrical wood or metal strips crossed and fastened together forming squares or diamond spaces in between) is also Eggers's special metaphorical choice to describe a type of horizontal social bonding.

> By producing links between individual readers on the basis of the alleged similarities between them, the editorial staff of *McSweeney's* boosts readers' identification with the virtual community of the magazine, which in turn, and like the myth of Timothy McSweeney, helps to build loyalty to the brand McSweeney's. (Bollen, Craps, and Vermeulen, 2013, p. 8)

In that sense, *McSweeney's* became a collective. So much so that, in 2001, when Shulevitz wondered whether any individual author published by the journal would be able to stand on their own, her answer was an unequivocal no.

It is paradoxical that interconnectedness became the paramount reference for the digital world that was also growing in San Francisco during those years. Unlike the lattice, though, the digital network was an abstract entity, removed from the physicality of the world.

The approach differential between both metaphors is revealed starkly by the rhetoric that accompanied the consolidation of the e-book, embodied in the emergence of the Kindle reader in November 2007. With its "The King is dead, long live the King"-sounding slogan: "The Book Lives On," Kindle heralded a new era of reading, consolidated with its "Books in 60 Seconds" from 2011. Reading and knowledge were moving into a nonphysical arena of ubiquitous existence and seamless, immediate circulation.

It is almost paradoxical that, looking back a quarter century since the first digital boom in Silicon Valley, *McSweeney's* physical, objectual nature and Eggers's circulation strategy (by subscription, individual sales through the website, and a few community bookstores) positioned the journal as the extreme opposite of Kindle and allowed it to endure the prevailing digitization of cultural objects and production.

In that sense, as a traditional printed object, *McSweeney's* can be seen as the flip side of the coin of the digital economy of knowledge. It was a stubborn, beautiful remnant that persisted during a time when physical bookstores started to cave under the pressure of digital distribution. As an object, *McSweeney's* was the physical rock in the virtual shoe of the e-book: slow, attention seeking, and durable. Eggers himself was concerned that e-books would eliminate physical books the way music streaming eliminated CDs, but he believed that if the physical magazine was beautiful enough, readers would continue to subscribe.

"To download the stuff was a crime compared to owning the tactile, luxurious physical object," Eggers said. "E-books are incredibly ugly. They have terrible design, they are crude, the books look terrible on the screen, and I'm a snob when it comes to type and design. I cannot stand the experience of looking at, reading a book on a screen" (Eggers, 2020).

Literary critic George Steiner discussed in his 1986 essay "Real Presences" an alternative mode to capitalistic consumption which, he argued, depletes the relationship between subject and object from its divinity. Steiner proposed a connection based on what he called "digestion," a dynamic in which access to the object requires the development and finessing of a certain skill, which is ultimately rewarding as the ability is mastered. A piano can be both a luxury object, consumed as a commodity, or an instrument mastered through the process of learning to play it, which ultimately allows for the achievement of a higher purpose, that of making music.

During the 2019 fires in Sonoma County, one of *McSweeney's* readers lost his entire collection—57 issues of the magazine—to the flames. Eggers and some of the staff helped him put it back together, regarding it as a "legacy collection" or heirloom to be passed along to his heirs (Eggers, 2020).

Figure 3.1 Issue 4 was presented as a white box featuring a robin with human arms and wooden boards as feet, with fourteen booklets inside. Courtesy of *McSweeney's*.

The Formatting

Starting with its first issues, *McSweeney's* aimed at separating itself from the look and feel of mass-market magazines. After his nine-month stint at *Esquire*, Eggers was determined to create a different experience for both readers and contributors. He based it on the design and voice of *Greenwich Street*, *Conjunctions*, and the *Paris Review,* but also eighteenth-century pamphlets. "The look of them . . . how the covers were very text-heavy and very personal, and sort of intimate in the way they were exhorting the reader." Eggers liked the old pamphlets' "exhortations, you know: 'Dear reader, here you have before you the greatest of all journals . . .' . . . kind of overzealous, and unintentionally comic intimate exhortation. But in terms of the interior we were trying to make it really distinct" (Dave Eggers, interview, February 2020).

And although the voice and the content direction had been present since Issue 1, it wasn't until *Issue 4* that formatting became a radical tool that allowed *McSweeney's* to swim against the stream of mass-market appeal.

Unlike the first three issues, which were published as single volumes, Issue 4 was presented as a white box with a color-illustrated cover featuring a robin with human arms instead of hands and wooden boards as feet. The box opened with a flap lid, and included fourteen booklets inside: a "Notes and Background" booklet, which serves as the "Editor's Note" to the volume, and thirteen individual notebooks with one story each. Each had a color cover and unique illustrations, selected or produced by their authors, in compliance with "The Author's and Book Enjoyer's Bill of Rights, at Least Insofar as the Book Jacket is Concerned." The manifesto, which discusses the input authors should have on their own book covers, is included in the second part of the first booklet, and lists thirty-two items and one sub-item (the last one is 31a) proclaiming the author's right to "guide the book cover creation process as much as she or he wishes. Or, if need be, control it completely" (*McSweeney's* No. 4, Late Winter, 2000).

McSweeney's printer for issue No. 1, Oddi, was based in Iceland. The island, which has no forests and cannot produce its own paper, had only two box-makers capable of manufacturing an object like the one Issue 4 required. Both the printer and the box-maker initially refused to produce the issue, complaining that the design was impossible to execute. But at Eggers's insistence both the printer and box-maker decided to get on board (Bollen, Craps, and Vermeulen, 2013, p. 4). "McSweeney's, at the start, was to be a sort of *refusalon*—a home for stories no one else wanted—so printing the magazine in Iceland made a certain amount of sense. I liked the sheer absurdity of it, and wanted badly to see Iceland myself," Eggers said (Eggers, 2020).

This was part of the decision he had made to "elevate" the *McSweeney's* design to the level of a collectible object.

> I always had been interested in "magazine as object," and when we started printing *McSweeney's* in Iceland, the printer was so good that they improved everything I did, and the object itself . . . and I give credit to them as the printer for choosing the materials. . . . I just enjoyed the process of winging that thing at them each time, and thinking about . . . well, what hasn't been done before, so that's been the goal ever since, and now we are on issue 57, and every few issues we try to come up with an object that has never existed and a format that has never existed before. (Dave Eggers, interview, February 2020)

The editorial rationale behind McSweeney's Issue 4 is expressed most clearly in the booklet "Notes and Background and Clarifying Charts and Some Complaining," which serves as a long editorial piece. It anticipates in tone and delivery Eggers's *A Heartbreaking Work of Staggering Genius*, with the same intimate and almost confessional stream of consciousness approach. The piece addresses head-on *McSweeney's* ideological separation from the world of the mass market discussing two ideas: the centrality of the literary artifact as an aesthetic object; and the desired new form of connection—fluid and horizontal—between publisher, authors, and readers (Bollen, Craps, and Vermeulen, 2013, pp. 3–4).

The Horizontal Voice

In more than one way, *McSweeney's* is a magazine for writers. That is, it presents itself as such in the editorial letters and is expected to be treated as such by its readers and writers. For *McSweeney's*, readers are also potential contributors.

The publication put in place two devices so anyone reading *McSweeney's* would assume that they could also write for the publication. These devices emphasized a horizontal connection between readers, authors, and publisher. This horizontal line was structurally emplaced by the letters section and reinforced by the magazine's voice at large.

In the No. 4 "Notes and Background" section, in the first of the fourteen booklets, the first page displays two textual exhortations to the reader, the first one about subscriptions and the second one about submission guidelines:

> SUBSCRIPTIONS are yours for the having, without condition or license—but requiring certain agreements (see card [the "Subscriber Agreement"] elsewhere in box)—and are now $36 for four issues. Yes, the price is ever-rising. First $20, then $28, then $30, now $36 . . . it's a bit like the Post Office. Oh, the Post

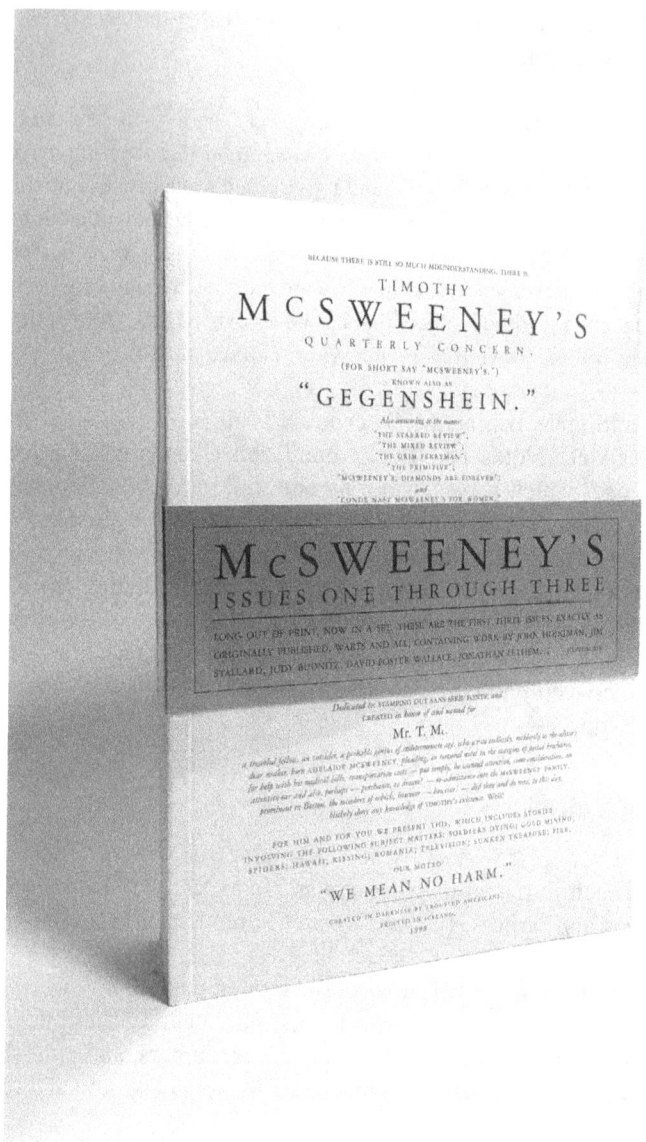

Figure 3.2 The first four issues of *McSweeney's Quarterly Concern* were printed in Reykjavik, Iceland, and assembled in Eggers's Brooklyn kitchen, then hand-delivered to local bookstores. Courtesy of *McSweeney's*.

Office. Oh. The reason for the price increase is fairly self-evident, and we hope you understand. From you we expect tolerance and understanding, for we knew your parents and know your children, and will be watching your movements closely. (*McSweeney's* No. 4, Late Winter, 2000)

The passage appeals to the reader in the second person, assumes the reader understands the reasons for the price increase, and points—albeit jokingly—at connections and networks of acquaintance.

Following the graph about subscriptions, there is one about submissions. The contiguity of these exhortations seems to imply that both statements are basically addressed to the same people. In fact, at least anecdotally, subscribers have in fact become part of *McSweeney's* roster of writers. But there's another, more oblique reference in the appeal for submissions:

SUBJECT MATTERS ENCOURAGED FOR SUBMITTERS OF SUBMISSIONS (use of one or more of these subject matters will endear you and your writing to our editors): Caves; balloons; balloons stuck in caves, and unhappy about it; balloons living in caves, and feeling good about it; large trees with people living in them; wind; gold; talking animals who only speak Spanish; men who live in caves; women who live in caves; chairs that are too big; houses that are too big; holes that people fall into; volcanoes; things that are round but flat; things that are small but emit loud noises; clouds that appear in bedrooms, over beds, during sleep; waterfoxes, landwhales, and/or riverkittens; planets covered with yellow water (if need be, you may substitute violet); old men who run very fast; old men with two-by-fours for feet; birds with arms instead of wings; people with very long fingers, the bones of which are too brittle to use; how things are made in factories; how things are made in factories in Africa; how things were made in factories in Africa between 1939–1945; giant people who carry small purses; small people who drag from place to place large knapsacks full of pillows; anything at all about the ocean monkeys of the former Upper Volta; anything at all about the Hand People of Franz Josephland; anything about the furry, self-propelling rocks of the Dakotas; anything at all about anyone named Lucy, Isabelle, Paulina, Geoffrey, or Will; anything mentioning the pre-1990 Jonathan Pryce or (tastefully) incorporating former Congressman Fred Grandy; and anything at all about the Swamp People of Lourdes. (*McSweeney's* No. 4, Late Winter, 2000)

Again, the language and phrasing imply horizontality and familiarity with the reader/writer, and a common sphere of shared knowledge. Bollen, Craps, and Vermeulen (2013, p. 6) suggest that the lack of hierarchy anchors an "anything goes" attitude toward literary topics and subject matters, but more importantly points in the direction of a certain intellectual quirkiness and a mocking self-referential quality that Eggers demands from the potential contributors to the magazine. However, that seemingly "anything goes" approach resembles a specific Jorge Luis Borges take on language and mimics his style of random enumerations in *The Universal History of Infamy* (1935) but specifically in the short story "The Analytical Language of John Wilkins."

As Eggers himself explained:

> I was going through a Borges, *Bartleby* and *Pale Fire* period I guess, so there was a lot of playfulness with the format. . . . I was trying to break the barrier between the reader and publisher. I was trying to have fun with that relationship a little bit. Keep it intimate and personal as opposed to aloof and professional. [. . .] To allow ourselves to speak directly, and also be reachable, and approachable, as opposed to, you know, on the tenth floor on a building on Fifth Avenue, Midtown Manhattan, that kind of a thing. To me it seemed that the professional sort of distance defeated the whole purpose of the enterprise. So being able to run it out of my apartment on Ninth Street, have people ring the doorbell to pick up their magazine, just brought it all back to what I'd been trying in the first place. (Dave Eggers, interview, February 2020)

The playfulness in the style not only delivers that proximity but also signals a few Borges passages from the early 1930s, a time when, as I have argued elsewhere (Calvi, 2019, 2015), the Argentine author flirted with a form of early mass-media populism. Borges wrote in the preface to the 1935 edition of *The Universal History of Infamy* that "good readers are even blacker and rarer swans than good writers" (Borges, 1999, p. 16).

The lack of hierarchy in the enumerations and lists, in that vein, appeals to a dual allegiance: an "anything goes" attitude, but also a direct reference to high literature and a canon that opens to both the mass media and to these black swans, the readers-writers of the hyperconnected late twentieth century.

CONCLUSIONS

In many ways, *McSweeney's Quarterly Concern* distanced itself from mass-market magazines and fast consumerism. Its approach started with a specific type of content (whatever, and whoever, wasn't receiving central attention in the mass-circulation spheres), mocking the processes of canonization of wider circulation magazines, and evolved into a visual and physical presentation that allowed the journal to endure as a singular, collectible, and desirable object. Still in publication today, this ethos continues to be tightly associated with *McSweeney's*.

Fast Company declared McSweeney's one of 2012's ten most innovative companies in media, and, to an extent, the journal championed a style and a format that opposed mainstream ideas at the dawn of the digital economy. This owes to *McSweeney's* objectuality, which turned the magazine into a coveted collector's item, to be preserved and treasured rather than consumed and discarded, an aura that Eggers himself meticulously conceived for his publication.

"The magazine does not so much reject commercial publishers' interest in economic gain as their lack of attention to graphic design and the aesthetic qualities of literary artifacts," Bollen, Craps, and Vermeulen argue (2013, p. 6). That skepticism about mass markets and common-ground ideas about circulation, the economy, and the publishing world consolidated *McSweeney's*' voice and made it the groundbreaking company it became, allowing it to face the most radical of digital trends, and move into the twenty-first century with the full force of the analog world.

REFERENCES

Amsden, David. 2005. "The Believer." *Salon*, March 9. https://www.salon.com/2005/03/09/eggers_37, last accessed February 29, 2020.

Bex, Sean. 2016. *Dave Eggers and Human Rights Culture*. Doctoral dissertation. Universiteit Gent.

Bex, Sean, and Craps, Stef. 2015. "An Interview with Dave Eggers and Mimi Lok." *Contemporary Literature*, Vol. 56, No. 4, pp. 544–67.

Bollen, Katrien, Craps, Stef, and Vermeulen, Pieter. 2013. "McSweeney's and the Challenges of the Marketplace for Independent Publishing." *Comparative Literature and Culture* Vol. 15, No. 4.

Borges, Jorge Luis. 1993. "The Universal Language of John Wilkins." Other inquisitions 1937–1952. Austin: University of Texas Press.

Calvi, Pablo. 2019. *Latin American Adventures in Literary Journalism*. Pittsburgh: University of Pittsburgh Press.

———. 2015. "From Journalism to Literature: Borges, Crítica and the Universal History of Infamy as an Experiment in Democratic Dialogue." *Australian Journalism Review*, Vol. 37, No. 2 (December 2015), pp. 109–21.

Crespo, Charles. 2013. *The McSweeney's Group: Modernist Roots and Contemporary Permutations in Little Magazines*. Doctoral dissertation. Florida International University. FIU Digital Commons.

Eggers, Dave. 2000. *A Heartbreaking Work of Staggering Genius*. New York: Simon & Schuster.

———. 2001. "Clarification." *McSweeney's*, February 14. web.archive.org/web/20010331103856/www.mcsweeneys.net/news/clar_nytimes.html, last accessed February 29, 2020.

———. 2020. Interview with author. January 31. Follow-up emails from February 25 and August 18.

Fitzgerald, Mary. 2009. "The United States of McSweeney's: Ten Years of Accidental Classics." *The New Statesman*, October 22. https://www.newstatesman.com/books/2009/10/american-mcsweeney-short last accessed, February 29, 2020.

Hamilton, Caroline. *One Man Zeitgeist: Dave Eggers, Publishing and Publicity*. New York: Continuum, 2010.

Heater, Brian, and Ha, Anthony. 2017. "A Decade of Amazon Kindle." *TechCrunch*, November 19, 2017. https://techcrunch.com/2017/11/19/a-decade-of-amazon-kindle/, last accessed February 29, 2020.

Hudes, Karen. 1997. "Magazines: 'Might' Has Fallen, But Not Without Leaving Its Mark: The Story of an Indie Magazine That Never Should Have Made It, But Almost Could Have, Then Didn't." *AdAge*, October 27. https://adage.com/article/news/magazines-fallen-leaving-mark-story-indie-magazine-made/70340, last accessed February 29, 2020.

Hungerford, Amy. 2012. "McSweeney's and the School of Life." *Contemporary Literature* Vol. 53, No. 4.

Kirkpatrick, David D. 2001. "Ambivalent Writer Turns His Memoir Upside Down; Denouncing Profits and Publishers While Profiting from Publication." *New York Times*, February 14. https://www.nytimes.com/2001/02/14/books/ambivalent-writer-turns-his-memoir-upside-down-denouncing-profits-publishers.html, last accessed February 29, 2020.

Kurowski, Travis. 2008a. "An Oral History of the Literary Magazine: 1953–Present." *Mississippi Review*, Vol. 36, No. 3, Literary Magazines (Fall 2008), pp. 212–17. University of Southern Mississippi.

———. 2008b. "Some Notes on the History of the Literary Magazine: 1953–Present." *Mississippi Review*, Vol. 36, No. 3, Literary Magazines (Fall 2008), pp. 231–43. University of Southern Mississippi.

McSweeney's Quarterly Concern. Number 4. Late Winter, 2000.

———. Number 23. 2007.

———. Number 38. 2011.

———. Number 46. 2014.

Rao, Leena. 2011. "New Amazon Kindle Commercial: 'The Book Lives On'." *TechCrunch*, February 21. https://techcrunch.com/2011/02/21/new-amazon-kindle-commercial-the-book-lives-on/, last accessed February 29, 2020.

Scott, Anthony O. 2005. "Among the Believers." *The New York Times Magazine*. September 11. https://www.nytimes.com/2005/09/11/magazine/among-the-believers.html, last accessed February 29, 2020.

Shulevitz, Judith. 2001. "Too Cool for Words." *The New York Times Books*, May 6. https://archive.nytimes.com/www.nytimes.com/books/01/05/06/bookend/bookend.html?_r=2&oref=login&oref=slogin, last accessed February 29, 2020.

Starre, Alexander. 2010. "'Little Heavy Papery Beautiful Things': McSweeney's, Metamediality, and the Rejuvenation of the Book in the USA." *Writing Technologies*, Vol. 3, pp. 25–41.

Stevens, Ashley. 2020. "Dave Eggers on Trump and the Perception of Truth in Unscripted Lies." *Salon*, January 21. https://www.salon.com/2020/01/21/dave-eggers-trump-captain-and-the-glory-interview/, last accessed February 29, 2020.

Uhle, Deborah. 2020. Interview with the author. February 25.

Worden, Daniel. 2006. "The Shameful Art: McSweeney's Quarterly Concern, Comics and the Politics of Affect." *MFS Modern Fiction Studies*, Vol. 52, No. 4 (Winter 2006), pp. 891–917.

Chapter 4

1960s American Folk Music Magazines

Counter-Hegemonic Voices of Social Transformation

Krystyna Henke

The American folk music revival of the late 1950s and early 1960s spawned a number of independently published folk music magazines that subverted the standard notions of what constituted a magazine's purpose and success. Unreliant on advertising and distributed informally, these folk music magazines were youth-driven, ragged in form, and provocative in content (Duncombe 1997). Often, like folk music itself, these publications engaged with current affairs.

Within this cultural niche, the revival also fostered the emergence of glossy, mainstream folk music publications, revealing the tension at large between those actively challenging the status quo and those upholding the established social conditions. Predominantly based in New York City—the heart of the urban folk music revival—these magazines and their readers responded to and reflected the times.

Folk musicians and their fans did not always have a progressive social agenda. Some folk music magazines advanced the notion of folk music as an apolitical art; others aimed for commercial success. Still, the category as a whole was more aligned with advocacy magazines than with other special interest magazines, like those focusing on sports, gardening, or carpentry. Although a rise in leisurely pursuits among a comfortable middle class in the decades after the Second World War had created a market for magazines that fed off and fostered such interests (Abrahamson 1996, 33), folk music magazines mostly avoided corporate interests in favor of advancing critiques of social problems.

During this time, the image and role of the folk singer were most distinctly personified by the iconic musician/activist Pete Seeger. But there were others who sang songs to advocate for change. The Freedom Singers effectively used protest songs during the fight for civil rights in the 1960s (Johnson Reagon 1983), much like the singing union workers who played a crucial role in boosting the labor movement in the early part of the twentieth century (Bierman 2013). A community feeling quickly developed, as the songs they sang were easy to learn and reminiscent of stirring hymns and popular songs. Linked by a common cause, like shared hardship, even those not directly affected by the circumstances they sang about would bond over the communal spirit of folk songs.

Operating as platforms and taste culture influencers, folk music magazines variously included or excluded, as well as encouraged or criticized folk singers for how and what they sang, ultimately underscoring the magazines' hegemonic or counter-hegemonic positions.

SONGS AS STORIES

Folk songs themselves often fulfilled a journalistic function. Among them were the "topical songs," which were used to spread news and information, embodying the "song as living newspaper" (Dunson 1965, 20). This was exemplified in Pete Seeger's 1958 and 1961 *Gazette* albums.

One of the topical songs performed by Seeger in his *Gazette, Vol. 1* album is "The Banks of Marble," originally written by apple farmer and farmers union president Les Rice around 1948 at a time of high unemployment during the first postwar U.S. recession. When Seeger's album was produced ten years later, the United States was facing another economic recession, with millions of people unemployed. The contrast of institutional wealth and the worries of the worker, now jobless, was again a concern, as these lyrics from "The Banks of Marble" illustrate:

I saw the weary farmer
Plowing sod and loam
I heard the auction hammer
A knocking down his home

But the banks are made of marble
With a guard at every door
And the vaults are stuffed with silver
That the farmer sweated for

I saw the seaman standing
Idly by the shore

> I heard the bosses saying
> Got no work for you no more
>
> But the banks are made of marble
> With a guard at every door
> And the vaults are stuffed with silver
> That the seaman sweated for (lines 5–20)

The folk singer as journalist was a function also advocated by singer-songwriter Phil Ochs, who combined what he had learned as a journalism major with folk music (Eliot 1989). *All the News That's Fit to Sing*, his 1964 debut album, consisted of topical songs, compositions that were directly informed by the news of the day.

"The Ballad of William Worthy," one of the songs written by Ochs on that album, is an example of Ochs creating and performing a folksong to comment on and highlight the news. In 1962, American newspapers reported on the troubles of African American foreign correspondent William Worthy, whom a federal grand jury had indicted for returning to the United States without a passport from Cuba. Worthy had interviewed Fidel Castro, and Worthy's favorable reporting on race relations in that country, his defiance of a travel ban to Cuba, his civil rights activism, along with his critical reporting of U.S. Cold War policies, made him into a lightning rod among American authorities.

Previously, the U.S. State Department had revoked Worthy's right to a passport, after he traveled to mainland communist China to do some reporting. Sentenced to prison for a supposedly illegal entry into the United States, Worthy, who as a journalist had been a Neiman Fellow at Harvard, had many supporters. Phil Ochs was one of them. Music and lyrics of "The Ballad of William Worthy" were published in March 1963 in the folk music magazine *Broadside*'s issue 22:

> Well, it's of a bold reporter whose story I will tell
> He went down to the Cuban land, the nearest place to hell
> He'd been there many times before, but now the law does say
> The only way to Cuba is with the CIA
> William Worthy isn't worthy to enter our door
> Went down to Cuba, he's not American anymore
> But somehow it is strange to hear the State Department say
> You are living in the free world, in the free world you must stay (lines 1–8)

In that same issue of *Broadside*, Ochs wrote an article explaining the need for topical songs:

Before the days of television and mass media, the folksinger was often a traveling newspaper spreading news through music. [. . .] Topical music is often a method of keeping alive a name or event that is worth remembering. [. . .] Every newspaper headline is a potential song, and it is the role of an effective songwriter to pick out the material that has the interest, significance and sometimes humor adaptable to music. (Ochs 1963b, 7–8)

Tom Paxton's album *Ain't That News!* was released in 1965. A review in the folk music magazine *Sing Out!* praised the songs on this album for their relevance to current affairs, "As songs of the moment, as passionate broadsides with a humanitarian point of view" (Silber 1966, 68).

Broadside, meanwhile, published music and lyrics of the title song of Paxton's album *Ain't That News!* in its December 20, 1964, issue 53. The song reflected the poor person's struggles against those with more money and power:

> In a hazard they're meeting at night
> Organizing, and doing it right
> And planning for a hell of a fight
> And they sure don't aim to lose
> In New York the tenants said no
> The slumlord ain't getting our dough
> They're fed up and I want you to know
> That's the very best kind of news
>
> And that's news, news, ain't that news?
> Ain't that something to see?
> News, news, you talk about your news
> It's mighty good news to me (lines 25–36)

Another topical song written and performed by Paxton on that album, titled "Lyndon Johnson Told the Nation," addressed the Vietnam War raging at the time, as well as the U.S. president's role in sending young men into military service to fight in a war that the public opposed and that Johnson escalated in 1965, the year the album was released:

> I got a letter from L. B. J.
> It said this is your lucky day.
> It's time to put your khaki trousers on.
> Though it may seem very queer.
> We've got no jobs to give you here.
> So we are sending you to Viet Nam.

Lyndon Johnson told the nation,
"Have no fear of escalation.
I am trying everyone to please.
Though it isn't really war,
We're sending fifty thousand more,
To help save Viet Nam from Viet Namese. (lines 1–12)

The song expressed the anxiety that many felt about the military draft. It also spoke about war as a make-work project, about a deceptive U.S. president, and about war as an absurd intervention. *Broadside*'s October 15, 1965, issue 63 mentioned the release of Paxton's *Ain't That News!* album in the magazine's "Notes" section along with announcements about other folk musicians' antiwar songs. In "Notes," coeditor Gordon Friesen noted that several of Paxton's songs on that album had been published in *Broadside*, including "We Didn't Know," "The Willing Conscript," "Goodman, Schwerner and Chaney," "Bottle of Wine," and "Georgie on the Freeway." Presciently, Friesen (1965) recognized the historical significance of these songs as a reflection of current affairs: "BROADSIDE will be studied seriously by scholars a hundred years from now looking for how things really were in the 1960's [sic]" (13).

CONDUITS FOR CRITIQUE

The concept of folk songs as a conduit for critique and change in an unjust society lay at the core of *Sing Out!* and *Broadside*, two related and highly influential folk music magazines. They were among the clearest examples of a counter-hegemonic approach in folk music magazines during the 1960s folk boom (Cohen 2002). Both publications were the brainchild of Pete Seeger, "generated by the people performing the music" (Dunson 2019) and established as much for fellow folk musicians as for nonmusicians with an interest in folk music.

Sing Out! had its roots in the *People's Songs Bulletin*, a quarterly publication of People's Songs, an organization Seeger cofounded in 1945 to "create, promote, and distribute songs of labor and the American people" (People's Songs Inc. 1945, 1). The *Bulletin* contained articles along with traditional and new songs meant to support various causes. Consisting of only four mimeographed pages, the *Bulletin*'s eight-by-ten format allowed recipients to fold it up and carry it with them in their back pocket or in a guitar case.

Folk musician Barbara Dane recalls seeing injured soldiers return to her Detroit neighborhood after World War II, where they faced rampant unemployment and racism. She looked to *The People's Songs Bulletin* for songs that she could learn and perform to make their plight heard: "I read it [the *Bulletin*] every which way, front and back and sideways and basically learned everything I knew from it that I was going to be doing. I learned the union songs that were there and the different histories of things" (Dane 2019). Dane called the *Bulletin* "a guide, with the tools, the inspiration" to connect people with each other and provide a common repertoire they could sing at rallies and protests. The continuity from old, traditional songs in a new, contemporary setting made people "feel the connection with an ongoing struggle" (Dane 2019).

When the *Bulletin* ceased publication in 1950 due to monetary challenges, *Sing Out!* was launched with a similar purpose: to support organizing and uniting workers for political and economic change and also to express labor grievances through collectively performed protest songs (Reuss and Reuss 2000). *Sing Out!* was nationally distributed, initially quarterly, then bimonthly. At its height, in 1965, a 100-page copy cost 75 cents, and its circulation was 25,000, making it the largest and eventually the longest-running independent folk music magazine. (It folded in 2014.)

Each issue of *Sing Out!* featured the music and lyrics of new and traditional songs, photographs, and in-depth articles, including interviews with musicians. Pete Seeger had a regular column, as did Izzy (Israel) Young, the owner of the Folklore Center, a store, concert venue, and meeting place for anything folk-related in New York City's artsy Greenwich Village neighborhood (Barretta 2013). Classified ads, a missing person announcement, letters, and brief reviews of new releases added a feeling of community to the publication. Over time, subscriptions to the magazine increased, attracting the attention of advertisers, including record companies, instrument makers and dealers, and other folk music magazines.

Sing Out!'s editor, Irwin Silber, was a member of the Communist Party until 1955, and even after that, continued to be a Marxist and a radical (Reuss 1975). This ideological kinship was not unusual among folk music enthusiasts before and after the war, fueling suspicion among some conservatives that folk music practitioners were subversive communists (Noebel 1974). Silber's political orientation was a source of contention among colleagues and readers of *Sing Out!* and while the legacy of *The People's Songs Bulletin* initially informed the overall character of *Sing Out!*, eventually letters from readers made clear that some subscribers were interested in music only and didn't care about labor conditions or political action for social transformation. Pressure arose that content in *Sing Out!* should reflect such attitudes as well, sparking disagreements within the editorial team over what to publish.

One such controversy erupted around Silber's "An Open Letter to Bob Dylan," published in *Sing Out!* in 1964. Silber criticized Dylan's transformation from a young folk singer concerned about social inequities to a celebrity preoccupied with existential angst and besieged by fans, and warned that "the American Success Machinery chews up geniuses at a rate of one a day and still hungers for more" (Silber 1964, 23). Readers wrote letters in response, expressing variously their support and dismay that Silber had publicly put Dylan's "notoriety, fast money, and status" on the spot (23). Ironically, Silber himself was straddling the fence between commercial mass appeal and left-wing grassroots ideology with *Sing Out!* as he sought to increase readership.

In the 1967 August/September issue, Silber announced a new chapter for *Sing Out!* Folk musician Happy Traum took over as the magazine's managing editor, and Silber left to work for the radical leftist newspaper the *National Guardian*, while Traum continued the mission of *Sing Out!* "to tell what we perceived was the truth [. . .] about justice and civil rights and anti-Vietnam sentiments and anti-nuclear. Nuclear war was a big threat in those days" (Traum 2019). To mixed reviews, Traum took readers of the magazine beyond the folk music genre: "My idea was to make it a little more broad-based musically. So, I got songs by people like Joni Mitchell and Jerry Jeff Walker and The Band. You know, more contemporary and sort of folk-rock artists" (Traum 2019).

While some enjoyed folk-rock and the new direction Traum offered readers of *Sing Out!* through his contacts in Woodstock, New York, where he had moved, he also continued to feature protest music by Pete Seeger, like the song "Waist Deep in the Big Muddy." However, there were those who wrote to the magazine to say, "Stick to traditional songs, we don't want any more of your politics" (Traum 2019). To reflect the times of the late 1960s, Traum felt it was only appropriate to include antiwar and antinuclear songs. There were others who felt that folk-rock, through its wide commercial appeal, lacked the same kind of political messaging as folk songs, indicating a fractured community of folk music enthusiasts and readers of *Sing Out!*

Broadside emerged out of a conversation between singer/songwriter Malvina Reynolds and Pete Seeger, who saw an urgent need for a magazine that would publish the latest political commentary on current affairs through songs. Agnes "Sis" Cunningham, a folk singer who had been involved with the People's Songs collective, offered to edit and publish *Broadside* with her journalist husband, Gordon Friesen. Like *Sing Out!*, *Broadside* followed in the footsteps of *The People's Songs Bulletin*.

Cunningham and Friesen were activists as well as artists. In 1941, they fled Oklahoma for New York City because civil liberties in their home state had been suspended, and suspected communists were being blacklisted, tried in court, and jailed (Cunningham and Friesen 1999).

Broadside, modeled after its namesake in Shakespeare's England (Seeger 2000), and calling itself "The National Topical Song Magazine" (*Broadside* 1964), launched in February 1962 as a biweekly mimeographed publication with a print run of around 500 copies. It consisted of a handful of stapled, single-sided pages, but was enormously influential, providing singer-songwriters with a serious forum in which to share their work. Bob Dylan published "The Talking John Birch Society Blues" in *Broadside*'s first issue, and "I Will Not Go Down Under the Ground" in its second issue, followed by "Blowin' in the Wind" in May 1962 and "Masters of War" in February 1963.

Getting a song printed in *Broadside* involved a visit to the humble Manhattan apartment of Cunningham and Friesen. Musicians like Tom Paxton, Len Chandler, Mark Spoelstra, and Phil Ochs would drop in and Cunningham would record their songs on a Revere reel-to-reel tape recorder, supplied by Pete Seeger. Cunningham transcribed these new and original songs and then, sometimes within mere days, printed them in *Broadside*.

Summing up the role of topical songs, Tom Paxton said, "What they really are is Op-Ed pieces" (Paxton 2019). In that regard, *Broadside* was an outlet not just for rousing songs, but especially for commentary that relied on music and song to inspire and empower a community of people that was in opposition to the prevailing social and political order. *Broadside* enabled musicians and fans to learn specific tunes and their lyrics, spreading their counter-hegemonic message through song.

FOLK MUSIC FANZINES

In August 1957, Lee Hoffman, a science fiction fanzine publisher and folk music enthusiast, launched *Caravan*. In the early 1950s, Hoffman had successfully put out a couple of folk music–themed science fiction fanzines, establishing an epistemological link between those interested in science fiction, folk music, and leftist politics (Van Ronk 2005, 63). Steeped in a genre known for its multitude of fan magazines or fanzines (Wertham 1973), it was not surprising that Hoffman envisioned *Caravan* as a fanzine.

Aided by a small group of unpaid folk music connoisseurs, Hoffman published and edited the fanzine, a de facto "club newsletter" and folk "forum" (Van Ronk 2005, 65, 66). *Caravan's* cover initially stated that the stapled, letter-size, fifteen-page publication was "free for the asking" (1). It featured a disclaimer: "Opinions expressed herein are not necessarily those of the editor-publisher and/or those other members of the staff, who come and go so rapidly" (1). Its content included articles, reviews, letters, gossip, concert notifications, and advertisements.

Figure 4.1 Cover of the folk music fanzine *Caravan*, Number 14, December 1958–January 1959, featuring folk singer Cynthia Gooding. Courtesy of Gary Hoffman.

The inaugural issue of *Caravan* featured a self-described "diatribe" by Blind Rafferty, a pseudonym for folk singer Dave Van Ronk (Van Ronk, 2005, 65). In "The Elektra Catalog: A Sarcophagus," he called out the record company for avoiding politically engaged folk singers in favor of innocuous musicians "to avoid frightening or offending anyone" (Blind Rafferty 1957, 3, 4). Van Ronk argued that folk music, the unpretentious and unvarnished music of ordinary people expressing their manifold struggles, had become co-opted into a harmless product of feel-good entertainment for mass consumption.

Caravan also published a regular column by British science fiction novelist and peace activist John K. H. Brunner about the folk music scene in Britain. Initially monthly, *Caravan*'s mimeographed press run consisted, at first, of 200 copies. Distribution was primarily a matter of Israel Young placing it on the counter at the popular Folklore Center, and Hoffman handing it out to friends and interested passersby in nearby Washington Square, where on Sunday afternoons folk musicians would gather and perform (Hoffman 2019).

A year later, the publication changed to a bimonthly basis, cost 35 cents, and was close to 50 pages thick with a press run of 2,000 printed through photo-offset. Like a true zinester, Hoffman was not interested in making money from the magazine, and charged only the minimum for advertising and subscriptions to cover the cost of printing and mailing (Hoffman 2019). Some of *Caravan*'s readers encouraged her to expand the publication, suggesting ways it could become a more successful magazine, but Hoffman preferred to keep the zine small and maintain a personal connection between the editor-publisher and the readers.

Hoffman's one-woman zine operation was a labor of love. She enjoyed being dependent on no one and answerable to no one. She saw her readers as fellow folk music–loving friends and acquaintances who didn't place any professional demands on her. To Hoffman, expanding the zine would have meant losing her sense of being on the same noncommercial, self-professed amateur level as her readers.

The now much more professional-looking magazine featured Appalachian dulcimer player and folk singer Jean Ritchie on the cover of *Caravan*'s August/September 1958 issue (number 12). Indicative of the concern with the increasing commercialization in folk music, contributor and assistant editor Roger Lass (1958, 6) wrote, "In today's commercial, manipulated, and artistically impure society, the preservation of anything as pure and lovely as Jean Ritchie's music is a rarity and quite possibly a brave stand in a losing battle." In another issue, *Sing Out!*'s editor Irwin Silber (1958, 9) wrote about his reaction to the Red Scare: "One of the favorite myths current in folk song circles today is that the 'political' folk song is a Communist invention."

Known for a brief period by her then-husband's last name, which was Shaw, Lee Hoffman chose a casual tone in her editorials, columns, and published responses to letters from her readers. This was in keeping with her intention to use the zine as a forum for a dialogue—a publication created with the help of a community of writers around her that loved folk music, many of whom hailed from the artsy and progressive Greenwich Village neighborhood in New York City.

In *Caravan*'s first issue, she announced: "CARAVAN will be published the first of every month, as long as reader-interest, my enthusiasm, and funds hold out. It may run small some months, but that's life. It isn't likely to run large any particular month, either" (Shaw 1957a, 2). In his memoir, folk musician Dave Van Ronk (2005), who was a good friend of Hoffman's, described it as a publication for local folkies who knew each other, "with gossip, in-jokes, and commentary about whatever was happening on the Village scene" (66).

Caravan was there to support, draw on, and interact with a community of performers and fans. A call for help to "EVERYBODY EVERYWHERE [*sic*]" (19) in the "New York Scene" section, written by Hoffman [Shaw] in *Caravan*'s November 1957 issue in response to a suggestion from a folk musician and reader, demonstrates the premium she placed on an engaged, personal relationship between herself and *Caravan*'s readers:

> Sandy Paton, who's travelled this wide world over, has come up with an interesting idea. Folksingers in general are a travelling lot, and many other them [*sic*] come into and pass through unfamiliar towns without knowing about interested people or active groups in such towns. So Sandy's suggested that we ask for, and publish information on who to contact. . . . So if you're in with an organized, unorganized or disorganized group that would welcome strangers, or would like to be contacted by folksingers passing through or living in your area, drop me a line, with your name and address and phone number, and in no time at all you may find road-weary travelling troubadors [*sic*] at your door. (Shaw 1957b, 19)

In its February/March 1959 edition (issue 15), readers learned that Hoffman had sold *Caravan* to professional banjo player and contributor Billy Faier. He put out four more issues before folding the magazine after the June/July 1960 issue.

After selling *Caravan*, Lee Hoffman started another mimeographed folk music fanzine in April 1959. She named it after the apocryphal story of eighteenth-century servants shouting the French phrase *gardez l'eau* ("mind the water") before dumping the contents of chamber pots into the street (P. Seeger 1959; Van Ronk 2005, 67). *Gardyloo*'s roughly 100 copies were locally distributed. The first issue consisted of twenty-four pages and announced *Gardyloo* could also be called *The Folkniks' Gazette* or *The New Lost City Ramblers Appreciation Magazine*. Costing 15 cents, each issue of *Gardyloo* featured articles, letters, concert announcements and reviews, advertisements, and polemical discussions. Like other zines, it was amateur and nonprofit, "somewhere between a personal letter and a magazine," and although others helped Hoffman, the zine was hers to do with as she pleased (Duncombe 1997, 10). The final issue came out in the spring of 1960, when Hoffman decided to end its publication (Hoffman 2019).

Figure 4.2   Cover of the folk music fanzine *Gardyloo*, **Issue 3, June 1959, featuring the Greenbriar Boys, an urban bluegrass group, first known for performances in Washington Square Park in New York City.** From left to right: Paul Prestopino, mandolin; Bob Yellin, banjo; John Herald, guitar. Courtesy of Gary Hoffman and Paul Prestopino.

ART AND COMMERCE

Paul Nelson and Jon Pankake, students at the University of Minnesota, launched *The Little Sandy Review* in March 1960, inspired by seeing Pete Seeger perform at a concert in Iowa in the summer of 1959. The form of the magazine was similar to other folk music magazines: it was self-published on "a high speed Gestetner mimeograph machine" (Pankake 1995, 106), collated on a friend's ping-pong table, and distributed to some 200 subscribers and 100 bookstores.

Strongly opinionated, the zine's founders were critical of the valuation of folk songs based solely on their use within the civil rights movement (Cunningham and Friesen 1999). Its reviews articulated the premium the two editors placed on traditional folk music as an art form, rather than contemporary folk songs written to voice dissent. Emulating film criticism's auteur theory in which the individual artist's creative expression was recognized above all else (Schudson 1991), they reviewed recently released recordings and rated the quality of folk music as a decontextualized traditional art practiced by specific musicians, rather than as a reflection of contemporary social struggles.

"Paul and I were just not political," recalled Pankake (1995, 108). In fact, Nelson's position and the multiple conversations he had with then fellow student Bob Zimmerman, soon to be known as Bob Dylan, helped convince Dylan of the direction of his career; after an initial foray into political songwriting, Dylan thereafter steered clear of political activism (Bell 2015, 125; Shelton 1986, 66).

Within the folk music community, *The Little Sandy Review*'s thirty issues caused a significant amount of commotion (Pankake 1995, 106), and it lasted about four years before petering out (Hansen 1995). To some extent Nelson and Pankake made it look like their magazine was operating within a capitalist structure; they even published unpaid advertisements for their favorite recordings (Pankake 1995). But they were adamant about editorial independence. Nelson and Pankake rejected making money from advertisements and declined to receive free records from recording companies, preferring to buy the records with their own money to avoid being beholden to the music industry and the commercial give and take of the cultural marketplace.

The Little Sandy Review did participate in the promotion of folk music by focusing on commercial recordings and professional singers (Cohen and Bonner 2018). But it also took a stance against capitalist hegemony. In a review of a Cisco Houston recording, Nelson and Pankake wrote: "It is sad to see a good folk singer like Cisco Houston make such a blatantly commercial LP such as this one" (*The Little Sandy Review* 1960, 15). The concern with commercialism was also heard in debates within the folk community

Figure 4.3 Cover of the folk music fanzine *The Little Sandy Review*, Number 5, 1960, featuring a drawing of folk music icon Woody Guthrie by Jon Pankake. Courtesy of John Pankake.

at large. Those who embraced folk music as a traditional art form and practice considered commercial success a form of selling out and abandoning authenticity, a core element of what the traditionalists valued and what in their view made folk music real. Ironically, by 1964, Nelson became managing editor of the leftist *Sing Out!* and eventually became a music critic at *Rolling Stone*.

Probably the most despised folk music magazine of the era, the slick *ABC TV Hootenanny* was a symbol of the media industry's greed and cultural co-optation. It was also short-lived, as was the television show on which it was based. Launched in January 1964, with a second issue in April and a final one in July, *Hootenanny* featured folk musicians who had been on the folk music television program, notorious for blacklisting Pete Seeger and The Weavers.

Magazine editor Linda Solomon was forbidden by the publisher from including stories on blacklisted folk musicians suspected of being communists, like Seeger; this was in the aftermath of the McCarthy era and the hearings before the House Un-American Activities Committee. But Solomon did manage to interview Phil Ochs and even Carolyn Hester for the magazine—a feat, since Ochs and Hester had been part of a large group of folk musicians who were boycotting the ABC TV *Hootenanny* show. This severely limited the content of quality folk talent available to appear on the show. Contributors to the magazine included folk musicians Oscar Brand, Theodore Bikel, Tommy Makem, and Columbia record producer John Hammond. The magazine was overtly commercial, and although she crossed paths with other magazine editors and writers on the folk scene, Solomon (2019) recalled that her job was different from that of the others: "I was on a *way* more commercial track."

Another *Hootenanny* magazine was the short-lived, glossy, and ambitious *Hootenanny: The National Folk Singing Magazine*, edited by *New York Times* writer Robert Shelton. Articles included a comparison between The Kingston Trio and The Beatles, and a history of the broadside ballad. Although the magazine featured superior writing and analysis, with Shelton receiving contributions from Nat Hentoff and Bob Dylan, he said: "There were two dreadful magazines called *Hootenanny*, including the late, unlamented monster I edited" (Shelton 1986, 128). After four issues published bimonthly in 1963 and 1964 by an advertising executive's company, the mass market–oriented *Hootenanny* folded (152).

END OF AN ERA

During the urban folk music revival of the late 1950s and 1960s, American folk music magazines articulated the concern of folk musicians and their fans with authenticity, noncommercialism, and protest. The discussions that took shape in these magazines were as important as the folk music that was sung anywhere from coffee houses to large concert hall stages. A forum for practical information, soul-searching debates about what folk music should be, and a rejection of the status quo, these often mimeographed publications were eagerly read, passed around, and discussed among folk music practitioners and enthusiasts.

Folk music magazines in operation during this era helped to build communities of readers and writers with varying reasons for their engagement, but always with a strong feeling of folkie identity (Mitchell 2007). The magazines solidified the sense of distinct belonging among folk music devotees that for many was based on a shared concern about social inequities, workers' rights, support of the civil rights and antiwar movements, and a belief that through folksongs they could make change for a better world. For others, folk songs represented a variety of musical traditions that were seen to be divorced from an ongoing political function.

Eventually, though, folk music succumbed to cultural changes, as a focus on individual well-being began to replace that of the collective. The critique of structural forces at the heart of contemporary social ills voiced through topical folksongs and freedom songs lost momentum. Folk music's relative mass appeal lost ground to the emergence of folk-rock.

Yet, the two most influential folk music magazines—*Broadside* and *Sing Out!*—endured beyond the 1960s. *Broadside* published its last issue in 1988. Until the end, its founding editors, Sis Cunningham and Gordon Friesen, believed in the power of topical songs. *Sing Out!* lasted until 2014. Over the years, a range of folk music genres shaped the magazine that at its height in the mid-1960s had a circulation of 25,000. Although the niche of folk music magazines of that era included some that rode the wave of folk's high public visibility and mass media interest driven by a purely commercial agenda, others that foregrounded social justice, and still others that placed a premium on aesthetic considerations, in the end the two magazines that survived owed their longevity to the idealism and commitment of their readers and editors.

REFERENCES

Abrahamson, David. 1996. *Magazine-made America: The cultural transformation of the postwar periodical*. Cresskill, NJ: Hampton Press.

Barretta, Scott, ed. 2013. *The conscience of the folk revival: The writings of Israel "Izzy" Young*. Lanham, MD: The Scarecrow Press.

Bell, John Frederick. 2015. "Time out of mind: Bob Dylan and Paul Nelson transformed." In *Refractions of Bob Dylan: Cultural appropriations of an American icon*, edited by Eugen Banauch, 125–34. Manchester: Manchester University Press.

Bierman, Benjamin. 2013. "Solidarity forever: Music and the labor movement in the United States." In *The Routledge history of social protest in popular music*, edited by Jonathan C. Friedman, 31–43. New York: Routledge.

Blind Rafferty. 1957. "The Elektra catalog: A sarcophagus." *Caravan*, August.

Broadside. 1964. "Broadside #37. 'The National Topical Song Magazine'." January.

Cohen, Ronald D. 2002. *Rainbow quest: The folk music revival & American society, 1940–1970.* Amherst and Boston: University of Massachusetts Press.

Cohen, Ronald D., and Bonner, David. 2018. *Selling folk music: An illustrated history.* Jackson: University Press of Mississippi.

Cunningham, Agnes S., and Friesen, Gordon. 1999. *Red dust and broadsides: A joint autobiography.* Amherst: University of Massachusetts Press.

Dane, Barbara. 2019. Interview with author. Toronto. August 26.

Duncombe, Stephen. 1997. *Notes from underground: Zines and the politics of alternative culture.* London and New York: Verso.

Dunson, Josh. 1965. *Freedom in the air: Song movements of the sixties.* New York: International Publishers.

———. 2019. Interview with author. Toronto. July 24, November 13, November 15.

Eliot, Marc. 1989. *Death of a rebel.* New York: Franklin Watts.

Friesen, Gordon. 1965. "NOTES." *Broadside,* October 15.

Hansen, Barry. 1995. "Folk magazines." In *"Wasn't that a time?" Firsthand accounts of the folk music revival,* edited by Ronald D. Cohen, 115–24. Metuchen, NJ: The Scarecrow Press.

Hoffman, Lee. 2019. "Lee Hoffman's biography: My folknik days." Accessed September 15, 2019. http://gary-ross-hoffman.com/Lee/bio-folknik.html.

Johnson Reagon, Bernice. 1983. "Movement songs that moved the nation." *The Civil Rights Quarterly Perspectives* 15, no. 3 (Summer): 27–35.

Lass, Roger. 1958. "Jean Ritchie." *Caravan,* August–September.

Mitchell, Gillian. 2007. *The North American folk music revival: Nation and identity in the United States and Canada, 1945–1980.* Burlington: Ashgate.

Noebel, David A. 1974. *The Marxist minstrels: A handbook on communist subversion of music.* Tulsa, OK: American Christian College Press.

Ochs, Phil. 1963a. "The ballad of William Worthy." *Broadside,* March.

———. 1963b. "The need for topical music." *Broadside,* March.

———. 1964. "The ballad of William Worthy." In *All the news that's fit to sing,* performed by Phil Ochs, Track 9. Elektra. EKS-7269. LP.

Pankake, Jon. 1995. "Folk magazines." In *"Wasn't that a time!" Firsthand accounts of the folk music revival,* edited by Ronald D. Cohen, 105–14. Metuchen, NJ: The Scarecrow Press.

Paxton, Tom. 1965. "Ain't that the news!" In *Ain't that the news!,* performed by Tom Paxton, Track 1. Elektra. EKS-7298. 1965. LP.

———. 1965. "Lyndon Johnson told the nation." In *Ain't that the news!,* performed by Tom Paxton, Track 3. Elektra. EKS-7298. 1965. LP.

———. 2019. Interview with author. Toronto. August 12.

People's Songs Inc. 1945. *People's Songs Bulletin* 1, no. 1 (February).

Reuss, Richard A. 1975. "American folksongs and left-wing politics: 1935–56." *Journal of the Folklore Institute* 12, no. 2/3: 89–111. DOI: 10.2307/3813920. https://www.jstor.org/stable/3813920.

Reuss, Richard A., with Reuss, JoAnne C. 2000. *American folk music and left-wing politics, 1927–1957.* Lanham, MD: The Scarecrow Press.

Rice, Les. 1948. "The banks of marble." In *Gazette, vol. 1*, performed by Pete Seeger, Track 2. Folkways Records. FW02501, FN 2501. 1958. LP.

Schudson, Michael. 1991. "The new validation of popular culture: Sense and sentimentality in academia." In *Critical perspectives on media and society*, edited by Robert K. Avery and David Eason, 49–68. New York: The Guilford Press.

Seeger, Anthony. 2000. Broadsides and Broadside magazine: A celebration of songwriters and their songs. Essay in accompanying book, *The best of Broadside 1962–1988: Anthems of the American underground from the pages of Broadside magazine*. Smithsonian Folkways Recordings SFW CD 40130.

Seeger, Pete. 1959. "Johnny Appleseed, Jr.: My favorite magazine title of the century." *Sing Out!*, December.

Shaw, Lee. 1957a. "Editorial & introduction & explanation: A FOLKMUSIC FANZINE? WHY . . . ?" *Caravan*, August.

———. 1957b. "New York Scene." *Caravan*, November.

Shelton, Robert. 1986. *No direction home: The life and times of Bob Dylan*. Milwaukee: Hal Leonard.

Silber, Irwin. 1958. "Politics and folk music." *Caravan*, May.

———. 1964. "An open letter to Bob Dylan." *Sing Out!*, November.

———. 1966. "Record Review: Topical song: Polarization sets in." *Sing Out!*, February–March.

Solomon, Linda. 2019. Interview with author. Toronto. October 29, November 4.

The Little Sandy Review. 1960. "Cisco Houston: The Cisco special." March.

Traum, Happy. 2019. Interview with author. Toronto. August 1.

Van Ronk, Dave. 2005. *The mayor of MacDougal Street: A memoir*. Cambridge, MA: Da Capo Press.

Wertham, Fredric. 1973. *The world of fanzines: A special form of communication*. Carbondale: Southern Illinois University Press.

Section 2

THE PRACTICAL AND THE PERSONAL

Chapter 5

Reaffirming the Pastoral Life
Reiman Publications 1970–2007
Sheila Webb

Over the course of almost forty years, from 1970 until 2007, the editors of the fifteen titles published by Reiman deliberately and successfully cultivated a community of readers who felt compelled to participate in the magazines. In doing so, Reiman created a unique model in two very important ways. First, 80 percent of published content was submitted by readers, evidence of a highly engaged and motivated community.[1] Second, the magazines carried no ads; this sole dependence on subscriptions was further testament to the engagement of their readership, and it provided a noncommercial environment in which submitters' interests and input were prioritized. This model, which made direct connections among "rurban" women across the country possible, prefigured the internet.

The fifteen magazines focused on food, crafts with a country flair, nostalgia, birds, and gardening.[2] The typical Reiman reader/submitter was a white Christian woman, married with children, with a median age of fifty-five. Submitters hailed from every area of the country, with the majority from the Midwest. Roy Reiman called his readers "rurban"—those who lived not in urban areas, but rather in the suburbs or the exurbs—and maintained that his magazines attracted those who felt left out in both interests and media venues by what he might call the supposed "elites on the coasts" (personal communication 2003). The company earned over $300 million a year and was valued at $760 million when it was bought by Reader's Digest in 2002 ("Rattled at Reiman," 2004, 45). In 2003, 15 percent of all American homes received Reiman publications. In 2005, the most popular title, *Taste of Home*, boasted a circulation of 3.1 million, greater than *Gourmet* and *Bon Appetit* together. In 2019, now solely under the control of Reader's Digest, *Taste of Home* is still the most popular food magazine in the world.

FILLING THE GAP

The first Reiman publication, *Farm Wife News*, premiered in 1970. Roy Reiman, founder and publisher, enjoyed telling the story of how he launched that title. Already working in publishing, he discovered that the country's two largest farm magazines were eliminating the sections devoted to women's issues because of the challenge of selling ads and the competition from TV and new magazines devoted to women. Reiman remembered thinking of his own mother, as well as millions of other farm wives, who would have no magazine tailored just for them. He reckoned that other media forms, including books, were financially viable without ads, so he decided to launch an ad-free magazine focused on farm women.

The reaction to that first issue was amazing—124,000 women subscribed to the initial offering sent to 400,000 potential readers. "It was a winner," Reiman said ("Reiman Publications," 2003). The cover of the first issue included comments from subscribers anticipating the magazine's publication. Mrs. James Renck wrote: "We farm women are a unique breed—we have a lot of things to share with each other, and this will give us a chance. You bet I'll subscribe!" Among the feature sections was "Sound Off," a special box on the front page that called for contributions, stating that the "primary goal of *Farm Wife News* is to provide a medium for exchange of good ideas among farm women . . . We want *your* ideas, *your* thoughts, *your* comments too" (emphasis in original). Inside articles included a farm wife rating tractor safety, the winning recipe of the month from a Wisconsin dairy man's wife, and an "ex-city gal" finding that the "farm is where the action is." Future issues promised stories on the dangers of farm chemicals and an exploration of whether 4-H was "all it's supposed to be."

The business model Reiman created—direct-mail, subscriber-based—was unprecedented in the magazine industry. As *Target Marketing* wrote: "The combination of a letter with order along with a sample copy is very risky and very expensive. Yet, Reiman Publications has made that model work" (Grossman, 1994, 11).

The instant success in subscriptions to *Farm Wife News* could also be attributed to its ability to reaffirm the resonant, pastoral beliefs in American culture in the 1970s (Gans, 2005). Despite the conflict engendered by the civil rights movement of the 1960s and the Vietnam War, this was a "good news" product, one that honored farm women's contributions and also endorsed their life choices.

The first issue also manifested the formula that continued to characterize the Reiman publications: a folksy style, an engagement with the reader/contributor, a focus on the exchange of information, and letters full of accolades for the publication. Although future titles tapped into nostalgia for farm life (as opposed to living that rural life), *Farm Wife News* provided the enduring template. Each element that characterized that first Reiman magazine sustained the company for almost forty years; directed at conventional American culture, the formula was repeated for the design and launch of all of the publications that followed. *Taste of Home*'s editor summed up the company's approach: "We are proud to be the comfortable shoe, not the stiletto, of food magazines" (Moskin, 2006). The appeal of this style was affirmed by readers; one described reading the magazines as "like visiting with people across the country for relaxing conversations among friends" (quoted on company website, www.reimanpub.com).

IMAGINED COMMUNITY AND CREATED IDENTITY

Appealing to a market largely ignored by other media companies—that is, rural women and suburban women with rural roots—Reiman editors were adept at creating community through narrative structures and rhetorical strategies. Their reader-centered model invited the reader in, asked the reader to contribute, reported on readers' interests, appeared to foster reader agency, and relied on reader submissions for the content.

In so doing, the magazines created an "imagined community" (Anderson, 1991) that framed and built core values, fulfilling the larger cultural role of providing an "essential social narrative" (Lule, 2002, 7, 278, 279–80), binding readers into a community and voicing shared values and a shared self-image (Kitch, 2003, 214). Like the "Seven Sisters"—the large, East Coast women's magazines—the Reiman titles served as guides to food, decorating, and creating a comfortable home. But unlike those elite publications, the Reiman magazines perfected a model of shared stories by providing a venue in which editors interacted with readers and shared reader-submitted anecdotes.

Further, as in other magazines directed toward women, the editorial stance crafted a setting in which its readers felt at home, both emotionally and culturally. What made the Reiman titles so compelling was the presentation of seemingly unedited direct testimony from readers in an ad-free environment. Due to the reader submissions, the editorial content nurtured and rewarded reader investment. This helped create a devoted following—readers who, by contributing, joined an imagined community and felt they were having a conversation with one another.

Much like Benedict Anderson's concept of French nationalism, this community of conservative women united geographic areas. Contributions came from all across the United States as well as Canada, yet the contributions were published within a context that assigned value to the presumed, shared pastoral

Figure 5.1 *Farm Wife News*, launched in 1970 after the country's two largest farm magazines eliminated their sections devoted to women's issues, was an immediate success and the first of the fifteen Reiman publications. Courtesy of Reiman Publications, LLC.

values of the Midwest. That community was one constructed and nurtured by the editors, who, by publishing curated narratives, provided submitters with a template or approach to follow if they wanted to see their contributions published. Because the edited and published stories portrayed a certain form of womanhood in contemporary America, and because submitters fashioned their stories to comply with that narrative, the magazines also functioned as sites for identity formation (see Steiner, 1991).

The imagined community constructed in the magazines was organized around core values, what Herbert Gans called "motherhood values"—family, community, church, reliance on small-town virtues, and idealizing the safety of the past—a construction that continues to resonate (Gans, 2005, 42). These deeply held, traditional values were embedded in the narrative structures of Reiman submissions, which presented the creation of meals and country crafts as a way to knit together family and community (see Webb, 2006). The magazines were vehicles through which a dialogue about those values was shared through reader submissions of stories that were shaped and shared with other readers (see Bird and Dardenne, 1988, 67–86).

Drawing from claims in the narratives and interviews with submitters, it is safe to say that the reader interpreted the modern world through a frame of "traditional" values and behavior. Through a nostalgic lens, these values were activated in material ways through a "country" aesthetic celebrating an aggressively "American taste" centered on country crafts, birding, and gardening. This taste was presented as "authentic" expression. The text, projects, and how-tos embodied an aesthetic that could be created by the readers themselves, in the process working to make them feel both validated and creative.

Given that the majority of content in the Reiman magazines was produced by readers, all of the publications thus deeply exemplify James Carey's concept of journalism as a dialogue between the reader and the producer—a mutual activity that is "a form of both cultural production and communal practice" (cited in Kitch, 2005, 4). Carey's model posits that through engagement in published stories, a modern society forms its "constitutive narratives" (Bellah et al., 1985, 153).

The comments of submitters to the Reiman magazines also show how dialogue between a media giant and its readers created a community of interests and values, and embodied Carey's "ritualized sharing" (Carey, 1989, ix). Carolyn Kitch (2005) called magazines the "most dialogic of all journalistic media" as they nurture readers' identification and foster their ability to "assess the meaning of American life and to define the 'imagined community of a nation'" (9).

Scholars of women's magazines regard the medium as "societal actors and institutions that form feminine public spheres where the objects, problems, and contradictions of women's everyday lives are dealt with.... [W]omen's magazines ... keep their readers updated on the latest social and cultural questions, create windows on the lives of contemporaries, help readers reflect on their own feelings, concerns, and hopes" (Törrönen and Simonen, 2015, 1139; see also Gill, 2009, 345–69). As Joy Jenkins notes, "Magazines create connections among readers based on shared interests, ideologies, and perspectives. Through these connections, magazines can construct identities for their audiences" (2016, 332).

Within this context, however, the Reiman publications were unique because they provided a forum in which Reiman readers shared testimony directly with one other. The editors presented themselves, somewhat disingenuously, as mere conduits in this process as they organized material into shared stories of a mother's recipe, a favorite prayer, or crafting of seasonal gifts. Due to the interactive nature of the reader submissions, the editorial content nurtured and rewarded reader investment.

This model created a devoted following—a group of readers who, by contributing their own stories, became participants who were encouraged to feel they were having a conversation with each other. By contributing to a community constructed in the pages of the magazines, women negotiated the stressors of changes in traditional norms. In reading and then contributing to the magazines, women were affirmed in their life choices. In this way, the magazines also became a site of identity formation, as the roles of wife, mother, and daughter were presented and honored.

A CAREFULLY CRAFTED SOCIAL BAROMETER

The Reiman editors worked to order the flux and chaos of life into a comforting narrative, approaching the task with a preconceived narrative structure that drew on a heritage of rural America as a site of traditional values. This encoding drove which submissions were selected and which writers were contacted for follow-up interviews. The narratives of cooking, crafts, and gardening presented these activities as integral to the roles of wife, mother, and grandmother, and at the same time structured these as essential strands to solidifying the family bond and participating in community. They ordered experience around family rituals of shared dinners, church potlucks, and the aesthetic of the everyday. These narratives told the story of ideal modern motherhood as rooted in the past, of the assumption of white Christianity as the default American identity, and of an authentic country aesthetic, all of which still play out more broadly in American culture today.

The concept promoted by the editors—of a community of readers for which Reiman served as merely a "clearing house"—was nurtured through language, story selection, and shaping of narratives. The editors produced an interactive product that encouraged readers to engage with the magazines at a broad and deep level. They asked readers to submit stories and recipes, to participate in contests, to advertise for pen pals, to find a picture of a toothpick hidden in the magazine, to send in a secret ingredient that made a dish special, to win a prize, to complete polls, to compete for prizes, to send in favorite photos, to share jokes and puns, and to submit a most embarrassing moment or a description of a favorite country character.

The appeal to the readership to submit is seen in the content of several of the magazines. *Taste of Home* featured repeating sections such as "Editor's Favorite Meal," "Mom's Favorite Meal," and "Men Who Run the Range" (in which men sent in recipes). *Country Woman* published seasonal crafts as well as repeating sections, such as "Quilters' Corner," "Grandma's Brag Page," and "Focus on Family Snapshots." The response was impressive: For example, in one recipe contest, the winning cookie recipe was one of 34,000 entries.

The Reiman publications were called a "social barometer" (Schrambling, 2002) of the taste of Middle America. If so, it was a carefully calibrated barometer. Although the construction of content was a collaboration between editors and readers, it was controlled by editors. The editors shaped the submissions into a seamless whole. For example, after submitters sent in a recipe or story, an editor called them, interviewed them, and completed the story. Despite this process, the editors portrayed themselves as mere "conduits" of an exchange: "It's not really a magazine. It's a conversation" ("Reiman Publications," 2003). This process "made the world make sense" (Manoff, 1987, 228) as published stories felt comfortable and seemingly familiar. The editors applied rhetorical devices that fostered agency on the part of the submitters, among them the insistent use of direct address, active verbs that were emotive (such as "relay" and "share"), punctuation that exclaimed, and the naming of submitters as "field editors," thus elevating them to "staff."

The Reiman magazines' narratives drew on American cultural resources to make sense of social and cultural change. They also tapped into the nostalgia trend and assuaged anxiety about the role of popular culture in contemporary life by portraying the nostalgic view that life was better, more relaxed, and more enjoyable in a previous era. As one commentator wrote: "The world of Reiman Publications is all benevolent rolling terrain, the sunshine always sparkles and there's nary a smokestack in sight" (Grossman, 1994, 48). Roy Reiman credited the magazines' popularity to their helping readers connect to their rural past: "Close to half of all people in America have rural roots at least through their grandparents. We're selling a two-hour escape to those people" (*American Demographics*, 1989, 15). This approach was intimately tied into identification as being an American, an identification crafted into every issue; Roy Reiman's stated goal was for American readers to put their "chins up, chests out" ("Reiman Publications," 2003).

This study examined narratives, in particular the longer profiles, in 231 issues of *Taste of Home*, the most popular title, and *Country Woman*. Of the fifteen magazines, these two had the highest circulations and provided content that captured two main content areas of the Reiman publications. They also represent a range of age demographics in submitters and published narratives of women's roles in the family. The narratives in these magazines told stories of individuals in their everyday lives. This presentation assigned value to the personal and the local, forming the image of a homogeneous social gathering foregrounded by geographic region. Thus, the private life was privileged over the public life, and that private life was one that any reader could duplicate through recipes and nonthreatening, familiar, country decorations.

The appeal to the local presented the contributor as an individual of a given place and of a given church. Under the pretext of the magazines being not theirs but the readers', the editors fostered the sense of agency that the submitter expressed in published stories. This process eased the strains of modern life that cut off community and created a product with which the targeted demographic felt comfortable. In this way, the magazines helped define contemporary thought—that of visualizing nostalgia for a country lifestyle (Webb, 2006).

These common narratives helped tie the publications together while at the same time providing a normative model for the ideal life. They also served as models for ways to order contemporary life and the proper stance to take toward the world. For the female reader, that model was to be a stay-at-home mom who devoted herself to her family. If that was not possible, the next best thing was to duplicate as much as possible her mother's life and to incorporate the demands of working into the pleasures of creating a comfortable home. In either case, the role of religion was a defining frame for volunteer activities, social values, and social networks.

An interesting aspect of this narrative style was the ability to adapt and "domesticate" societal changes that might threaten this comfortable nostalgic view, including demands on working women, changing roles of women and men in the home, and divorce. There was the sense of modern life made palatable; in spite of changing norms, stresses on family life, and threats to traditional family structures, the old values held. These narratives, then, of the woman as the heart of a nuclear family, of marriage as the norm, and the assumption of Protestant Christianity, negotiated the tension in the lives of women leading contemporary lives but whose values were traditional. The narratives affirmed that although she could not stay home like her mother, the contemporary mother could still make dinner from scratch; despite the divorce rate in the United States, traditional marriage was the norm; despite growing levels of immigration, the heartland was still a white, Christian world.

One irony in studying the company is that the model it perfected prefigured media sites on the internet—in the submission of shared stories, the shared tips, and the sense of community. Of all magazine publishers, the Reiman company was well-positioned to exploit the new media landscape. The model the company established engendered a great deal of loyalty. Given their relationship with their readers, going onto the web should have been "natural" for them.

However, despite the editors' stated expectation (personal interview, 2009) that the magazines would continue to foster the community of like-minded readers, this did not bear fruit. With the sale to Reader's Digest, the magazines began to carry ads in the mid-2000s, and the space once devoted to women's contributions became a branded one. With the full ownership in the hands of Reader's Digest, the company moved to make the titles part of the so-called enthusiast brands, primarily a marketing ploy. Only seven of the original fifteen titles are now available.

It seems that the comfortable and comforting space so successfully realized in the print form did not migrate along with the new ownership. None of the new, interactive features promoted in 2009—chat groups, blogs, forums—is evident on the websites in 2019. In *Taste of Home*, space formerly devoted to reader narratives is now mainly occupied with recipes. The narratives of women's lives built on pastoral values and the community built around them are, thus, now a thing of the past.

REFERENCES

Abrahamson, David. 2002. "Beyond the Mirror Metaphor: Magazine Exceptionalism and Sociocultural Change." *The Journal of Magazine and New Media Research* 4, no. 1.

American Demographics. 1989. "Almost Heaven." February.

Anderson, Benedict. 1991. *Imagined Communities: Reflections on the Origin and Spread of Nationalism.* London: Verso.

Bellah, Robert N., Richard Madsen, William M. Sullivan, Ann Swidler, and Steven M. Tipton. 1985. *Habits of the Heart: Individualism and Commitment in American Life.* Berkeley: University of California Press.

Bird, Elizabeth, and Robert Dardenne. 1988. "Myth, Chronicle, and Story: Exploring the Narrative Qualities of News." In *Media, Myths, and Narratives: Television and the Press*, edited by James Carey, 67–86. Newbury Park, CA: Sage.

Carey, James. 1989. *Communication as Culture: Essays on Media & Society.* Boston: Unwin Hyman.

Gans, Herbert J. 2005. *Deciding What's News: A Study of CBS Evening News, NBC Nightly News, Newsweek, and Time*, Twenty-Fifth Anniversary Edition. Evanston, IL: Northwestern University Press.

Gill, Rosalind. 2009. "Mediated Intimacy and Postfeminism: A Discourse Analytic Examination of Sex and Relationships in a Woman's Magazine." *Discourse & Communication* 3 (4): 345–69.

Grossman, Gordon. 1994. "The Best-Kept Secret in Publishing," *Target Marketing*, November.

Jenkins, Joy M. 2016. "The Good Life: The Construction of Imagined Communities in City Magazines." *Journalism Studies* 17 (3): 319–36.

Kitch, Carolyn. 2003. "'Mourning in America': Ritual, Redemption, and Recovery in News Narrative After September 11." *Journalism Studies* 4 (2): 213–24.

———. 2005. *Pages from the Past: History and Memory in American Magazines.* Chapel Hill: University of North Carolina Press.

Lule, Jack. 2002. "Myth and Terror on the Editorial Page: The *New York Times* Responds to September 11, 2001." *Journalism & Mass Communication Quarterly* 79 (2): 275–93.

Manoff, Robert Karl. 1987. "Writing the News (By Telling the 'Story')." In *Reading the News*, edited by Robert Karl Manoff and Michael Schudson, 197–229. New York: Pantheon Books.

Moskin, Julia. 2006. Quoted in "Food for the People, Whipped up by the People." *New York Times*, December 27, sec. D, p. 3, col. 3.

"Rattled at Reiman: A Look at *Reader's Digest* Two-Year Record." 2004. *Folio*, October.

Reiman, Roy. 2003. Personal communication. July.

"Reiman Publications." 2003. Reiman Company film, Reiman Publications Visitor Center in Greendale, Wisconsin, and personal communication.

Schrambling, Regina. 2002. "'Mixed Media' America's Real Foodie Bible (It's Not What You Think)." *New York Times*, March 20, sec. F, p. 1.

Steiner, Linda. 1991. "Evolving Rhetorical Strategies / Evolving Identities." In *A Voice of Their Own, The Woman Suffrage Press, 1840–1910*, edited by Martha M. Solomon, 183–97. Tuscaloosa: University of Alabama Press.

Törrönen, Jukka, and Jenni Simonen. 2015. "The Exercise of Symbolic Power by Women's Magazines from the 1960s to the Present: The Discursive Construction of Fields, Positions, and Resources in Alcohol-Related Texts." *Media, Culture & Society* 37 (8): 1138–57.

Webb, Sheila M. 2006. "The Narrative of Core Traditional Values in Reiman Magazines." *Journalism & Mass Communication Quarterly* 83, no. 4 (Winter): 865–82.

Chapter 6

Tilling Fertile Ground

The Trailblazing Role of Farming Magazines

Catherine M. Staub

Nearly 6 million. That was the number of farms in the United States at the beginning of the twentieth century (Spielmaker 2018). Of the approximately 75 million people who populated the nation, more than 29 million lived on farms. Farm magazines and papers were just as ubiquitous. In 1900, fifty farm publications were headquartered in Illinois alone (Evans 1969). By the close of the twentieth century, farmers were less than 0.6 percent of the United States population (Nordin and Scott 2005, 176; Rasmussen 1960, 304). In the early 1900s, farmsteads were typically small family operations. By the year 2000, many farms were massive corporate-owned entities; yet a movement toward small, sustainable, often organic farming practices was afoot as well. What transpired in the intervening years was a transformational change in farming.

Throughout the twentieth century, farm magazines were a source of practical information for farmers and farm families on a range of topics from crops and livestock to the latest farm implements and developments. The fictional stories and poetry featured in these publications entertained farm families who were isolated from neighbors. For decades, farm magazines also included tips for farmers' wives on homemaking, personal care, sewing, parenting, and domestic tasks. And as a complete source of information for the farm families, the magazines often tackled relationship issues and provided political news relevant to their readers. In short, the farm magazine was a go-to guide for virtually all aspects of farm life for much of the century. As U.S. agriculture changed, so too did the farm magazine. And yet the farm magazine continued to counsel farmers as well as chronicle the evolution of this changing landscape.

INFLUENCE OF FARM MAGAZINES

Agriculture magazines have long been a key source of information for farmers (Thomas and Evans 1963; Fett 1984; Vincent 1980; Walter 1996; Marti 1980; Evans and Salcedo 1974; Ford and Babb 1989; Lauters 2009). They deserve attention "as an acknowledged major influence in American agriculture" (Evans and Salcedo 1974, vii) and as a key form of communication in agricultural communities.

"In order to be successful, a farmer must have access to new information. Three major sources of information for farmers are other farmers, farm magazines, and extension agents" (Sachs 1983, 111). For women living on farms between 1910 and 1960, "Reading, and the mass media, were critical not only to the education of youth on those farms but also to keeping the family abreast of the world outside the farmhouse door" (Lauters 2009, 35). Farm magazines were "virtually farmers' only source of sustained journalistic coverage of agricultural issues, rural life, and the business of farming" (Walter 1996, 595).

Given their prevalence in farm households, farm periodicals' portrayals of farmers and farming likely influenced farming practices and farmers' roles and identity (Evans and Salcedo 1974; Walter 1996). A U.S. Department of Agriculture (USDA) survey of farmers' reading habits in 1913 found 66 percent reported they were "influenced by agricultural magazines" (Nordin and Scott 2005, 43). By 1920, the average farm home received two to three commercial farm periodicals (Evans and Salcedo 1974). One-third of farmer respondents reported farm papers and home magazines to be their preferred source of printed information (U.S. Department of Agriculture 1928). By 1965, farm households received an average of 6.7 farm magazines (Walter 1996). And by 1970 more than 24 million copies of 386 commercial farm periodicals were delivered to American mailboxes each month (Evans and Salcedo 1974).

Agricultural publications and their editors are credited with "urging better farming methods" and "promoting education and research as a means to further progress" (Evans and Salcedo 1974, vii). The first issue of *Successful Farming*, for instance, included an article counseling a farmer to "not forget that true science is always true" ("How to Make" 1902, 2). (See figure 6.1 *Successful Farming* magazine cover, October 1902.) That same issue included information about an experiment conducted at the Iowa research station to "test the value of soft corn versus mature corn in fattening steers" ("A Practical Experiment" 1902, 7). And new pest control methods are detailed in a 1934 *Farm Journal* article ("Pst!" 1934, 7). This wealth of information about new research and best practices is evidenced by one study that suggests agricultural publications were five to fifteen years ahead of agricultural colleges "in making transitions and additions in subject matter" (Evans and Salcedo 1974, viii).

In an address to editors, Edwin T. Meredith, founder of *Successful Farming* magazine, underscored the importance of agriculture publications, stating, "You constitute one of the most effective channels through which the people of the country can secure the information in the possession of the Department of Agriculture" (Meredith 1920).

Agricultural publications are credited with fostering pride in farming, offering low-cost access to industry information, informing farm families about nonfarm affairs, and marketing supplies (Evans and Salcedo 1974, viii). A *Successful Farming* article, for instance, addressed a concern that the country church, which formerly had been a "community center for all the people round," was now "falling into decay and the congregation is small and discouraged or has disappeared altogether" (Newcomb 1910, 72). The first of a series of banking-related articles delved into the safety of "money placed in banks" by examining bank deposit insurance (Secor 1926, 5). And a *Farm Journal* article explained how readers will pay less taxes thanks to a bill passed by Congress and signed by President Eisenhower ("You'll Pay" 1954, 18).

Meredith explained the purpose of his own farm magazine in this way:

> Every issue of *Successful Farming* amounts practically to a good-sized book of up-to-the-minute literature for farm people. *It covers the whole range of agricultural subjects and interests of every member of the farm family* [emphasis original]. (Score Card n.d.)

In an address at the Associated Advertising Club of the World, Meredith reiterated the importance of farming magazines, stating, "The farm paper is developing and fostering the agriculture of this country . . . making farm life more pleasant by the introduction to the farmer of many modern conveniences" (Meredith 1916).

Dave Kurns, editorial content director, *Successful Farming*, explains the purpose of the magazine in this way:

> *Successful Farming* was really started to serve American farmers in a time when one-third of us lived on farms. In 1900 there were many changes happening in agriculture. *Successful Farming* was there to educate, to teach and to share new practices that farmers needed when mechanization was just coming in agriculture in the 1910s and '20s. . . . It's always been a practical guide to help farmers in the field, in the shop, in the office. Very practical, everyday ideas to make them more money, make them smarter, make them more successful. (Kurns 2019)

Practical advice abounds in nearly every issue of farm magazines. Service articles include explanations of how to rotate crops and the resulting benefits

Figure 6.1 *Successful Farming* magazine cover, October 1902. Courtesy of Meredith Corporation.

(Synder 1913, 10), methods for preventing soil loss (Wood 1925, 15), and how to correctly hitch a plow to a tractor ("Hitching the Plow" 1926, 34).

When Meredith launched *Successful Farming* magazine in October 1902, farm families had little opportunity to share news, information, and ideas—a ripe opportunity for farming publications. *Successful Farming* established a Subscribers Information Bureau designed as "a personal consultation service for all subscribers" (Score Card n.d.). The Bureau personally responded to "any inquiry on any subject sent in by subscribers or their friends" (Score Card n.d.). The letters poured in at a rate of more than 15,000 annually. Neither the inquiries nor the replies were limited to farm operations. Of the 1,722 inquiries in the month of February 1919, for instance, 15 were about autos, 31 about etiquette, and 191 about income tax (Score Card n.d.). Some reader questions were featured in the magazine itself. The August 1925 issue, for instance, included responses to questions about the legality of verbal rental agreements, burning limestone, a lack of water pressure in a bathroom, and the best finish for old softwood floors, in addition to agriculture-specific questions about rotating crops for sandy loam soil, feeding skimmed milk to hogs, eliminating granary weevils, and inoculating alfalfa crops ("Answers to Questions" 1925, 13).

Farming magazines provided service to their readers in other ways as well. *Successful Farming* organized a Rural Schools Service Bureau as a "service aide in the teaching of practical agriculture and in the upbuilding of rural life" (Score Card n.d.). Its *Rural Schools Bulletin* included lesson plans and monthly question sheets for use in agricultural classes. The lessons relied on the use of elements from the current issue of *Successful Farming* and were designed for children of multiple ages in grades one through eight, as would commonly be found in rural one-room schoolhouses. Most questions included a page reference from that month's issue of *Successful Farming* on which students could find the answer (*Rural Schools Bulletin* 1931). For instance, students in seventh and eighth grade were told to read the article on page 8 of the April issue of *Successful Farming* and then answer the question, "Why do you think the county was more successful in getting rid of weeds than individual farmers would have been working alone?" Students were encouraged to refer to pages 8 and 87 in crafting their responses (*Rural Schools Bulletin* 1931, 13).

In the 1940s, *Successful Farming* again extended its brand, this time by offering a series of home plans. Readers were encouraged to submit snapshots so editors could select homes to be featured in the magazine (Fox 1947). The June 1944 issue of *Successful Farming* showcased the winning ideas submitted to the 1944 "Successful Homes Contest." The article included photos of the winners along with house plans for Mr. and Mrs. Theo Nelson of Cylinder, Iowa, first-prize winners in the remodeling category; and Mr.

and Mrs. Dike Johnson of Bristol, Wisconsin, first-prize winners in the new building category ("Here Is the Way" 1944, 24–25).

LEVERAGE OF ADVERTISEMENTS

Revenue from ad sales is key to the affordability of most consumer magazines, a truth that applies to farm magazines, too. In 1970, for instance, 80 percent of agricultural marketers' media budgets went to advertising in farm journals (Evans and Salcedo 1974). Despite this, E. T. Meredith displayed a reader-friendly warning to advertisers in the first issue of *Successful Farming*. The magazine would reimburse any financial loss experienced by a paid subscriber as a result of a deliberately false advertisement in the pages of *Successful Farming*. The policy stated, in part, "we will make good any loss to paid subscribers sustained by trusting any deliberate swindler advertising in our columns, and any such swindler will be publicly exposed" (Cooper 1999, 41).

The first issue of *Successful Farming* included ads for agriculture-related products such as wagons, dairy separators, seeds, sweep mills, and incubators, but also included an ad for a luxury item—a musical organ—as well as a liniment touting its health benefits. Subsequent early issues included promotions for similar products, in addition to advertisements for cures for ailments including baldness, kidney trouble, and blindness. Ads in more recent farm magazines typically promote tractors, diggers, trucks, pesticides, and other products directly related to the business of farming.

Ads not only generated valuable revenue for publishers; they also conveyed information to farmers. Farm magazines were a natural vehicle by which agricultural-related companies publicized their products to their target audience of farm families, informing them about new technology, equipment, and other offerings. In fact, in a letter to readers, E. T. Meredith explained the value of advertisement, stating, "When you are thinking and planning ahead, isn't it easier to see where you can save time, reduce labor or improve a method by adopting a suggestion you find in the advertising columns?" (Meredith 1926, 3). Similarly, the title of a column in the April 1934 issue of *Successful Farming* proclaimed, "Our Advertisers Are Honest" (60).

In one study, an analysis of a year's worth of advertisements in three conventional farming magazines from 2010 found a shift away from representations of a "rugged, strong, solitary farmer, who dominates nature through his manual labor, to depictions of a 'businessman' farmer, who farms in collaboration with certain qualified partners (i.e., company representatives)" alienating the farmer from the land and ultimately resulting in deskilling (Bell, Hullinger, and Brislen 2015, 285). This shift in messaging encourages farmers to become less self-reliant and more dependent on the expertise and products offered by advertisers.

Messaging in editorial content was largely consistent with farm magazine advertisements, pointing to a generally cozy relationship between advertising and editorial in farm magazines. Hays and Reisner, for instance, gathered data from AAEA (The Agricultural Communicators Network) members who responded to a questionnaire about the influence of advertisers on farm journals in the late 1980s. Sixty-two percent reported hearing from advertisers who threatened to pull advertisements because they were displeased with editorial copy. Almost half reported advertisements had been pulled by advertisers unhappy with editorial copy (Hays and Reisner 1991).

While the magazines were launched as a means to provide information to farmers, they became "an important medium for communicating to farmers the commercial applications of agricultural science and technology" (Walter 1996, 594). Success stories portrayed in farm magazines from 1934 through 1991 analyzed by Walter "have used agrarian imagery to further advertiser interests" (Walter 1996, 594).

REGIONAL AND NATIONAL REACH

The Progressive Farmer, its first issue appearing February 10, 1886, as a newspaper, was published by Leonidas L. Polk to serve the "various needs and interests of the South's farmers and their families" (Lauder 2007, 186). Polk intended for the magazine to be "a forum for promoting the goals of a better rural way of life, a more scientific agriculture, and an improved educational system for farm people" (Wilson 2008, 190). From the beginning *The Progressive Farmer* championed issues including "better public education not only for rural white children, but also for blacks; for women's right to vote; for soil conservation and for two-armed farming—a rotation of cotton with corn, as well as with cover crops" (Deterling 2011, 72). In large part, these progressive views stemmed from a shared dedication to addressing issues faced by farm families and also "reflected the close proximity in which black and white farmers lived" (Creech 2006, 74). "These farmers were not just poor; they were angry, and as Polk made clear, their anger had a target: economic, political, and religious centralizers who had captured the levers of state and local government through 'class legislation'" (Creech 2006, 48). Polk saw black farmers as allies in his movement to improve life for the Southern farmer. By 1960, the magazine had a circulation of 1.4 million—the largest of any Southern farm publication (Lauder 2007; Deterling 2011).

Farm Journal was launched in 1877, and has been in uninterrupted publication ever since then. Unlike *Successful Farming*, which served farmers in the

Midwest, and *Progressive Farmer*, which served the Southern farmer, *Farm Journal* was a national magazine. Even though it was initially conceived for farmers "within a day's ride of Philadelphia" (Quebral 1970; "Farm Journal" n.d.), when its founder, Wilmer Atkinson, received letters from outside the region, he worked to achieve national circulation ("Farm Journal" n.d.). By 1882, the magazine "claimed more subscribers than any other 'legitimate agricultural paper'" in the United States (Quebral 1970).

To serve the wide-ranging needs of farmers with diverse crops, livestock, soil conditions, and more, in 1952 the magazine divided circulation into three regional editions: Central-East, West, and South (Reuss 1973). In the 1960s, as farm production became more specialized and as *Farm Journal* executives weren't satisfied the geographic approach was allowing them to effectively reach livestock subscribers, *Farm Journal* collected information about the specific crops and livestock each of its readers produced, allowing the magazine to develop special dairy, hog, and beef sections directed only to specific livestock producers ("Farm Journal" n.d.; Reuss 1973). Former *Farm Journal* editor Lane Palmer indicates it wasn't until the 1960s that advertisers "discovered the advantages of geographic editions and pressed the publishers into offering more and more of them" (Reuss 1973, 6). The magazine responded. With computer technology, *Farm Journal* became the first magazine to bind issues electronically, which meant it could produce magazines customized by size of readers' farms, types of crops or livestock, and readers' region. By 1999 *Farm Journal* had more than 2,000 demographic versions of each issue (Callahan 1999).

FARM MAGAZINE CONTENT THROUGHOUT THE TWENTIETH CENTURY

In the first two decades of the twentieth century, referred to as a "golden age" for farming by some agricultural historians, farmland values soared and commodity prices rose steadily (Nordin and Scott 2005, 25). In farm magazines, farmers found plenty of information about the newest farm implements and developments in farming practices. Farm magazines touted advances in livestock breeds, herd management, and new equipment (Evans and Salcedo 1974, 8). For example, "Improving the Farm Draft Horse" (1910, 4) advised farmers how to select and breed a horse that will "do his work best or prove most profitable in his particular market." "How and Why of Crop Rotation" (1913, 10) addressed challenges faced by Midwest grain farmers.

Publishers in the early twentieth century benefited from at least two government programs: The Hatch Act of 1887 and Smith-Lever Act of 1914. The Hatch Act established funding for agricultural experiment stations—science research centers dedicated to ag-related research. The Smith-Lever Act expanded many of these into extension services as a mechanism for sharing the work of the experiment stations with farmers and other interested parties. Farming publications, too, were a natural vehicle by which to share the resulting information and advances (Evans and Salcedo 1974, 9). While the extension services could have been a threat to farming magazines, the U.S. Department of Agriculture stated, with irony, "the agricultural press would seem to be at present the most efficient of our agricultural extension agencies in reaching the farmer" (Smith and Atwood 1913, 25).

World War I brought prosperity for many U.S. farmers as they were tasked with providing food for the nation's allies. Commodity prices rose along with ag production rates. For instance, exports increased 10 percent per year from 1916 to 1919, while prices for crops and livestock doubled (Henderson, Gloy, and Boehlje 2011). The resulting rise in farm income led to an increase in farmers' spending.

The 1920s, however, saw falling commodity prices coupled with farmers struggling with excessive debts (Nordin and Scott 2005, 53). By 1922, export levels fell to prewar levels, while commodity prices dropped 40 percent from 1919 to 1921 (Henderson, Gloy, and Boehlje 2011). The article "Shall I Quit the Farm? Why One Family Is Going to Stick" was one attempt to encourage *Successful Farming* readers. In it, farmer R. D. Willis acknowledged the "call of the city" some of his neighbors had heeded while detailing the reasons he and his family would remain on the farm (Willis 1925, 13).

But the exodus from farm to city was occurring. The Great Depression forced many farmers into foreclosure. In 1933 alone, more than 200,000 farms were foreclosed (Alston 1983). Those who retained their farmsteads experienced a collapse of commodity prices and higher debts relative to assets. Hired hands, once common on farms, couldn't be paid. Technological advances, expanding farm operations, and mechanized operations led to a decrease in diversified farm operations. As a result, the Great Depression caused farmers to be less self-sufficient, since they now depended on others for food. In response, women on farms returned to cost-saving measures such as canning, raising poultry for eggs, planting and harvesting vegetables, as well as sewing and mending clothes (Nordin and Scott 2005).

Farm magazines already were providing farmers with practical advice regarding successful agricultural operations. Content during this time included articles about best practices to maximize yields and increase profitability. "The Biggest Farm Waste" in *The Farm Journal* detailed the loss of potential soil nutrients from mismanagement of manure and encouraged the use of a manure spreader, which the magazine assured cost-conscious readers would "pay for itself" (Stephenson 1934, 5). Other articles also touted the benefits of new implements, despite rising farm debt. "New Equipment for the Farm" (1934,

14) recommended larger model rotary tillers, wind-electric plants, manure spreaders, stainless steel separators, and power spray outfits—right next to a two-thirds page advertisement for the latest McCormick-Deering tractors. Homemakers, too, encountered cost-cutting content, such as a reader submission about a home economics bulletin that explained how to make cleaning products from materials in the home ("Reducing Cleaning Costs" 1934, 41).

Despite optimism in the pages of many farm magazines, the Dust Bowl of the 1930s furthered the plight of farmers in affected regions. It also led to an interest in soil improvement (Kelly 1992). This and Victory Gardens—fruit and vegetable gardens planted by nearly 20 million Americans during wartime to help offset food shortages—provided an opening for alternative farming publications.

In the early 1940s, J. I. Rodale, "founder and father of the organic movement in America," launched *Organic Farming and Gardening* magazine to share information about organic practices (Boehmer 2003; Rodale 2019, 2010; Gross 2008).

During this timeframe, nearly a third of traditional farming magazine content was directed to the farm wife. While much of the information focused on recipes, child-rearing, homemaking, sewing, and fashion, an article in *The Farm Journal* detailed "farm women helping individually and collectively in an effort to increase and conserve farm incomes and to build better community life" (Temple 1934, 11). More typical fare in the "woman's section" of the magazine were articles such as "Seven Budget Recipes" (Howe 1935, 7), "How to Can Like a Champion" (Williams 1944, 42), and "Easier Upkeep for Men's Summer Suits" (Richard 1953, 104).

The Farmer's Wife is unique in that it was an entire magazine for farm women. The Webb Company published this national monthly magazine from 1905 to 1939. "Through its fiction, editorial content, and, most especially, its write-in forums, *The Farmer's Wife* revealed its dedication to the notion that farm women had distinct, valid views on both farm and domestic culture" (Casey 2004, 183). By 1930, it boasted more than one million subscribers. Despite or perhaps because of its healthy circulation numbers, *The Farmer's Wife* was purchased by *Farm Journal* in 1939 and folded into it (Casey 2004). The cover of the merged publication included both titles.

In the 1940s *Successful Farming* magazine included a recurring section of the magazine, "Successful Homemaking." Articles featured more color photos and illustrations than the rest of the magazine. Family and farm wife–related content was evident in other ways as well. The Pattern Department of *Successful Farming* published *Successful Farming Fashion Catalogue*. The spring and summer 1920 catalog, for instance, featured "five hundred and fifty designs of Ladies, Misses' and Children's Garments in Current Fashions" (*Successful Farming Fashion Catalogue* 1920).

U.S. entry into World War II saw a rise of women taking on roles previously limited to men (Jellison 1993; Bradley 1989). The USDA called on farm women to raise food for the war cause (Jellison 1993). Farm magazines highlighted such efforts. In "The Thorps Farm Without Manpower," the author wrote, "The fact that the Thorp farm has remained in full production can be entirely attributed to the work done by Laura, her sister and their mother" (1945, 6). The April 1944 cover of *Successful Farming* featured a mother–son "poultry improvement team," and the September 1944 cover of *The Farm Journal* portrayed a woman driving a farm truck delivering food. Images of women actively doing farm work—particularly highlighted on the cover—were rare outside war years.

Wartime content also encouraged resourcefulness. In "Smart Clothes from Feed Sacks," farm women were told, "you want to do your patriotic bit by using what you have" (Reynolds 1944, 66). Women weren't the only ones called upon to do their part to help the war effort. "Who Wants a 'Hired Man'" relayed the success of a program in which county extension agents delivered "town boys" to farms in most need of assistance (Schultz 1945, 20).

The following years saw a steady decline in the number of farmers and farms—a trend that would continue through the end of the twentieth century. More than 2,000 farms per week were lost between 1945 and 1978 (Coughenour and Swanson 1983). In the 1950s, it was commonplace for members of a farm family, particularly the women, to take a "town job" to generate additional income (Jellison 1993, 166). Farm magazine content, however, did not reflect this trend, instead focusing on the interests and needs of those who stayed on the farm.

Concerns about air and water pollution were making their way into the contents of traditional farm magazines by the late 1960s. An August 1967 issue of *Successful Farming*, for instance, covered the impact of new water pollution control permits on agricultural operations. Readers were urged to "check with your state department of health to review any pollution regulations. Then, make sure your facilities comply with them" (Malena 1967, 31).

As early as 1967, farming magazines were addressing the topic of big ag. "Will We See More Corporate Farming?" (Brantley 1967, 52) projected farm debt would at least double or triple by the 1980s, resulting in more corporate farming. Already, the magazines were changing their editorial mix, with diminished family-related stories. As E. T. Meredith III, grandson of *Successful Farming*'s founder, acknowledged, "Around 1968, we moved *Successful Farming* from a newsprint publication to slick paper. We took women's interest out of the magazine and made it a farm management magazine" (Meredith III 2001). Kurns concurs. "We used to devote a lot of space to family issues, to family lifestyle, to cooking, to keeping a farm home" (Kurns 2019).

By the 1970s and early 1980s, farm production was becoming more concentrated with fewer farms producing most agricultural products (Coughenour and Swanson 1983). Farm magazine content reflected that change. Now *Successful Farming* has "become more of a business-focused brand and a business-focused publication" (Kurns 2019). Similar to its counterparts, *The Farm Journal* has also become a business publication. "We provide production, marketing and policy information for businessmen who happen to farm," says Sonja Hillgren, former *Farm Journal* editor in a 1999 interview (Callahan 1999).

Content—both editorial and advertisements—about pesticides and herbicides became common in farming magazines beginning in the mid-1970s as farmers expanded operations and were more reliant on chemical treatments. At the same time, public concern about the environment and pollution was rising (Kroma 2002).

The 1980s ushered in a tough time for farmers who faced a sustained economic downturn and adverse market conditions. Farming magazines in this decade associated "commercial orientations with explicit references to success" (Walter 1996, 604).

While consolidation meant a decrease in the overall number of farms in the 1990s, the U.S. Department of Agriculture shows the number of certified organic farms increased from 2,753 in 1991 to 4,856 in 1995 (Klonsky and Tourte 1998). In a study of feature articles that portray successful farmers as central characters, if alternative farming practices were mentioned, they were framed in terms of their "contribution to profitability or production" (Walter 1995, 64), while concern for the environment is "manifested more in terms of controlling the environment in the name of higher production than working in harmony with nature to reduce environmental degradation" (Walter 1995, 66). In general, traditional farm magazines largely omitted sustainable agriculture and nonconventional farming practices (Walter 1995).

ALTERNATIVE PRACTICES GET COVERAGE

Alternative farming practices did have roots in twentieth-century farming magazines, though not in the likes of *Successful Farming* and *The Farm Journal*. J. I. Rodale was keenly interested in natural agricultural practices, such as composting and cover crops, written about by agriculturalist Sir Albert Howard in the early 1940s. Inspired by Howard's writings, Rodale "decided that we must get a farm at once and raise as much of our family's food by the organic method as possible" ("Our Story" n.d.; Gross 2008, 56). After conducting numerous experiments and noticing improvements to the land as well as his own health, he launched *Organic Gardening and Farming* to spread the word (Rodale 2019; "Our Story" n.d.; Klonsky and Tourte 1998). In May 1942, Rodale printed about 14,000 copies of his new magazine and mailed them to farmers in hopes of generating subscriptions; only 12 responded (Gross 2008, 62). But he eventually found interest from gardeners—primarily Victory Gardeners in the early days—and grew the circulation of the magazine to approximately 260,000 by 1960 and to 1,300,000 by 1980 (Gross 2008; Kelly 1992).

As for the impact of magazines such as Rodale's flagship *Organic Gardening and Farming*, his granddaughter Maria Rodale—formerly the CEO and chairman of Rodale, Inc.—stated, "My grandfather created a community. . . . It [*Organic Farming and Gardening* magazine] planted a lot of seeds all over the world that are now growing and producing their own seeds" (Rodale 2019).

Rodale's magazine was not alone in serving the needs of twentieth-century farmers interested in alternative agricultural practices. *Acres U.S.A.* magazine launched in 1971 as "a comprehensive guide to sustainable agriculture" ("About Acres" n.d.). While Rodale's *Organic Gardening* may have been tailored to smaller-scale operations, *Acres U.S.A.* included information applicable to larger-scale farms.

Mother Earth News, founded by John and Jane Shuttleworth in 1970, went beyond farming practices to encompass an entire lifestyle—perhaps not unlike the content of early 1900s farming magazines that addressed farming, home, family, and lifestyle. But *Mother Earth News* was driven by a mission to address environmental problems (Hill III 2019). In part, *Mother Earth News* was founded in response to the problems John Shuttleworth saw in agribusiness: its reliance on pesticides and the loss of small family farms to large corporate operations (Shuttleworth 1975a). Five years after its founding, *Mother Earth News* enjoyed a circulation of 250,000 from its initial subscription list of just 147 (Shuttleworth 1975b).

Like other successful magazines, *Mother Earth News* took its message beyond the covers of the magazine. It offered world tours so "readers could see for themselves that the planet was worth saving" (Hill III 2019). In the early 1980s, 20,000 people each summer attended seminars put on by the magazine, listeners could tune in to its syndicated radio show, and *Mother Earth News* alternative-fuel vehicles made media appearances across the country (Hill III 2019).

Traditional farming magazines weren't covering organic practices. Whether influenced by advertisers whose products were counter to the organic movement or focused on proven methods for increasing yields on large-scale commercial farms, traditional ag publications didn't educate readers about organic farming practices. An analysis of the coverage of organic agriculture in *Farm Journal*, *Successful Farming*, and *Progressive*

Farmer from 1985 to 2005 found "so little discussion about organic farming in farm trade publications, readers of those magazines may have never been adequately informed of the potential benefits of organic farming practices" (Thomas 2011, 92).

FARMER SUCCESS STORIES

Farmer success stories illustrate the influence of farming magazines throughout the twentieth century. A staple of editorial content since the early 1900s, farmer success stories typically describe how a farmer's "management skill or use of technology has enabled him to increase crop or livestock production, improve labor efficiency, or solve some other common farming problem" (Walter 1996, 595). From the 1930s, the farmers selected for portrayal generally have operated larger-than-average farms that are "more highly capitalized and industrialized" (Walter 1996, 601). In the 1930s and 1940s, success stories referenced a farmer's "hard work and appreciation of farming as a way of life" (Walter 1996, 601).

During the 1950s and 1960s, those portrayed as successful farmers were "businessmen first and foremost, achieving higher yields by controlling nature and farming more acres than ever before" (Walter 1996, 602–3). Such messages both influenced and underscored a period of rapid technological advancement. While the impact on readers and their farming practices can't be proven, these stories suggest mainstream farming magazines provided a specific model for readers looking for guidance in successful farming practices (Walter 1996). These stories are further evidence that traditional farm magazines advocated and celebrated the farmer's triumph over nature, while alternative publications advocated and celebrated a harmony with nature—a fundamental rift between two farming ideologies, each with their own magazines to define, inform, educate, and reinforce their ideals.

GROWING PUBLISHING HOUSES

Several farm magazines provided the impetus for their publishers to expand and reach new audiences. According to Steve Lacy, chairman of the board, Meredith Corporation, in *Successful Farming*'s earliest days its salespeople called on family farms to sell subscriptions and were consistently greeted by the farmer's wife. Recognizing an opportunity for growth, E. T. Meredith launched *Better Homes and Gardens* magazine in 1924 (Lacy 2018). Fast-forward almost 100 years, and with the acquisition of Time, Inc., in 2018, Meredith Corporation became the largest magazine company in the world.

The Progressive Farmer had impact beyond its print editions, too, leading a reorganization of North Carolina's Department of Agriculture and the founding of North Carolina State University (Wilson 2008). In 1912 it was the first Southern farm magazine to hire a full-time home department editor (Deterling 2011) and was responsible for the creation of *Southern Living* magazine when the "Country Living" section of *Progressive Farmer* was expanded into its own magazine in 1966 (Wilson 2008; Lauder 2007; Deterling 2011). The new magazine was launched in part because a growing shift to agribusiness meant lifestyle content was no longer seen as having much relevance in a farming magazine (Lauder 2007).

Successful Farming magazine not only provided the launchpad for Meredith Corporation; Agriculture.com—*Successful Farming*'s website, which launched in 1995—was the first agriculture media site in the United States and one of the earliest magazine websites. According to Kurns (2019), who led the efforts to launch Agriculture.com, the website was "an early sign of the transformation of the entire business, a transformation of farming, the transformation of media. It was truly a tectonic shift in our world."

ROOTS OF CONTENT MARKETING

Traditional publishers weren't the only ones to address farmers' need for information. John Deere's magazine, *The Furrow*, is widely recognized as one of the first content marketing publications (Edgecliffe-Johnson 2014; Pulizzi 2011, 2012; Palmieri 2013; Triantafyllis 2013). Content marketing utilizes "the writing standards of conventional journalistic products" but the "content is designed on behalf of an organization with an aim to engage their customers and/or members, deepen the relationship, which shall ultimately lead to loyalty, and—in the case of profit-oriented organizations—increased sales" (Haeusermann 2013, 104). Launched in 1895, *The Furrow* reached four million readers by 1912. While its North American circulation today has dropped from that number to "well over a half million" it remains influential (Jones 2019). Existing John Deere customers are the only ones eligible to receive the magazine. This approach to distribution has been the model all along, says editor David G. Jones. "You can't sign up for a subscription. You can't go to the store to buy one. Ninety-five percent of the audience is involved in production agriculture full-time somehow" (Jones 2019).

It is worth noting that most business-to-business magazines follow a similar controlled circulation distribution model in which only readers who meet certain criteria—typically certain senior job titles with spending authority—receive the magazine. In the case of a business-to-business magazine, advertisers typically pay a premium to reach a highly focused and therefore highly desirable audience. In the case of John Deere, *The Furrow* is part of the company's overall marketing strategy. According to Jones, one year of *The Furrow* exposes readers to 65 million print advertising impressions. "Readership surveys tell us 40 percent of recipients read every single word, including the ads, in every single magazine" (Jones 2019).

The editorial content in *The Furrow* makes virtually no mention of John Deere or its products; the ad pages do the work of promoting the company and its products. Nor do editorial photos include John Deere tractors or other equipment; again, ad pages feature John Deere equipment. "If you look back at 70 years of *The Furrow*, you won't see the words John Deere more than half a dozen times [in editorial content]" (Jones 2019).

In an industry that has experienced advancements over the years, the mission of *The Furrow* is "exactly the same today" as it was when Charles Deere, son of John Deere, started the magazine. *The Furrow* is designed to help sell John Deere equipment by "giving the farmer something he or she needs; information they need to run their operations better . . . accurate, unbiased information" (Jones 2019).

And that's the purpose of every twentieth-century farm magazine.

CONCLUSION

Since their debut, farm magazines have been a source of practical information for farmers and farm families. Chock-full of recommendations for improved crop yield, better animal health, and higher prices at market, ag magazines guide those in the business of farming. The magazines were a vehicle by which the latest research developments from the Department of Agriculture could make their way to farmers in the fields.

And yet, for much of the twentieth century, farm magazines served a more expansive role in the lives of their readers. The magazines developed academic lessons for children in rural schools; home plans to shelter farmers and their families; explanations of how the latest government policies would impact farmers; poetry and fiction to entertain readers; recipes for farm wives; and information bureaus that not only answered farming-related questions, but a bevy of inquiries about relationships, personal care, automobiles, and more.

So, too, were these magazines a means of delivering readers to advertisers. Farm magazines in the twentieth century were subsidized by advertising dollars just as most consumer magazines are today. As such, advertisers seem to have had an outsized, if mostly unspoken, role in shaping the content of the magazines. Even in some of the darkest periods for agriculture—the 1930s and 1980s for instance—editorial content encouraged readers to invest in new equipment and other enhancements for their farms.

Traditional farm magazines rarely featured organic farming practices. Rather, articles encouraged the use of herbicides, pesticides, and modified seeds along with the latest tractors and implements, all in the name of successful agricultural practices. A look at the advertisements throughout the magazines shows a collection of fertilizer, seed, and machinery companies. Were these messages simply best practices for running a farm business, or the influence of advertisers who needed to continue selling, no matter the economic outlook or environmental impact?

Farming magazines and their reader-engagement techniques serve as a model for today's magazines as all-encompassing brands. More than monthly print publications, farm magazine brands extended their reach into all aspects of farm life. In addition to editorial content that went beyond the fields and into the home, these magazines offered syndicated radio shows, seminars, and tours, all creating robust brands prevalent in the lives of farm families.

Content that catered to the entire farm family certainly provided reader service. Yet it also reinforced gendered stereotypes about roles on the farm. Women's content in farm magazines focused on recipes, child-rearing, home keeping, and fashion. It was largely men who were shown working in the fields, tending to the animals, and making the decisions. Rather than simply a reflection of reality, these gendered portrayals served to reinforce masculine hegemony of U.S. farm culture.

Alternative farming practices debuted in magazines during the twentieth century, though not in the pages of traditional farm magazines. These practices needed their own magazines, because traditional ag magazines covered traditional farming practices. The first "alternative" farming magazine launched in the 1940s, with more to follow in the 1970s. These magazines came into being, in part, because of social, cultural, and environmental movements of the time. They were an important counterpoint to the advertiser-driven messages promoting herbicides and pesticides for farm success found in the pages of traditional farming publications. And while these alternative farming cultures were initially small, they steadily grew.

The impact of farm publications of the twentieth century extends beyond the magazines and their brands in other ways. Several magazines highlighted in this chapter—*Successful Farming*, *Progressive Farmer*, and *Organic Farming and Gardening*—were the foundations on which publishing houses were built.

Farming publications may seem a narrow, and perhaps even quaint, niche category in the world of magazines. Yet throughout the twentieth century they played a crucial role in agricultural communities throughout rural America. In addition, this genre of magazines, as well as their founders and publishers, had a much broader impact: a lasting impact on farming practices, with equally consequential influence on magazine publishing in the United States.

REFERENCES

"A Practical Experiment." 1902. *Successful Farming*, October 1902: 7.

"About Acres U.S.A. Magazine." n.d. Acres USA, Swift Communications. Accessed June 28, 2019, https://www.acresusa.com/pages/about-acres-usa-magazine.

Alston, Lee J. "Farm Foreclosures in the United States During the Interwar Period." 1983. *The Journal of Economic History* 43 (4): 885–903.

"Answers to Questions of General Interest." 1925. *Successful Farming*, August 1925: 13.

Bell, Shannon Elizabeth, Alicia Hullinger, and Lilian Brislen. 2015. "Manipulated Masculinities: Agribusiness, Deskilling, and the Rise of the Businessman-Farmer in the United States." *Rural Sociology* 80 (3): 285–313.

Boehmer, Stephanie M. 2003. "Organic Gardening: A Guide to Resources: 1989–September 2003." Alternative Farming Systems Information Center, National Agricultural Library, U.S. Department of Agriculture, https://pubs.nal.usda.gov/sites/pubs.nal.usda.gov/files/org_gardening.0.htm.

Bradley, Harriet. 1989. *Men's Work, Women's Work*. Cambridge: Polity Press.

Brantley, Bill. 1967. "Will We See More Corporate Farming?" *Successful Farming*, February: 52.

Callahan, Sean. 1999. "Farm Journal." *Business Marketing*. 1 (March): 20. *Academic OneFile*, http://link.galegroup.com/apps/doc/A54104720/AONE?u=drakeu_main&sid=AONE&xid=939ed6e3.

Casey, Janet Galligani. 2004. "This Is YOUR Magazine": Domesticity, Agrarianism, and The Farmer's Wife." *American Periodicals* 14 (2): 179–211.

Cooper, Gael L. 1999. "Edwin Thomas Meredith." *The Serials Librarian* 37 (2): 33–58.

Coughenour, C. M., and L. Swanson. 1983. "Work Statuses and Occupations of Men and Women in Farm Families and the Structure of Farms." *Rural Sociology* 48 (1): 23–43.

Creech, Joseph W. 2006. *Righteous Indignation: Religion and the Populist Movement*. Urbana: University of Illinois Press.

Deterling, Del. 2011. "The Progressive Farmer Turns 125." *Agri Marketing* (April): 72.

Edgecliffe-Johnson, A. 2014. "The Invasion of Corporate News." *Financial Times*, September 19.

Evans, James F. 1969. *Prairie Farmer and WLS: The Burridge Butler Years*. Urbana: University of Illinois Press.

Evans, James F., and Rodolfo N. Salcedo. 1974. *Communications in Agriculture: The American Farm Press*. Ames: Iowa State University Press.

"Farm Journal." n.d. *Farm | Journal AgWeb*, AgWeb. Accessed July 5, 2019. https://www.agweb.com/farmjournal/magazine/.

"Farm Topics in Season: Now Is the Time to:" 1944. *The Farm Journal*, June: 23.

Fett, John. 1984. "Agricultural Market and Outlook Information in U.S. Newspapers, Radio, Television, Magazines and Farmers' Newsletters and Farmers' Newslines." Department of Agricultural Journalism Bulletin 42, University of Wisconsin-Madison.

Ford, Stephen, and Emerson Babb. 1989. "Farmer Sources and Uses of Information." *Agribusiness* 5 (September): 465–76.

Fox, Kirk. 1947. Letter to Reader, Editor, *Successful Farming*, December. Original document.

Gardner, B. L. 2002. *American Agriculture in the Twentieth Century: How It Flourished and What It Cost*. Cambridge, MA: Harvard University Press. Retrieved from http://search.ebscohost.com.cowles-proxy.drake.edu/login.aspx?direct=true&db=nlebk&AN=282275&site=ehost-live&scope=site.

Gross, Daniel. 2008. *Our Roots Grow Deep: The Story of Rodale*. Reading, PA: Rodale, Inc.

Haeusermann, T. 2013. "Custom Publishing in the UK: The Rise of a Silent Giant." *Publishing Research Quarterly* 29 (2): 99–109.

Hays, Robert, and Ann Reisner. 1991. "Feeling the Heat from Advertisers: Farm Magazine Writers and Ethical Pressures." *Journalism Quarterly* 67: 936–942.

Henderson, Jason, Brent Gloy, and Michael Boehlje. 2011. "Agriculture's Boom-Bust Cycles: Is This Time Different?" *Economic Review* 96 (4). Retrieved from https://go-gale-com.cowles-proxy.drake.edu/ps/i.do?id=GALE%7CA301775815&v=2.1&u=drakeu_main&it=r&p=AONE&sw=w.

"Here Is the Way WE Want to Live!" 1944. *Successful Farming*, June: 24–25.

Hill III, Oscar H. 2019. "50 Years of Mother Earth News and Counting." *Mother Earth News*. April/May 2019. https://www.motherearthnews.com/nature-and-environment/50-years-and-counting-zm0z19amzrrog.

"Hitching the Plow to the Tractor." 1926. *Successful Farming*, March: 34.

"How and Why of Crop Rotation." 1913. *Successful Farming*, April: 10.

"How to Make Farming Profitable." 1902. *Successful Farming*, October: 2.

Howe, Eleanor. 1935. "Seven Budget Recipes." *The Farm Journal*, February: 7.

"Improving the Farm Draft Horse." 1910. *Successful Farming*, December: 4.

Jellison, Katherine. 1993. *Entitled to Power: Farm Women and Technology, 1913–1963*. Chapel Hill: University of North Carolina Press.

Jones, David G. 2019. Interview with author. July 1.

Kelly, William. 1992. "Rodale Press and Organic Gardening." Proceedings of the Workshop on the History of the Organic Movement on 24 July 1991 at The Pennsylvania State University. Published in *HortTechnology* 2 (2); DOI: https://doi.org/10.21273/HORTECH.2.2.261.

Klonsky, Karen, and Laura Tourte. 1998. "Organic Agricultural Production in the United States: Debates and Directions." *American Journal of Agricultural Economics* 80 (5), Proceedings Issue (December 1998): 1119–24. Stable URL: https://www.jstor.org/stable/1244215. Accessed June 26, 2019.

Kroma, Margaret M. 2002. "Gender and Agricultural Imagery: Pesticide Advertisements in the 21st Century Agricultural Transition." *Culture and Agriculture* 24 (1): 2–13.

Kurns, David. 2019. Interview with author. June 27.

Lacy, Steve. 2018. "Address to Meredith Apprentices" (speech). Meredith Corporation. April 12.

Lauder, Tracy. 2007. "The Southern Living Solution: How the Progressive Farmer Launched a Magazine and a Legacy." *The Alabama Review* 60 (3) (July): 186.

Lauters, Amy Mattson. 2009. *More than a Farmer's Wife: Voices of American Farm Women, 1910–1960*. Columbia: University of Missouri Press.

Malena, Dave. 1967. "Laws to Control Farm Wastes—Are They Coming?" *Successful Farming*, August: 31.

Marti, Donald B. 1980. "Agricultural Journalism and the Diffusion of Knowledge: The First Half-Century in America." *Agricultural History* 54 (January): 28–37.

Meredith, Edwin T. 1916. Manuscript of address delivered at the Associated Advertising Club of the World. (June).

———. 1920. Abstract of Remarks of E. T. Meredith, Secretary of Agriculture, at meeting of Agricultural Editors' Association, Hotel Harrington, Washington, D.C., June 17.

———. 1926. "Getting the Most Out of Advertising." *Successful Farming*, June 1926: 3.

Meredith III, Edwin T. 2001. (interview audio recording). Des Moines Oral History Project. *Oral History Interviews of the Des Moines Oral History Project, 1998–2001*. Recorded January 2001.

"New Equipment for the Farm." 1934. *The Farm Journal*, April: 14.

Newcomb, Ozro R. 1910. "Problems of the Country Church." *Successful Farming*, December: 72–75.

Nordin, Dennis and Roy Scott. 2005. *From Prairie Farmer to Entrepreneur: The Transformation of Midwestern Agriculture*. Bloomington: Indiana University Press.

"Our Advertisers Are Honest." 1934. *Successful Farming*, April: 60.

"Our Story." n.d. *Rodale Institute*, Rodale Institute. Accessed June 28, 2019. https://rodaleinstitute.org/about/.

Palmieri, M. 2013. "Help vs. Hype." *Landscape Management* 52 (10): 6.

"Pst!—Bad News for Pests." 1934. *The Farm Journal*, April: 7.

Pulizzi, Joe. 2011. "Content Marketing Has Arrived. Should Publishers Be Worried? Nine out of 10 Organizations Are Using Content Marketing, per CMI." *Folio: The Magazine for Magazine Management* 40 (10): 43.

———. 2012. "The Rise of Storytelling as the New Marketing." *Publishing Research Quarterly* 28 (2): 116–23. doi:10.1007/s12109-012-9264-5.

Quebral, Nora C. 1970. "Wilmer Atkinson and the Early *Farm Journal*." *Journalism Quarterly*, Spring 1970, 47, 1; Periodicals Archive Online, 65.

Rasmussen, W. D. 1960. *Readings in the History of American Agriculture*. Urbana: University of Illinois Press.

"Reducing Cleaning Costs." 1934. *Successful Farming*, February: 41.

Reuss, Carol. 1973. *Editorial Involvement in Regional/Split Run Editions*. Paper presented at the Annual Meeting of the Association for Education in Journalism. Ft. Collins, Colorado. August.

Reynolds, Mary R. 1944. "Smart Clothes from Feed Sacks." *The Farm Journal*, March: 66.

Richard, Tracy. 1953. "Easier Upkeep for Men's Summer Suits." *The Farm Journal*, May: 104–5.

Rodale, Maria. 2010. *Organic Manifesto: How Organic Farming Can Heal Our Planet, Feed the World, and Keep Us Safe*. New York: Rodale, Inc.

———. 2019. Interview with author. July 9.
Rural Schools Bulletin. April 1931. Rural Schools Bureau of Successful Farming. Des Moines, Iowa.
Sachs, C. E. 1983. *The Invisible Farmers: Women in Agricultural Production.* Totowa, NJ: Rowman & Allanheld.
Schultz, Howard. 1945. "Who Wants a 'Hired Man'?" *Successful Farming*, April: 20–21.
Score Card Test of Farm Papers. n.d. *Successful Farming.* Score card test of Successful Farming as a medium for the advertising of standard merchandise, 1917–1919.
Secor, Alson. 1926. "Insuring the Security of Bank Deposits." *Successful Farming.* June: 5.
Shuttleworth, John. 1975a. "John Shuttleworth, Founder of *Mother Earth News*, Interview Part I." *Mother Earth News*, January/February. https://www.motherearthnews.com/nature-and-environment/interview-with-the-mother-earth-news-founder.
———. 1975b. "John Shuttleworth, Founder of *Mother Earth News*, Interview Part II." *Mother Earth News*, March/April. https://www.motherearthnews.com/nature-and-environment/the-plowboy-interview-john-shuttleworth-zmaz75mazgoe.
Smith, C. Beaman, and H. K. Atwood. 1913. The Relation of Agricultural Extension Agencies to Farm Practices, USDA, Bureau of Plant Industry. Circular number 117, March 15: 25
Spielmaker, D. M. 2018, March 21. "Growing a Nation Historical Timeline." Retrieved from https://www.agclassroom.org/gan/timeline/index.htm.
Stephenson, R. E. 1934. "The Biggest Farm Waste." *The Farm Journal*, July: 5.
Successful Farming Fashion Catalogue. 1920. Spring and Summer. *Successful Farming.* Des Moines, Iowa.
Snyder, A. H. 1913. "How and Why of Crop Rotation." *Successful Farming*, April: 10–11.
Temple, Charlotte M. 1934. "Rural Club Women Lead." *Farm Journal*, April: 11.
"The Thorps Farm without Manpower." 1945. *Successful Farming*, October: 6.
Thomas, Robert Z. 2011. "Tilling New Soil: Coverage of Organic Agriculture in Farm Journal, Successful Farming, and Progressive Farmer from 1985 to 2005." Thesis presented to the Scripps College of Communication of Ohio University. March.
Thomas, Su Ann, and James F. Evans. 1963. "Where Farmers Get Information." *Agricultural Communications Research Report* 14, University of Illinois.
Triantafyllis, J. 2013. "Sponsored Content Programs all the Rage with Young People. (Greek television)." *Video Age International* 33 (5): 1.
U.S. Department of Agriculture. 1928. *Yearbook of Agriculture, 1928.* Congressional document.
Vincent, Gary. 1980. "Where You'll Get Information in the '80s." *Successful Farming*, December 1980: 21–22E.
Walter, Gerry. 1995. "A 'Curious Blend': The Successful Farmer in American Farm Magazines, 1984–1991." *Agriculture and Human Values* 12 (3): 55–68.

———. 1996. "The Ideology of Success in Major American Farm Magazines, 1934–1991." *Journalism and Mass Communication Quarterly*, Autumn, 73 (3): 594–608.

Williams, Miriam. 1944. "How to Can Like a Champion." *The Farm Journal*, June 1944: 42–43.

Willis, R. D. 1925. "Shall I Quit the Farm? Why One Family Is Going to Stick." *Successful Farming*, February 1925: 13.

Wilson, Charles Reagan. 2008. "Progressive Farmer." In *The New Encyclopedia of Southern Culture: Volume 11: Agriculture and Industry*, edited by M. Walker and J. Cobb, 190–92. Chapel Hill: University of North Carolina Press. *JSTOR*, www.jstor.org/stable/10.5149/9781469616681_walker.59.

Wood, Ivan D. 1925. "More Ways to Stop Soil Washing." *Successful Farming*, May: 15.

"You'll Pay Less Taxes." 1954. *The Farm Journal*, September: 18.

Chapter 7

Magazine as Gay Lifeline

AIDS and the Emergence of POZ

Gary R. Hicks

"Despair to hope. Fear to knowledge." With these words of empowerment, gay activist Sean Strub welcomed readers to the first issue of his new magazine, *POZ*. Newly diagnosed with AIDS himself, and discouraged by mainstream media coverage of the crisis, Strub launched the magazine in 1994 to reach a highly stigmatized, marginalized, and often-hidden community.

"Almost no one knew what *POZ* meant when we launched," Strub wrote. "It had the advantage of serving as a double entendre, meaning both 'HIV positive' as well as 'thinking positive and taking control of one's life,'" which was central to the magazine's message (Green 2019).

While *POZ* was meant for all people living with an HIV or AIDS[1] diagnosis, this chapter specifically considers its value to the gay male reader. From the epidemic's beginning, arguably no group suffered from as much discrimination, blame, ostracism, and hatred as did the gay male community. People who had already been told in large part by society's institutions that their sexuality was unnatural, a perversion, illegal in most parts of the country, even an abomination, became the obvious targets of the hysteria that was fomented by typical mainstream media coverage of the time.

At a time when most HIV-positive people only saw themselves depicted in the media as "diagnoses," and when the limited resources available to them for information were more often than not clinical and dispassionate, *POZ* provided a corrective. Glossy, and colorful in both style and content, the magazine addressed its audience as multidimensional individuals, people for whom HIV/AIDS was central to their lives but did not define their lives. Along with health advice were personality profiles, art and theater reviews, political coverage, and tips on dating with HIV (exactly the kind of content that would be expected from a general-interest magazine). It was designed to be read not only by those with HIV/AIDS, but also their family members, caregivers, and anyone with an interest in the biggest untold story of the preceding decade. But it was to the marginalized that it really spoke, mainstreaming their concerns and including them in the conversation.

EMERGENCE OF AN ACTIVIST

Strub, born in 1958 in Iowa City, Iowa, did not come out of the closet until he moved to Washington, D.C., in 1976 to attend college at Georgetown University. Beginning with his part-time work operating the elevators in Senate office buildings, he quickly developed a passion for politics and started cultivating professional relationships with people in power. In 1990 he became the first openly HIV-positive person to run for federal office when he ran for a seat in the U.S. House of Representatives. A long-term AIDS survivor, Strub has spent his career advocating for the rights of the LGBTQ^2 community and has been one of the nation's most outspoken and most often cited AIDS activists, appearing in numerous news articles on the issue. He currently serves as mayor of Milford, Pennsylvania (Strub 2014).

In his autobiography, Strub titled the chapter about founding *POZ* "Creating Communities" and discussed the magazine's reach to all people affected by HIV/AIDS. "*POZ* was a way for people with HIV to get together, in its pages, every month," he wrote (Strub 2014, 298). The magazine was available on newsstands, in bookstores, and through mail subscriptions, but it was also distributed free to doctors' offices, HIV clinics, correctional facilities, and anywhere else Strub and his staff knew the HIV community existed. To fund the venture, Strub sold his house and borrowed heavily. Few advertisers were interested.

The magazine not only survived, it thrived, in print and online. By 2020, the circulation was 125,000. And since 2016, POZ.com has offered all of the editorial content of the magazine, along with special features including videos, slideshows, community forums, and an online social network that has more than 150,000 registered members (*POZ* 2021).

MEDIA AND THE NEW "UNTOUCHABLES"

For decades following the 1981 *New York Times* article, "Rare Cancer Seen in 41 Homosexuals" (Altman 1981), HIV/AIDS was indelibly linked to the nation's gay male population. The *Times* story reported on a new, mysterious, and deadly ailment predominantly affecting gay men. The illness didn't even have a name at that point, but soon researchers and the media began calling it GRID, for gay-related immune deficiency.

GRID was the primary term used in a 1982 *New York Times* piece with the headline "New Homosexual Disorder Worries Health Officials" (Altman 1982). Though mentioning that some victims of the illness were heterosexuals and intravenous drug users, the story overwhelmingly linked the disease to gay men and their sexual behavior. Though future medical research—as well as the overall progression of the illness—would prove that what later became known as the AIDS crisis was not limited to any one community, "AIDS hysteria became a familiar term in the media and public life and its truth was borne out in shocking examples" (Mustich 2011). This connection further demonized what was arguably the most marginalized group in society at the time. "Gay men's sexuality, again, became an insidious curse and, in the context of AIDS, a life-threatening experience" (Kyle 1989).

News coverage of AIDS did change in character following high-profile cases such as those of Ryan White, the thirteen-year-old hemophiliac who contracted AIDS through a blood transfusion and was subsequently barred from attending public school (MacNeil 1985), and Wimbledon champion Arthur Ashe, also believed to have contracted the virus during a blood transfusion (Rhoden 1992). When basketball star Earvin "Magic" Johnson appeared on the Arsenio Hall show in 1991, one day after revealing in a *Sports Illustrated* column that he was HIV-positive, he received uproarious applause from the studio audience when he told Hall, "I'm far from being homosexual, you already know that" (Johnson 2016).

Instances of violence against gay men increased as media coverage of the epidemic expanded (Greer 1986), with the perpetrators, if caught, oftentimes saying that they acted in response to those responsible for AIDS. In his 1987 account of the illness's impact on the gay community, *San Francisco Chronicle* reporter Randy Shilts recalls news reports of attackers calling their victims "plague-carrying faggots" and "diseased queers" (Shilts 1987, 311). "If we don't kill these fags, they'll kill us with their fucking AIDS disease," one assailant told the police after being arrested. "So-called 'gay-bashing'— incidents of violence against homosexuals—increased and they had a decidedly AIDS theme" (Cimons 1991).

Even with the rapidly expanding disease, it took almost two years from the original 1981 *New York Times* article for a story about AIDS to actually run on the paper's front page—even in a city experiencing some of the largest numbers of new cases and fatalities. In a 2018 review of the paper's coverage of the early AIDS crisis, *New York Times* features editor Kurt Soller noted that the paper's coverage was often stigmatizing and dismissive.

Information about the spread of illness was often scant, judgmental or distressingly vague—even while reporters on the Science desk were trying their best with an ever-evolving story. The social and emotional toll of AIDS and the resulting queer movement were, when covered, often buried in the back of the newspaper (on a page called Styles of the Times), far from national news stories that were deemed important enough for the front page. (Soller 2018)

THE "PERFECT" DISEASE

For some, the early framing of AIDS as a gay issue served both political and cultural interests. Following the nascent stage of the gay rights movement at the Stonewall uprising in 1969, the gay community experienced a decade of progress both in public opinion and in representation in social and cultural institutions. Leaders of the gay and lesbian movement learned from the civil rights and anti-Vietnam War protests of the preceding decade the most effective means of shifting public opinion and policy—particularly the need to be public and vocal (Suran 2009).

They had a lot of work to do. A Harris public opinion poll taken just after Stonewall showed that 63 percent of Americans said homosexuals were more harmful than helpful to society. "This balance of opinion at the time put homosexuals in similar esteem as prostitutes and atheists—although not as negatively viewed as Americans who were members of the Communist Party" (Motel 2013). The 1970s, however, proved a period of growth and transformation for the community, in terms of political and economic clout and increased public visibility. Major cities began passing ordinances protecting gay citizens, the first Pride events were held, positive storylines began appearing in films and on TV, and even mainstream news media ran stories sympathetic to gays and lesbians.

On November 1, 1972, the ABC television network presented its viewers with a groundbreaking episode of the popular "Movie of the Week": *That Certain Summer*, a made-for-TV movie about a divorced man and his gay lover. The gay couple was portrayed by well-known actors Hal Holbrook and Martin Sheen, both of whom were advised by their agents not to take on a gay role. Though largely well-received, and ultimately nominated for seven Emmys, network executives insisted that the writers include dialogue indicating the widely held belief that homosexuality was a sickness (McDonald 2014). Still, it was the first time that gay men were presented on national television from a sympathetic viewpoint.

Movies also broke through tired and stigmatizing stereotypes of homosexuality in the 1970s. In his 1981 book *The Celluloid Closet: Homosexuality in the Movies*, Vito Russo documents and decodes the tropes of homosexuality that Hollywood had used for years. He, too, noted the beginnings of a change in the direction of 1970s films, with pressure from gay rights groups sometimes prompting the changes. Demeaning dialogue about homosexuality in 1973's *The Laughing Policeman*, for example, was changed after complaints by gay rights activists (Russo 1981). Even in comedies, screenwriters began to abandon worn-out jokes about gay people.

In 1973, the board of the American Psychiatric Association voted 13–0 in favor of removing homosexuality as a psychiatric disorder in its diagnostic manual (Drescher 2015).

News media also began to take a more nuanced look at homosexuality, and started paying attention to the social and cultural issues surrounding gay life, though not always in a positive way. Newspapers, news radio, and TV news operations began placing reporters on beats that included—but were certainly not exclusive to—covering the gay community. While almost entirely restricted to major cities with large gay populations, this move represented a major shift in how editors and producers viewed the newsworthiness of gays. Even the notoriously homophobic then-editor of the *New York Times*, A. M. Rosenthal, who denied his reporters' requests to cover the gay community, occasionally acquiesced when the story met his designation of newsworthiness (Atwood 1996, 166).

While the decade of the 1970s brought greater influence to the gay community, many of the strides were short-lived. AIDS, along with its coverage in the media, brought about a backlash that some community activists have said ultimately changed the direction of the movement from a focus on gaining civil rights to saving lives. "The goal prior to the AIDS crisis was to get the government out of our lives," Jeff Levi, executive director of the National Gay and Lesbian Task Force, told the *New York Times* in 1987. "Now, because of AIDS, we were asking the government to help save our lives. The objective of the movement is no longer just to see a right to privacy, but also to get the government and society to affirm our lives just like they do for heterosexuals" (Morgan 1987).

States and the federal government were slow to address the issue through research funding and care for those impacted. Ronald Reagan, who was president at the time of the first reported cases, only publicly said the word AIDS five years into his presidency—well into his second term. And gays continued to be blamed for the suffering AIDS caused them. As conservative columnist Patrick Buchanan wrote in 1983, "The poor homosexuals; they have declared war on nature and now nature is exacting an awful retribution" (Cimons 1991). Cleve Jones, an AIDS activist and founder of the NAMES Project AIDS Memorial Quilt, recalled in an interview with the PBS show *Frontline* (2006) seeing a bumper sticker that read, "AIDS: It's killing all the right people."

"ACT UP! FIGHT BACK! FIGHT AIDS!"

Some members of the gay community, particularly those in large cities, responded to the media coverage of AIDS, the backlash against gay men, and government inaction through organization and protest. Activist organizations like ACT UP and Queer Nation were founded during this time, and names like Larry Kramer, Randy Shilts, Vito Russo, and Michel Foucault entered the public conversation about AIDS and the meaning of gay male sexuality (Thompson 1994, 211, 321, 224, 265).

This was long before the Supreme Court's decision legalizing same-sex marriage and nullification of state sodomy laws. Remaining in the closet was a reasonable, if ultimately unsustainable, retreat from the new pressures AIDS posed to openly gay men. Outing, the unsanctioned public identification of a closeted individual as gay, came into being. "Everyone of privilege, everyone who'd gotten by somehow—either by testing negative or by sitting in a powerful position in this society—was obligated now to do whatever she or he could to end this disease," wrote Michelangelo Signorile in his 1993 pro-outing manifesto (Signorile 1993, 65). Gay men turned on gay men. The once sacrosanct right to decide when, or if, to come out as gay, was now being questioned by some gays themselves as a response to AIDS and the media. Publications like Signorile's *OutWeek* fueled these debates.

If AIDS served to push some gay men back in the closet, media coverage at the time certainly indicated that was the right direction to go. Some news organizations, while tentative in their commitment to serious coverage of the crisis, were more than willing to cover the more salacious side of gay male sexuality. "The Case for Closing Bathhouses: Night Visit by Post Reporter Reveals Shocking Evidence," was the headline of a *New York Post* article on one of the city's gay bathhouses. The story began, "It is midnight and inside the atmosphere is dark, steamy and sad. It is the Skid Row of gay sex. And every form of sex—anal and oral and anonymous—that the city and state wants to outlaw continues to go on" (Esposito 1985).

Compare this story with one published by *Life* magazine in 1964 to "introduce" mainstream American readers with homosexuality. Within the first paragraph, the story used the words "social disorder" in describing homosexuality and accused homosexuals of "openly admitting, even flaunting, their deviation" (Welch 1964, 66). More than twenty years separated the *Life* and *Post* stories, yet their common themes of the dangers gay men pose to society were amazingly similar.

It was as if two decades of public opinion progress for the gay community had been wiped out in the backlash brought on by AIDS. Meanwhile, the suffering continued in private lives. "I know there are some who die because they give up," a man sick with AIDS in rural Minnesota told *St.*

Paul Pioneer Press reporter Jacqui Banaszynski for a story called "AIDS in the Heartland," which won the 1988 Pulitzer Prize in Feature Writing. "They have no hope, no reason to fight. Everything they're faced with is so desperate and dismal. . . . I believe the biggest obstacle for us who have AIDS or an AIDS-related complex is fighting the fear and anxiety we have over the whole thing. Every positive thing, every bit of hope, is something to hold on to" (Banaszynski 1987).

While highlighting the lives of a committed gay couple far outside the city-dwelling stereotypes of gay man perpetuated by mainstream media, Banaszynski's story was really representative of the many gay men with AIDS living lives often isolated from family, community, and reliable, non-judgmental sources of information.

FINDING COMMUNITY IN PRINT

From the earliest stirrings of what could be called a gay "community," the dearth of coverage in mainstream media led gay men to alternative publications. *One Magazine*, published in the 1950s, contained essays and editorials by openly gay writers, mostly calling for assimilation into, and tolerance by, the heterosexual mainstream. Founded in 1967, *The Advocate*, a magazine that in 2020 billed itself as the leading source of LGBTQ news content in the world, began as an activist newspaper before becoming a glossy lifestyle magazine. While also covering the lesbian community, the magazine paid disproportionate attention to gay males and the consumerism of the gay "lifestyle." According to Sender, the magazine "consolidated the image of the ideal gay consumer, his (occasionally her) tastes, pleasures, and concerns, for readers and advertisers alike" (2006, 73).

When the AIDS epidemic struck, *The Advocate* robustly covered the crisis as a public health issue—an example of wide-scale governmental failings—and gave voice to a generation of both gay and AIDS activists. Early articles dealt with many issues that had been ignored by the mainstream press. Articles titled "Etiquette for an Epidemic: What to Say and Who to Tell When Someone Has AIDS," and "Your HIV Status, Should You Take the Test?" were examples of early articles that provided information useful to those living with an AIDS diagnosis. The magazine routinely ran pieces on safer-sex practices—information that even health professionals oftentimes failed to discuss with their gay patients.

In his 1996 book, *Straight News: Gays, Lesbians, and the News Media*, Edward Alwood credited *Advocate* coverage of AIDS with providing the kind of specific and direct information unavailable in the mainstream press. "As mainstream reporters and editors continued to search for language that would be acceptable to a broad-based readership, the gay press began describing the suspected methods of transmission in explicit terms, without relying on the vague euphemisms used in daily newspapers and broadcast news" (Alwood 1996, 222).

AGAINST THE ODDS

In his memoir, *Body Counts: A Memoir of Politics, Sex, AIDS, and Survival*, Strub recounts the initial doubts about the chances of a magazine named *POZ* succeeding. "One trade publication made a crack about readers not living long enough to renew subscriptions," Strub writes. Even the owner of *The Advocate*, Sam Watters, told the trade publication *AdAge* that he doubted that Strub's new magazine would make it. "What advertiser would want to advertise in a magazine on such a grim topic?" (Strub 2014, 286).

Strub, however, did not see the magazine in such bleak ways. "I envisioned *POZ* as a general-interest magazine reflecting the way we lived our lives with AIDS—pursuing careers, falling in love, raising our children, everything life entails—not just the death and dying that defined us in mainstream media" (Strub 2014, 286).

POZ had an initial audience of subscribers to a newsletter Strub and his partner created in the early 1990s for people on AIDS medications, including them on his own medical journey with AIDS. When *POZ* launched in April 1994, Strub made sure that his status was known to his expanded base of readers, too. He even ran pictures of his own lesions from Kaposi's sarcoma (a form of cancer that plagued many AIDS patients). His readers, he argued, were all members of his community.

Other media took note. A 1995 *New Yorker* story noted what it called "one of the strangest columns in American journalism: a page reproducing, with commentary, the latest lab report analyzing its publishers blood" (Lubow 1995). The blood report mentioned was Strub's T-cell test, which indicates how many infection-fighting white blood cells are present. "It's very freeing," Strub told the reporter. "People don't have to ask me how I am. They know. They've read it in the magazine."

From its beginning, Strub referred to *POZ* as a lifestyle magazine, an inspirational moniker for a publication marketed to people with a disease whose mortality rate just a few years earlier was eighteen months from an AIDS diagnosis. The first issue included advice columns, along with columns on the arts, media, even sex advice, all designed to, as staff writer Richard Perez-Feria (1994) wrote, "simultaneously provoke, inform and entertain in the vast arena that is AIDS."

Magazine as Gay Lifeline

Figure 7.1 The cover of the first issue of *POZ* (April–May 1994), which welcomed readers with the promise to help them move from "despair to hope" and from "fear to knowledge." Courtesy of POZ/CDM Publishing LLC.

The information—and entertainment—that *POZ* provided was as diverse as its readership. The first issue's cover story was on Ty Ross, the openly gay and HIV-positive grandson of 1964 Republican presidential candidate Barry Goldwater. Strub hired Kevin Sessums, a big-name celebrity interviewer for *Vanity Fair*, to interview Ross. "Kevin was already well known, and Ty's famously conservative Republican grandfather was as far removed from the popular impression of AIDs as could be" (Strub 2014, 289). The issue even teased readers with partially nude photos of Ross, not a feature necessarily associated with a magazine all about a "terminal illness."

All 30,000 newsstand copies sold out, and the publication increased its press run for its second issue from 100,000 to 150,000 (Kelly 1994). Half the copies were distributed free to people living with an HIV or AIDS diagnosis at doctors' offices and clinics. Reviews were strong: The *Los Angeles Times* called it "literate and provocative" (George 1995). *Utne Reader* (1995) hailed it as a publication that transcended the expected, given its name and audience:

> Despite its highly specialized subject matter, or perhaps because of it, leafing through *POZ* is in some ways a glance at American culture in the age of demographic pluralism. From one angle, it's a glitzy, over commercialized billboard stripe featuring lavish full-page color ads for drugs, vitamins, T-shirts, and, most prominently, insurance brokers offering viatical settlements. But tilt your head just a few degrees in another direction, and *POZ* is a poignant attempt at community building, offering its readers real services: information on medical developments; advice on financial matters; and even short autobiographical essays and sketches. The aesthetic bottom line, though, is the magazine's inspirational stories on individuals who, despite HIV, are persevering in the arts, sports, business—in every kind of human activity.

From its inception, Strub wanted *POZ* to be more about life and less about death. Yet, providing a readership with potentially lifesaving information is at the core of the magazine's purpose, and advertising space in *POZ* during this time was dominated by pharmaceutical industry ads promoting the use of newly developed drugs.

> Through *POZ*, we hope to shed light on the policies, people and practical issues involved with AIDS and, in the process, help people with AIDS lead longer and healthier lives. In my view, for a newly-diagnosed person with AIDS, information is a more important first step than any pill, potion or prayer. (Strub 1994)

Even publishers in the gay press recognized the importance of *POZ*. "*POZ* filled an incredibly important market niche," Ronald Kraft, the editor of *Genre*, a gay lifestyle magazine, told the *Los Angeles Times*. "A lot of gay magazines have been trying to cover AIDS, but it has been pretty piecemeal since AIDS is not the only issue affecting the gay community" (George 1995).

In keeping with Strub's desire that the magazine address all parts of its readers' lives, and not just their diagnoses, early issues contained such varied features as reviews of films and TV shows with AIDS themes; photo essays; profiles of scientists, politicians, and celebrities involved in AIDS awareness; and even a sex column with advice on cruising while in the hospital. Strub's approach proved popular among his readers. Sample letters to the editor following the first issue included:

> "Thank you. I can't express how good it feels to see a magazine that celebrates the purposefulness of our lives as people with HIV/AIDS. The interviews were interesting, humorous, and even titillating. I look forward to your next issue and the next."

> "I am a PWA (Person With AIDS) involved with AIDS since the beginning. I have gone through the whole spectrum of feelings and involvement. I have seen support groups evolve from fear, anger, gurus, emotional support and education; and now something else. Here comes POZ to show that there are other sides to AIDS than sickness and death."

> "Your magazine has afforded me the strength I need to carry on. I look forward to each issue as if I were waiting for a friend. The insightfulness of your articles and the humor and love each issue holds is wonderful. I feel so renewed with each issue, and the range of your articles and information is so usable. I keep all the issues and pore through them from time to time."

The magazine's relationship with its readers, one that Strub often referred to as one of trust, was aided by its style guidelines. Articles usually began by quoting a person with HIV or AIDS, and "doctors, scientists, and elected or government officials came later." Strub had a rule against the use of stock photography, always using real people with HIV or AIDS. "Survey research showed that *POZ* readers trusted the magazine more than they did AIDS organizations, other media, even their own doctors" (Strub 2014, 292).

POZ AND THE CHANGING FACE OF AIDS

With the introduction of protease inhibitors and other drug "cocktails" in the 1990s, the progression from HIV to AIDS began to slow and, in some cases, was prevented entirely (Quinn 2009). Magazine content evolved in response to growing acceptance of gays, recognition of their buying power, and the diminished threat AIDS posed to their survival.

A 2007 study of more than 400 articles on AIDS in *The Advocate* showed that beginning in the 1990s, the number of articles on health care, particularly AIDS, went down dramatically, while coverage of gay culture, gay celebrity, and gay consumerism increased (Tian 2007). This decrease in coverage may have been in response to the emergence of other glossy gay lifestyle magazines, such as *Out*, *Genre*, and *Attitude*, all of which wanted to take advantage of Wall Street's and Madison Avenue's discovery of the gay consumer. Corporations and advertisers previously disinclined to even acknowledge the gay audience were interested in cashing in on what many considered an untapped market. Perhaps fueled by the idea that all gay people have loads of disposable income—a myth that ignores the reality of life for most gay people—magazines like *The Advocate* saw a huge uptick in the amount of mainstream advertising coming their way. For some, the images of AIDS seemed incompatible with the images of consumerism.

As the face of HIV/AIDS changed, *POZ* continued to provide the most up-to-date information for the newly diagnosed and the connections they need to one another. Its digital version includes blogs, advice columns, and personal ads. But mostly, it continues to provide its readers a space for community. As stated on the magazine's current website:

> From the newly diagnosed to long-term survivors, from very young people to people aging with the virus, from people in the highest tax bracket to those on disability, POZ provides a platform for the HIV community to speak to one another, and the world at large. (*POZ* 2021)

POZ was a leader in helping shape our understanding of HIV/AIDS, and along the way became an important player in the story itself.

REFERENCES

"About Us." 2021. *POZ*, https://www.poz.com/page/about-us.

Altman, Lawrence. 1981. "Rare Cancer Seen in 41 Homosexuals." *New York Times*, July 3. https://www.nytimes.com/1981/07/03/us/rare-cancer-seen-in-41-homosexuals.html.

———. 1982. "New Homosexual Disorder Worries Health Officials." *New York Times*, May 11. https://www.nytimes.com/1982/05/11/science/new-homosexual-disorder-worries-health-officials.html.

Alwood, Edward. 1996. *Straight News: Gays, Lesbians, and the News Media*. New York: Oxford University Press.

Banaszynski, Jacqui. 1987. "AIDS in the Heartland." *St. Paul Pioneer Press*, June 21. http://www.jacquibanaszynski.com/bylines-2/aids-in-the-heartland/.

Cimons, Marlene. 1991. "Column One: AIDS: 'It's Changed Us Forever': Over a Decade the Crisis has Brought Out Society's Best and its Worst. It Has Also Galvanized Gays, Energized Researchers and Made Scientists More Accountable." *Los Angeles Times*, May 31. https://www.latimes.com/archives/la-xpm-1991-05-31-mn-2779-story.html.

Clarke, Juanne, N. 2007. "Homophobia Out of the Closet in the Media Portrayal of HIV/AIDS 1991, 1996 and 2001: Celebrity, Heterosexism and the Silent Victims." *Critical Public Health* 16(4):317–30. doi:10.1080/09581590601091620.

Drescher, Jack. 2015. "Out of DSM: Depathologizing Homosexuality." *Behavioral Sciences* (4):565–75. doi: 10.3390/bs5040565.

Esposito, Richard. 1985. "The Case for Closing Bathhouses: Night Visit by Post Reporter Reveals Shocking Evidence." *New York Post*, October 31.
Galambos, Colleen M. 2004. "The Changing Face of AIDS." *Health & Social Work* 29(2):83–85. doi.org/10.1093/hsw/29.2.83.
George, Lynell. 1995. "A Positive Vision: Through His Year-Old Magazine POZ, Sean O'Brien Strub Is Challenging the View of AIDS as a World of Suffering and Hopelessness." *Los Angeles Times*, January 30. https://www.latimes.com/archives/la-xpm-1995-01-30-ls-25969-story.html.
Golebiowska, Ewa A., and Thomsen, Cynthia J. 1999. "Group Stereotypes and Evaluations of Individuals: The Case of Gay and Lesbian Political Candidates." In *Gays and Lesbians in the Democratic Process*, edited by Ellen D. B. Riggle and Barry L. Tadlock, 194. New York: Columbia University Press.
Green, Alicia. 2019. "Life After POZ." *POZ Magazine*, September 1. https://www.poz.com/article/life-poz.
Greer, William. 1986. "Violence Against Homosexuals Rising, Groups Seeking Wider Protection Say." *New York Times*, November 23. https://www.nytimes.com/1986/11/23/us/violence-against-homosexuals-rising-groups-seeking-wider-protection-say.html.
"HIV and Gay and Bisexual Men." 2018. CDC Report, https://www.cdc.gov/hiv/group/msm/index.html.
Johnson, James. 2016. "Magic Johnson on 'The Arsenio Hall Show 1991." YouTube video, 16:50. May 1, https://www.youtube.com/watch?v=CkbaBnzmQIY.
Johnson, Magic. 1991. "I'll Deal with It: HIV Has Forced Me to Retire, But I'll Still Enjoy Life as I Speak Out About Safe Sex." *Sports Illustrated*, November 18. https://www.si.com/vault/1991/11/18/125420/ill-deal-with-it-hiv-has-forced-me-to-retire-but-ill-still-enjoy-life-as-i-speak-out-about-safe-sex.
Kelly, Keith. 1994. "Healthcare Fuels Magazine Growth: Mainstream Advertisers Latching on in Numbers." *Advertising Age*, May 30. https://adage.com/article/news/healthcare-fuels-magazine-growth-mainstream-advertisers-latching-numbers/86931.
Koegler, Erica, Thomson, T. J., Speno, Ashton G., and Teti, Michelle. 2018. "Image-Sharing Via Social Media: Reflections from an Ethnically- and Age-Diverse Sample of People Living with HIV in the Midwest." *Journal of HIV/AIDS & Social Services* 17(4): 249–62. doi.org?10.1080/15381501.2018.1519479.
Kyle, Garland. 1989. "AIDS and the New Sexual Order." *The Journal of Sex Research* 26(2): 276–78. doi:10.1080/00224498909551513.
Leiken, Jessie. 2006. "The Changing Face of AIDS: Eradicating AIDS in the U.S. Will Require Special Attention from One Community – and Help from an Unlikely Source." *Mother Jones*, June 26. https://www.motherjones.com/politics/2006/06/changing-face-aids/.
Lubow, Arthur. 1995. "Positive Thinking." *New Yorker*, May 1. https://www.newyorker.com/magazine/1995/05/01/positive-thinking.
"The Many Faces of HIV." 2011. AIDS Foundation of Chicago. November 4. https://www.aidschicago.org/page/inside-story/the-many-faces-of-hiv.

MacNeil, Christopher. 1985. "School Bars Door to Youth with AIDS." *Kokomo Tribune*, August 31. https://www.hemophiliafed.org/news-stories/2014/03/1985-ryan-white-banned-from-school-because-of-aids/.

McDonald, James. 2014. "Today in History: That Certain Summer," *Out*, November 1. https://www.out.com/today-gay-history/2014/11/01/today-gay-history-hal-holbrook-martin-sheen-loving-partners-certain-summer.

Morgan, Thomas. 1987 "Amid AIDS, Gay Movement Grows but Shifts." *New York Times*, October 10. https://www.nytimes.com/1987/10/10/us/amid-aids-gay-movement-grows-but-shifts.html.

Motel, Seth. 2013. "On Stonewall Anniversary, a Reminder of How Much Public Opinion Has Changed." Pew Research Center, June 26. http://www.pewresearch.org/fact-tank/2013/06/26/on-stonewall-anniversay-a-reminder-of-how-much-public-opinion-has-changed/.

Murr, Andrew. 2004. "The New Face of AIDS." *Newsweek*, December 5. https://www.newsweek.com/new-face-aids-123319.

Mustich, Emma. 2011. "The History of AIDS Hysteria." *Salon*, June 5. https://www.salon.com/2011/06/05/aids_hysteria/.

Perez-Feria, Richard. 1994. "POZ, Day One: The Human Touch." *POZ*, April 1. https://www.poz.com/article/poz-day-one-25400-8748.

Quin, Thomas. 2008. "HIV Epidemiology and the Effects of Antiviral Therapy on Long-Term Consequences." *AIDS* 22(Suppl 3): S7–12. doi: 10.1097/01.aids.0000327510.68503.e8.

Rhoden, William. 1992. "An Emotional Ashe Says That He Has AIDS." *New York Times*, April 9. https://www.nytimes.com/1992/04/09/sports/an-emotional-ashe-says-that-he-has-aids.html.

Russo, Vito. 1981. *The Celluloid Closet: Homosexuality in the Movies*. New York: Harper & Row, 215.

Sender, Katherine. 2001. "Gay Readers, Consumers, and a Dominant Gay Habitus: 25 Years of the Advocate Magazine." *Journal of Communication* 51(1): 73–99. doi.org/10.1111/j.1460-2466.2001.tb02873.x.

Shilts, Randy. 1987. *And The Band Played On*. New York: Penguin.

Signorile, Michelangelo. 1993. *Queer in America: Sex, the Media, and the Closets of Power*. New York: Doubleday.

Smit, P. J., Brady, M., Carter, M., Fernandes, R., Lamore, L., Meulbroek, M., Ohayon, M., Platteau, T., Rehberg, P., Rockstroh, J. K., and Thompson, M. 2012. "HIV-Related Stigma within Communities of Gay Men: A Literature Review." *AIDS Care* 24(4): 405–12. https://doi.org/10.1080/09540121.2011.613910.

Soller, Kurt. 2018. "Six Times Journalists on the Paper's History of Covering AIDS and Gay Issues." *New York Times*, April 27. https://www.nytimes.com/2018/04/27/t-magazine/times-journalists-aids-gay-history.html.

Strub, Sean. 1994. "S.O.S." *POZ*, April/May. https://www.poz.com/article/S-O-S-1869-8182.

———. 2014. *Body Counts: A Memoir of Politics, Sex, AIDS, and Survival*. New York: Scribner.

Suran J. D. 2009. "'Out Now!': Antimilitarism and the Politicization of Homosexuality in the Era of Vietnam." In *Gender and Sexuality in 1968*, edited by L. J. Frazier, D. Cohen. New York: Palgrave Macmillan. https://doi.org/10.1057/9780230101203_2.

Taggart, Tamara, Grewe, Mary Elizabeth, Conserve, Donaldson F., Gliwa, Catherine, and Isler, Malika Roman. 2015. "Social Media and HIV: A Systematic Review of Uses of Social Media in HIV Communication." *Journal of Medical Internet Research* 17(11): e248. doi: 10.2196/jmir.4387.

"The Age of AIDS: Interview Cleve Jones." 2006. *Frontline*, May 30. https://www.pbs.org/wgbh/pages/frontline/aids/interviews/jones.html.

Thompson, Mark. 1994. *Long Road to Freedom: The Advocate History of the Gay and Lesbian Movement*. New York: St. Martin's Press.

Tian, Yi. 2007. "AZT, Safe Sex, and a 'Widow's' Story: A Content Analysis of Aids Coverage in The Advocate, 1981–2006." Master's thesis, Ohio University. https://etd.ohiolink.edu/.

Utne Reader. 1995. "Magazines: Recommended Readings." January/February, 125.

Welch, Paul. 1964. "Homosexuality in America." *Life*, June 26.

Chapter 8

From Marginal to Mainstream

Vegetarian Magazines vs. the Standard American Diet

Sharon Bloyd-Peshkin

In 1970, Paul Obis, a nurse in Chicago, had an epiphany while eating a hamburger in a local Burger King: "A lot of people in the world don't eat meat. How many cows will I eat in my lifetime? I don't have to contribute to this." But it wasn't obvious what he should do next. There were few vegetarian cookbooks or convenience foods (Bohan 2018). Obis placed signs in the windows of local health-food stores—"Vegetarians: Lettuce Unite"—and assembled a group of vegetarians who ate potluck meals together (Henderson 1987). Obis then wrote an article he titled "Being a Vegetarian Is Never Having to Say You're Sorry—to a Cow," which no editor accepted. So he created a four-page newsletter, called it *Vegetarian Times* (tagline: "a publication for non-meat eaters"), created 300 mimeographed copies, and delivered it to local health-food stores and other locations on his green Schwinn Varsity bicycle (Kinch 2019). With that, a magazine that charted an emerging movement was born.

Obis's timing was fortuitous. In the late 1960s and early 1970s, American youth were challenging traditional forms of authority. Interest in vegetarianism played an important role in the countercultural movement, reinforced by numerous spiritual, environmental, and ethical concerns. Young people drawn to Zen Buddhism and yoga adopted a meatless diet as part of their spiritual path. Frances Moore Lappé's best-selling *Diet for a Small Planet* (1971) linked meat-eating to environmental degradation and food scarcity, motivating people with environmental and ethical concerns to give up meat. Peter Singer's *Animal Liberation* (1975) galvanized and expanded the animal rights movement. As part of a general overthrow of conventional arrangements, communes and other intentional communities were founded during this period, many of them embracing a vegetarian diet (Puskar-Pasewicz 2010, xiv). One of the more famous and long-lasting was begun in 1970 in San Francisco by Stephen Gaskin, whose traveling caravan attracted adherents and eventually settled in Summertown, Tennessee, to establish The Farm, a pacifist vegan commune (The Farm, n.d.).

Still, among the general public, vegetarians were subjected to stereotyping as "hippies" and "health food nuts." Being considered odd for eating a meatless diet was not a social stigma to many of those who adopted the lifestyle; it was a badge of pride. Still, lack of acceptance could be isolating for vegetarians when they were invited to food-based gatherings with nonvegetarian friends and family, and all vegetarians were frustrated by lack of access to recipes, restaurant meals, and sound nutritional advice. Moreover, vegetarians in the United States were relatively small in number and spread out geographically.

Vegetarian Times helped connect them during the early years and rapidly expanded in size and reach. By 1977, the magazine was bimonthly, with 56 pages and 10,000 readers. During this period, the influence of vegetarians extended beyond those who adopted a meatless diet, leading to some backlash. "Public interest in vegetarianism also sparked renewed concerns about the safety of America's system of mass food production" and prompted "large-scale, industrial meat companies and associations to portray vegetarianism as extreme and even unhealthy" (Puskar-Pasewicz 2010, xiv–xv). Most nutritionists also discouraged vegetarian diets, particularly for children (Maurer 2002, 29). And physicians, who received little education about nutrition, remained skeptical that a plant-based diet was adequate for good health (Iacobbo and Iacobbo 2006, 173). This wasn't helped by the since-debunked notion of the need for "complementary proteins" promoted in Frances Moore Lappé's *Diet for a Small Planet*, which suggested that vegetarian diets could be risky without careful meal-planning (Maurer 2002, 37).

Against this backdrop, *Vegetarian Times* was essential reading. It provided articles documenting the many arguments against eating meat—environmental, agricultural, animal rights, and nutritional—and correcting the misconceptions spread by the meat industry and uninformed health professionals. It also published dining guides, recipes, and advice on cooking and traveling as a vegetarian. It wasn't the only vegetarian magazine of its time, but *Vegetarian Times*, as a consumer magazine with a rapidly growing subscriber base, quickly became the must-read of a growing movement.

A NEW TWIST ON OLD IDEAS

Vegetarianism didn't emerge in the 1970s. In fact, its roots in the United States go back to the mid-nineteenth century, when it was embraced along with other social movements related to moral reform, such as temperance, women's suffrage, and abolitionism (Puskar-Pasewicz 2010, xiv). At the American Vegetarian Convention of 1850, the Chicago Vegetarian Society was formed with a declaration that "the adoption of a Vegetarian Diet is calculated to destroy the strife of antagonism, and to sustain life in serenity and strength." The founders were convinced that "there are mental feasts, and a moral being, which to the flesh eater can never be revealed, and moral happiness of which as such he cannot fully participate." Membership was $1 per year (*American Vegetarian and Health Journal* 1850, 1).

In 1893, vegetarians met as part of the World's Congress at the World's Columbian Exposition in Chicago. "Live on Vegetables: Men and Women Who Eat No Meat Open a World's Congress," declared the *Chicago Daily Tribune* (*Live on Vegetables* 1893). Still, vegetarians were regarded as dietary fringe characters, and in many ways they were. "Nineteenth-century vegetarians were often considered too radical, too naïve, or, simply speaking, wacko. They were called 'half-crazed,' 'sour-visaged,' 'infidels' and 'food cranks'" as they sought to establish vegetarian cities and proclaimed puritanical views of not only diet but also physical pleasure. The blandness of vegetarian meals of the time didn't help, either. "To upper, aristocratic classes, with their taste buds trained on gourmet feasts, vegetarian food must have been impossibly boring. To lower, aspiring classes, it offered nothing to aspire to" (Zaraska 2016, 129).

By the beginning of the twentieth century, advocates of a vegetarian diet emphasized evidence of a meatless diet's health benefits more than moral claims (Puskar-Pasewicz 2010, xiv). This contributed to the withering of the nascent movement during the first half of the twentieth century, when some early leaders of the movement died of communicable diseases, undercutting their arguments for the health benefits of a meatless diet. Meat gained nutritional and social status during the two world wars, when they were the centerpiece of army rations, and civilians with means demonstrated their ability to afford and obtain meat during wartime. "War scarcity, human suffering that left no place for caring about animals, meat-loaded army rations—that would have been enough to stamp out the vegetarian movement. But it also didn't help the movement's PR that Hitler was a vegetarian" (Zaraska 2016, 132). The meat-and-potatoes nutritional doctrine of 1950s America cemented this decline.

And yet, there was still an undercurrent of vegetarianism in the United States. The Seventh-Day Adventist (SDA) Church, which includes the belief that "a well-balanced vegetarian diet that avoids the consumption of meat . . . will promote vigorous health" (Seventh-Day Adventist Church, n.d.) established the Loma Linda Sanitarium in 1905, which grew to Loma Linda University Medical Center in 1967. It began graduating nursing students in 1907 and over the years expanded to offer medical education in a variety of fields, from certificates to doctoral degrees (Loma Linda University, n.d.). Members of the church served as subjects for epidemiological studies on health and vegetarian diets, starting with the SDA Mortality Study of 1958–1966 (Banta et al. 2018, 12).

The American Natural Hygiene Society (renamed in 1998 to the National Health Association) also published journals and later a quarterly magazine for members. Between 1954 and 1960, the society published first *The Journal of Natural Hygiene* and then *Natural Hygiene* magazine. In 1977, it launched *Health Science* as a quarterly magazine, which "regularly featured in-depth articles on all aspects of the NHA Health program including healthy eating, healthy living, fasting for the recovery of health and the latest health news" (National Health Association, n.d.). For adherents of natural hygiene, a vegetarian diet was one aspect of the pursuit of a healthy life. But like the SDA publications, these magazines were circulated to members and were not widely available on newsstands. Thus their influence was primarily on those who followed the society's principles and not on society at large.

Seventh-Day Adventists of the twentieth century and members of the Hygiene Society, like members of the American Vegetarian Convention, were motivated by religious conviction and health concerns to abstain from meat along with alcohol and other intoxicants. But while studies of SDA members provided evidence that a vegetarian diet was nutritionally sound, most of America wasn't paying attention. The dietetics program at Loma Linda University was not accredited by the American Dietetic Association until 1957, "in part due to a belief that one could not be a real dietitian if not able to prepare a typical meat-based American diet" (Banta et al. 2018, 16). American vegetarians who weren't associated with these institutions didn't have many places to turn for support or community until the 1970s.

BUILDING IDENTITY AND COMMUNITY

This is the vacuum that *Vegetarian Times* filled. It provided its readers motivation, practical information, and validation. As author Ellen Sue Spivack wrote in the October 1975 issue:

> The more I embodied vegetarianism, the more I realized that it was not merely a diet. It became a spiritual / ethical / compassionate / political / health issue. In short, it became my lifestyle. I could no longer separate my vegetarianism from other aspects of my life. I realized that no matter which of the schools of vegetarian thought a person came in by, or which "group" he/she belonged to, they all seemed to embody their vegetarianism as a way of life.

Whereas members of the SDA church embraced a vegetarian diet because of their religion, these new vegetarians were finding in their diet something like a spiritual path. "For some vegetarians, the choice symbolizes their entire political, social and ecological posture. Vegetarianism is their ideology" (Lawrence 1993, 998).

Vegetarian Times also provided these readers with a sense of community. When Obis died in 2018, comments on his memorial website attested to the role the magazine played during those early years in connecting readers who otherwise felt isolated:

> "Vegetarians were few and far between in the early 1970s and excluding meat from a diet was viewed in a freakish light. There was no internet or social media for folks to connect."—Craig Kinch

> "*VT* was a lifesaver for me, especially as an early teen with no vegetarian contacts or connections."—Kay Stepkin

> "When I first became vegetarian nearly two decades ago, *Vegetarian Times* was a lifesaver to me. I knew no other vegetarians and got no support from my family, so it was the highlight of my month to get my copy in the mail."
> —Shell Jess

> "I was raised vegetarian but didn't have any veg friends. This magazine, which I started reading as a teen, really helped me not feel so isolated or as the kids in school said, 'weird.'"—Ali Burrito

Letters from readers published in the early issues of *Vegetarian Times* also reflect how people found a connection and a community through the magazine. As one new subscriber from West Virginia wrote in the February 1982 letters column: "I received my first copy of *Vegetarian Times* and I am thrilled with it. Tears of joy came to my eyes while reading it because now I don't feel so alone" (*Vegetarian Times* 1982, 4).

The sense of connection also fostered a sense of ownership. Readers sometimes chastised the editors for perceived lapses. In the March 1981 issue, a reader complained about an ad for the airline Laker Skytrain: "Did you notice the picture showing full meals depicts a tray with a piece of chicken and other unmentionables? . . . Please don't offend your readers, as I was, by such an unsightly oversight." The editors replied that she was not the only one to express outrage, but went on to explain that "although we value our health food type advertisers greatly, it's nice to know that advertisers in other fields (such as air travel) view the vegetarians as a large enough 'market segment' to warrant advertising to them" (*Vegetarian Times* 1981, 8).

Figure 8.1 The covers of *Vegetarian Times* reveal an evolution from a lifestyle publication to a food magazine. In the early 1970s, covers reflected the countercultural lifestyle of its readers. In the 1980s, covers primarily featured the celebrities, athletes, and activists who exemplified what vegetarians could be: healthy, successful, influential, and admirable. By the mid-1980s, food occasionally replaced people on the covers, and in 1989, people were consistently relegated to a small box in the upper-left side. Throughout the 1990s, high-quality food photography on the covers made the case that vegetarian food can be just as appealing and satisfying as meat-based meals. Courtesy of Janeen Obis.

Researchers also turned to *Vegetarian Times* to connect with readers. In 1980, the magazine published a letter from an author working on a book about diet and health among Black Americans, asking to "hear from others who have an interest in this area of study" and providing a street address in New York. Similarly, the Vegetarian Information Service asked readers to send "ideas for effective projects designed to promote vegetarianism on a national level," and offered $10 each for the five top ideas (*Vegetarian Times* 1980, no. 40, 63). Readers reached out to each other through the letters, too; one requested recipes for vegan hair conditioners and provided her home address for other readers to respond to (*Vegetarian Times* March 1981, 86).

As editor Val Weaver wrote in 2004, the magazine "created a sense of community among vegetarians.... It became a virtual meeting place for the veg community decades before anyone used 'virtual' in this sense" (Iacobbo and Iacobbo 2006, 61).

MAKING THE ARGUMENT

Vegetarian Times was not the only consumer magazine for American vegetarians in the 1970s. Another, short-lived magazine, *Vegetarian World*, published fourteen issues between 1974 and 1978. It, too, offered practical and inspirational articles, including guidance on plant sources of vitamin B12 and protein, profiles of vegetarian celebrities and athletes, and articles about links between diet and disease, but also more controversial topics like world hunger and vivisection. The two magazines merged in the late 1970s.

During the decade after *Vegetarian Times* was launched, numerous vegetarian organizations emerged and gained national attention, including the North American Vegetarian Society (NAVS) in 1974, People for the Ethical Treatment of Animals (PETA) in 1980, and the nonprofit Vegetarian Resource Group (VRG) in 1982. NAVS launched *Vegetarian Voice* magazine in 1975, and VRG launched *Vegetarian Journal* in 1982. "These canonical texts and organizations helped to establish a vegetarian community by constructing a vegetarian identity rhetorically, an identity that is both personal and social, and by advocating a common set of goals and beliefs" (Malesh 2005, 24). Those goals and beliefs included protecting the environment and opposing animal cruelty.

Vegetarian Journal, a quarterly publication, emphasized scientific as well as practical information to help people adopt or maintain a vegetarian diet (Vegetarian Resource Group, n.d.). With the tagline, "The practical magazine for those interested in health, ecology and ethics," it also started as a typewritten four-page newsletter. Unlike *Vegetarian Times*, however, it was entirely vegan (no dairy or eggs) and eschewed ads for supplements—a mainstay of *Vegetarian Times*'s advertising support. "In general the vegetarian movement felt that people were being charged a lot of money for something they don't need," explained Charles Stahler, co-founder of the Vegetarian Resource Group. "We're not just promoting products. It was a different mindset" (Stahler 2019). *Vegetarian Voice* was also quarterly and nonprofit—a member benefit—and its tagline was "perspectives on healthy, ecological and compassionate living."

In the early 1980s, *Vegetarian Times* reflected the breadth of interests of the vegetarian community, regularly publishing stories about health, nutrition, agriculture, and the environment. Some of the edgier material appeared in the "News Digest" in the front of the magazine, but feature stories also explored controversial topics such as whether a macrobiotic diet could help the body fight cancer or whether homeopathic remedies could treat illnesses. "Carrot & Stick" applauded or criticized organizations, institutions, and individuals for their food policy and treatment of animals and the environment. (In November 1983, *Vegetarian Times* gave a stick to cover celebrity William Shatner for buying his wife "a mink wrap, lynx jacket and Blackglama full length coat," as reported in *Variety* magazine [p. 57].)

The covers of the magazine primarily featured people who were profiled or figured prominently in stories, such as actress Betty Buckley, entertainer Kinki the Clown, marathoner and bodybuilder Gayle Olinekova, musician Michael Jackson, and, of course, "America's favorite neighbor," Fred Rogers. These were the celebrities, athletes, and activists who exemplified what vegetarians could be: healthy, successful, influential, and admirable. Kay Stepkin, founder of the National Vegetarian Museum, viewed "the early *Vegetarian Times* as focusing more on the vegetarian community. It was everything that was binding us together as a group and learning about things we didn't know because there were so many aspects about being a vegetarian" (Stepkin 2019).

MEATLESS GOES MAINSTREAM

Vegetarian Times's 1981 Laker Skytrain advertisement controversy was a portent of things to come. In the early 1980s, most of the magazine's ads were still for cotton clothing, juicers, organic and cruelty-free products, vitamins, and other supplements. As the magazine grew in circulation, eventually surpassing 250,000, mainstream advertisers did start to "view the vegetarians as a large enough 'market segment' to warrant advertising to them," as the editors had suggested years earlier. By 1990, ads for national brand supplements and cruelty-free cosmetics predominated, along with organic and natural foods, such as Lundberg Rice and Fantastic Foods. And by 2000, the ads were predominantly for products related to cooking and health, including a large array of dietary supplements, mass-market vegetarian foods (e.g., Silk and Vitasoy soy milks, Nasoya tofu, Gardenburger, Eden organic pasta, Colavita olive oil), Tempur-Pedic mattresses, and KitchenAid mixers (*Vegetarian Times*, May 2000).

During the 1980s, the magazine assumed that readers included "new vegetarians, near vegetarians, and people just cutting back on meat," and Obis was convinced that "people don't want to be preached to" (Henderson 1987). They also came to the magazine for a variety of reasons, and the magazine sought to serve them all while avoiding putting any of them off. "The magazine refuses to be drawn into the more-vegetarian-than-thou game, with a tone that rarely hectors and is often humorous" (Henderson 1987).

The covers of *Vegetarian Times* reveal an evolution during this period from a lifestyle publication to a food magazine. Starting in the mid-1980s, food occasionally replaced people on the covers, and in 1989, people were consistently relegated to a small box in the upper-left side. Throughout the 1990s, high-quality food photography on the covers made the case that vegetarian food can be just as appealing and satisfying as meat-based meals. The food was bountiful, seasonal, and beautiful. As Obis wrote in issue 155, July 1990, the magazine was on newsstands next to *Cooking Light* and *Bon Appetit* and needed "to look as good as they do and to show that vegetarian food is as attractive as nonvegetarian food" (*Vegetarian Times* 1990).

At this point, it diverged from *Vegetarian Journal*, which, as a nonprofit, had a specific mission to make institutions more vegetarian-friendly by providing information about vegetarian nutrition and recipes for professionals and organizations: school cafeterias, physicians and hospitals, food manufacturers, and restaurants (Iacobbo and Iacobbo 2004, 216). *Vegetarian Journal* also provided information of special interest to vegans (vegetarians who don't eat eggs and dairy, and sometimes also honey, and avoid leather products). This included extensive coverage of nutrition, along with cooking tips, product guides, and practical information for vegan travelers (Vegetarian Resource Group, n.d.).

Vegetarian Journal remained fairly consistent throughout the 1990s, its mission and focus driven by the nonprofit organization and not by the marketplace and changes in American consumer behavior. By contrast, *Vegetarian Times* underwent a seismic change in the early 1990s. First, Obis sold the magazine to Cowles Enthusiast Media in 1992. The new owners—publishers of other niche titles including *Teddy Bear and Friends*, *Doll Reader*, *Civil War Times*, and *Bow Hunter* magazines—viewed *Vegetarian Times* not as a lifestyle magazine, but as a meatless eating magazine.

By late 1993, even the small photos of people rarely appeared on the covers, and with the exception of three people covers in 1995 and 1996—mega-celebrities Paul and Linda McCartney, and two celebrity chefs who appeared on the cover with food—all the covers were dominated by enticing photographs of vegetarian meals. That remained the cover strategy through several redesigns of the logo and the magazine, and even a few changes of ownership. The magazine was often found on newsstands with other food magazines, and enticing food photography was essential to its success.

The editorial content reflects this shift, too. Where the magazine once exposed the hazards of a meat-based diet, it now supported a vegetarian diet with recipes and service pieces (articles that help readers accomplish their goals). For example, in the April 2000 issue (chosen because it did not have a theme, like fitness or kids), the articles were almost exclusively about health and food, from "American Classics" (vegetarian versions of meat dishes) to "Beating the Blood Sugar Blues" (preventing and treating diabetes). The only exception was a story about the rewards of socially conscious investing—in an issue that has full-page ads from the socially conscious Parnassus Investment Fund and Domini Social Investments, and a half-page from Pax World Funds Family.

In the early 2000s, the magazine was not only providing an enticing environment for advertisers; it was also avoiding unpalatable topics it formerly emphasized (such as vivisection) that might offend advertisers as well as mainstream readers. The News Digest (now called "In The News") in this issue has one Earth Day-related story along with the food and health stories. "Carrot & Stick" applauds the Canadian health minister for proposing graphic images of smoking-related diseases on cigarette packs, gives a stick to a professor who claims everyone can learn to tolerate lactose, and offers another carrot to the U.S. EPA for new automobile emissions rules (*Vegetarian Times*, April 2000, 20). There is nothing in the magazine resembling the old *Vegetarian Times*'s advocacy for animals, ethics, and the environment. "*Vegetarian Times* . . . transformed from an independent publication, primarily covering philosophy and politics of vegetarianism, to a commercial periodical oriented toward cuisine and health" (Iacobbo and Iacobbo 2006, 61). The magazine was no longer agenda-setting; it was table setting.

This reflected the fact that attitudes toward vegetarianism had changed. The founders of the Vegetarian Resource Group noted the difference when they traveled to events around the country. "In the 1970s and early 1980s when we did outreach booths, often people would ask us, 'Why be a vegetarian?' We almost never hear that question now. Instead, people come by and say, 'I wish I could do that.' They are looking for information on how to eat more vegetarian meals" (Stahler 1994).

Vegetarians still comprised a small percentage of the American population; a variety of surveys suggest that in the late 1970s and early 1980s, between 1 percent and 2 percent of Americans were vegetarian, and by the end of the century, the percentage may have increased to between 4 percent and 6 percent (Šimčikas 2018). But their influence surpassed their size; by the turn of the century, vegetarians and meatless meals were gaining widespread acceptance.

By 1988, the American Dietetic Association began supporting a "properly planned" vegetarian diet, and in 1993, its official statement read: "A considerable body of scientific data suggests positive relationships between vegetarian diets and risk reduction for several chronic degenerative diseases and conditions, including obesity, coronary artery disease, hypertension, diabetes mellitus, and some types of cancer" (ADA Reports 1993, 1317). This acceptance by the ADA (now the Academy of Nutrition and Dietetics) was accompanied by a more general acceptance in American society. "Today vegetarian diets are much more widely accepted than they were two decades ago" (Maurer 2002, 148). This is also evidenced by the explosion in vegetarian offerings at restaurants, vegetarian foods in supermarkets, and the U.S. Department of Agriculture's 2000 ruling that the federal school lunch program would allow the protein component to come from nonmeat sources (Maurer 2002, 135).

Vegetarian magazines, including *Vegetarian Times* and *Vegetarian Journal*, contributed to this acceptance through awareness and advocacy. Their writers and readers influenced the variety of meals served in restaurants and on airplanes; the advice provided by the nation's dieticians about the nutritional adequacy of a meatless diet; and awareness of the environmental and ethical consequences of the mainstream, meat-based American diet. In the end, the magazines' evolution reflected that accomplishment. *Vegetarian Journal* remained a nonprofit education and advocacy magazine with a niche appeal, and its circulation peaked at 10,000. Other small vegetarian magazines specific to animal rights concerns also continued advocating for an end to animal testing, and fur and factory farming. *Vegetarian Times* went mainstream, shedding its more provocative content and catering to the growing number of people striving to eat less meat as well as the advertisers seeking to reach them. But by shedding its advocacy for a specific community of readers for whom vegetarianism was an identity, not just a diet, *Vegetarian Times* became just another food magazine helping readers eat less meat—a competitive and ultimately unsustainable enterprise.

In the end, both magazines contributed to a twentieth-century revival of vegetarianism in the United States. "The winds of change during the countercultural era of the 1960s and 1970s helped blow it back onto a steady course that continues to the present day" (Iacobbo and Iacobbo 2004, 234).

REFERENCES

ADA Reports. 1993. "Position of the American Dietetic Association: Vegetarian Diets." *Journal of the American Dietetic Association* 93(11), 1317–19. Accessed December 5, 2019. https://www.sciencedirect.com/sdfe/pdf/download/eid/1-s2.0-0 00282239391966T/first-page-pdf.

American Vegetarian Society. 1850–1852. *American Vegetarian and Health Journal*, vol. 1, Philadelphia: American Vegetarian Society. Accessed December 6, 2019. https://babel.hathitrust.org/cgi/pt?id=mdp.39015013165181&view=1up &seq=1.

Banta, Jim E., Lee, Jerry W., Hodgkin, Georgia, Yi, Zane, Fanica, Andrea, and Sabate, Joan. 2018. "The Global Influence of the Seventh-Day Adventist Church on Diet" *Religions* 9(9), 251. https://doi.org/10.3390/rel9090251.

Bohan, Peter. 2018. "Innovator and Free Thinker." The Interactive Memorial of Paul L. Obis, Jr. Accessed November 17, 2019. http://paulobis.com/timeline/innovator-and-free-thinker/.

Health Science Association. n.d. "Health Science Magazine." Accessed December 10, 2019. https://www.healthscience.org/health-science-magazine.

Henderson, Harold. 1987. "These Are Vegetarian Times: And the World's Leading Meatless Magazine, Based in Oak Park, Is Starting to Rake in the Green Stuff." *Chicago Reader*. December 10. Accessed November 15, 2019. https://www.chicagoreader.com/chicago/these-are-vegetarian-times/Content?oid=871525.

Iacobbo, Karen, and Iacobbo, Michael. 2004. *Vegetarian America: A History*. Westport, CT: Praeger Publishers.

———. 2006. *Vegetarians and Vegans in America Today*. Westport, CT: Praeger Publishers.

Kinch, Craig. 2019. "The Interactive Memorial of Paul L. Obis, Jr." Accessed November 17, 2019. http://paulobis.com/timeline/innovator-and-free-thinker/.

Lappé, Frances Moore. 1971. *Diet for a Small Planet*. New York: Ballantine Books.

Lawrence, Valerie. 1993. "Is Vegetarianism a Diet or an Ideology?" *Canadian Medical Association Journal* 148(6), 998–1002.

Levitt, Aimee. 2018. "The National Vegetarian Museum Uncovers the Movement's Chicago Roots." *Chicago Reader*, March 6. https://www.chicagoreader.com/chicago/national-vegetarian-museum-kay-stepkin-vegetarianism/Content?oid=42547547.

"Live on Vegetables: Men and Women Who Eat No Meat Open a World's Congress. Vegetarians Assemble at the Art Institute and Expound Their Views—Prison Reform Congress Is in Session—Discusses the Old and New Methods of Discipline—Non-Partisan Temperance Women Listen to an Address On Womanliness—Catholic Opponents of the Saloon Meet." 1893. *Chicago Daily Tribune* (1872–1922), June 9. Accessed November 20, 2019. https://colum.idm.oclc.org/login?url=https://search.proquest.com/docview/174854604?accountid=10231.

Loma Linda University. n.d. "History." Accessed November 20, 2019. https://home.llu.edu/about-llu/history.

Malesh, Patricia Marie. 2005. "Rhetorics of Consumption: Identity, Confrontation, and Corporatization in the American Vegetarian Movement." PhD diss., University of Arizona.

Maurer, Donna. 2002. *Vegetarianism: Movement or Moment?* Philadelphia: Temple University Press.

National Health Association. n.d. "Historic Publications and Books." Accessed December 10, 2019. https://www.healthscience.org/heritage/natural-hygiene-movement/books-and-publications.

Obis, Janeen. 2018. "Entrepreneur, Insightful and Provider." The Interactive Memorial of Paul L. Obis, Jr. Accessed November 17, 2019. http://paulobis.com/timeline/entrepreneur-insightful-and-provider/.

———. 2018. "Innovator and Free Thinker." The Interactive Memorial of Paul L. Obis, Jr. Accessed November 17, 2019. http://paulobis.com/timeline/innovator-and-free-thinker/.

———. 2019. Interview with the author. November 26, 2019.

Puskar-Pasewicz, Editor. 2010. *Cultural Encyclopedia of Vegetarianism*. Santa Barbara, CA: Greenwood Press.

Seventh Day Adventist Church. n.d. "Living a Healthful Life." Accessed November 20, 2019. https://www.adventist.org/en/vitality/health/.

Šimčikas, Saulius, 2018. "Is the Percentage of Vegetarians and Vegans in the U.S. Increasing?" Accessed December 4, 2019. https://animalcharityevaluators.org/blog/is-the-percentage-of-vegetarians-and-vegans-in-the-u-s-increasing/#review.

Singer, Peter. 1975. *Animal Liberation: A New Ethics for Our Treatment of Animals*. New York: HarperCollins.

Spivack, Ellen Sue. 1975. "Vegetarianism as a Way of Life." *Vegetarian Times*. Vol. 12. Accessed November 21, 2019. https://ivu.org/congress/wvc75/life.html.

Stahler, Charles. 1994. "How Many Vegetarians Are There?" Accessed November 16, 2019. https://www.vrg.org/nutshell/poll.htm.

———. 2019. Interview with the author. December 2.

Stepkin, Kay. 2019. Interview with the author. December 4.

The Farm Community. n.d. "Celebrating 47 Years of Life in Community!" Accessed December 1, 2019. https://thefarmcommunity.com/.

Vegetarian Resource Group. n.d. Accessed November 21, 2019. https://www.vrg.org/journal/vj2012issue3/2012_issue3_notes_from_coordinators.php.

Wasserman, Debra, and Stahler, Charles. 2012a. "It's the 20th Anniversary of the Vegetarian Resources Group!" Accessed November 17, 2019. https://www.vrg.org/journal/2002issue3/2002_issue3_special.php.

———. 2012b. "The VRG Celebrates 30 Years of Activism." Accessed November 17, 2019. https://www.vrg.org/journal/vj2012issue3/2012_issue3_notes_from_coordinators.php.

Zaraska, Marta. 2016. *Meathooked: The History and Science of Our 2.5-Million-Year Obsession with Meat*. New York: Basic Books.

Chapter 9

Read Them for the Articles

Masculinity, U.S. Men's Magazines, and the Tension between Niche and Mainstream Audiences

Kevin M. Lerner

Before the launch of *Esquire* in 1933, men were not seen as a demographic niche that magazines could target so much as they were *the* demographic niche that almost all magazines targeted. There were women's magazines, and then there were magazines.

Men's magazines here refer to cultural and lifestyle magazines—the publications meant not just to appeal to men, but to teach them, in a way, how to *be* men of a particular kind. The story of men's magazines in the United States over the course of the twentieth century shows how a group of people who were once seen as synonymous with the mainstream—heterosexual, cisgender, mostly white men—came to be discovered, and to discover themselves, as a niche. At the same time, these magazines have defined American masculinity and men's relationships with women and with each other in ways that have changed significantly over time.

The definitions of masculinity that these magazines both created and reflected have influenced the way that American men and even the culture itself—through the hegemonic predominance of men—see themselves and behave in public. This is the man who was successful in business, who appreciated expensive watches, who hunted and fished and worked with wood, but who also moisturized and knew which scotch to serve to his guests and business partners. It is the masculinity satirized in *Mad Men*, the television series set in a 1960s advertising agency. And while there have been many different shades of masculinity represented in and promulgated by these men's lifestyle magazines, the overriding mode of manliness in these magazines has been one that in the twenty-first century would be seen as retrograde and even toxic, no matter how much of a veneer of sophistication they put on what they viewed as an essentially animal drive at the heart of American men.

DISCOVERING MEN AS A NICHE

Magazines aimed at attracting an audience of women first began appearing in the United States as early as the 1790s, and they were one of the prime categories for publishers during "the great magazine explosion" of the middle third of the nineteenth century. More than a hundred magazines for women were launched by the beginning of the Civil War (Tebbel and Zuckerman 1991, 27). All of the other categories—literary magazines, art magazines, political magazines, and even "general interest" magazines—assumed men as their primary, if not their sole, audience.

To be sure, there were magazines that appealed to men prior to the launch of *Esquire,* but they were largely relegated to the low-cost and generally lowbrow pulp magazines, including *Argosy*, which Frank Munsey revamped into a magazine of adventure stories—all fiction—in 1896 (Tebbel and Zuckerman 1991, 340). Some of these pulp magazines appealed specifically to men, either with tales of rugged adventure in the jungle, the western frontier or the mountains, or with titillating, but not obscene, erotic fiction. But as a category, they still attempted to appeal to as broad an audience as possible, and fell far short of being the sort of men's lifestyle magazine that *Esquire* would invent.

But the first issue of *Esquire* noted that general-interest magazines had begun to tip too much toward attracting women readers and the ad revenue that they brought with them. "Esquire aims to be the common denominator of masculine interests," a mission statement in the first issue read. *Esquire,* the statement said, would be a pointed rebuke to the "mad scramble" for female readers (and their advertising dollars) by the general-interest magazines of the day, which provided features for men only "after the manner in which scraps are tossed to the patient dog beneath the table" (Williams 2017).

While *Esquire* did not begin life as a magazine about men's fashion, that was a major aspect of its editorial content. In fact, the founding publisher, David Smart, intended to sell the magazine primarily in men's clothing stores; of the 105,000 copies of the original press run, only 5,000 were intended for newsstand sales. But demand for the magazine was far higher than Smart and his partner, editor Arnold Gingrich, anticipated, and even with 100,000 copies eventually going to newsstands, the first issue sold out (Polsgrove 1995, 24).

The formula that sold so many copies included fiction, journalism, humor, sports writing, poetry, cartoons, and photography—with authors and artists getting credit on the cover. In part, that was because the bylines were already famous ones. In that very first issue, readers would find nonfiction by Ernest Hemingway, Ring Lardner, Jr., and Nicholas Murray Butler, who was the president of Columbia University at the time. Fiction authors included John Dos Passos and Dashiell Hammett. William Steig, who was at the time primarily a cartoonist for adults, but would go on to be best known for his children's books, contributed drawings. This list of names ran down the right side of the front cover, which was illustrated with a painting of four men on a lake—perhaps one of the Great Lakes, since the far shore is beyond the horizon—transferring their baggage from a seaplane to a canoe or vice versa.

All of this speaks somewhat to the intended audience: a cosmopolitan, cultured, but rugged man who has money to spend on clothes, but who also loves boxing and golf, and perhaps a cheekily risqué cartoon featuring a woman. But the advertisement on the back cover might be even more telling. It is for Budweiser, but the artwork depicts a gentleman in jodhpurs, tie, and tails atop a polo pony, and the tagline reads, "For those with a Flair for Good Living" (*Esquire #1* 1933). This is a far cry from the ragged, cheap pages of the pulps. And the cover price was 50 cents, which was a tremendous amount of money to charge for a magazine at one of the lowest points of the Great Depression. Tebbel and Zuckerman (1991) compare this to Henry Luce's audacity in charging a dollar for his *Fortune* magazine at a time when the general-interest *Saturday Evening Post* was selling for a nickel (p. 186). Despite the high cover price—or perhaps because of it—*Esquire* was an immediate hit. By 1937, circulation hit 675,000 copies (Polsgrove 1995, 24). The magazine's mascot, a dapper but randy mustachioed, bug-eyed gentleman named Esky, stood as an avatar for the reader and also as an aspirational goal.

GQ, the magazine that would eventually become *Esquire*'s primary competition in the men's lifestyle category in the United States, actually traces its roots two years earlier than *Esquire*, and it was founded by the same partners who started *Esquire*. Some histories of the magazine industry confuse the timeline, but the magazine that would become the contemporary *GQ* began its life as *Apparel Arts*, a trade publication for the menswear industry, in 1931 (Sterlacci and Arbuckle 2009). When Smart and Gingrich added *Esquire* to their stable of publications, they were attempting to bring some of their knowledge of haberdashery to a consumer audience, but blend it with the cultural coverage that made *Esquire* such an instant success. *Apparel Arts* was distributed entirely to menswear stores (which explains why the founders thought *Esquire* could be distributed the same way).

The two magazines published in tandem for decades, with *Apparel Arts* focusing on fashion, and *Esquire* bringing fashion and the rest of its editorial content to a consumer audience. In 1957, *Apparel Arts* added the subtitle "Gentleman's Quarterly" with an announcement that the magazine would focus entirely on fashion. In an introductory note, the editors described their mission to "be the male counterpart of *Vogue Magazine*, possessing both trade and consumer appeal" (Christian 2013). In 1967, the magazine rebranded to its familiar two-letter title, and it became a monthly publication in 1970. In 1983, the magazine was sold to the Condé Nast company, and *GQ* began publishing a mix of editorial content that mirrored its former stablemate, now a full-fledged competitor in the upscale men's lifestyle category (Sterlacci and Arbuckle 2009).

SKIN SELLS

Esquire always relied on sexualized images of women as part of its appeal, but that reliance reached a new peak in the 1940s, as the magazine emphasized pin-up girls in an attempt to win the favor of lonely American servicemen during World War II. At a time when illustration played a far larger role in magazine publishing than it does now, the emblematic figure of *Esquire*'s World War II–era sex appeal was an artist named Alberto Vargas. The Peruvian-born Vargas made a name for himself painting watercolors of chorus girls in the teens and 1920s, doing his most notable work for the Ziegfeld Follies. David Smart, the publisher of *Esquire*, hired Vargas to paint his women for the magazine in 1940, on the eve of the U.S. entry into the war, and persuaded Vargas to drop the "s" from his last name, leading to what would become known as the "Varga Girl." Magazine scholar Carol Holstead describes the Varga Girl as "an idealized version of the American woman. The Varga Girl had eggshell skin, long limbs, and breasts that defied gravity. She was both sensual and wholesome. Although the girls were scantily clad, their eyes were always averted" (Holstead 2000).

Vargas painted 180 portraits in his six years at *Esquire*, an incredible pace of production that was made even more hectic by the other work he was doing at the time, including calendars, playing cards, and mascots for military units—the last of these a commission Vargas never declined (Holstead 2000). The magazine's more louche approach to sex during the war, however, led the U.S. Postal Service to decline to continue *Esquire*'s discounted mailing rate on the assertion that its distribution served no public good. Essentially, the Postmaster General's decision to revoke this rate amounted to a kind of censorship, and with the support of public protests in the magazine's favor, *Esquire* challenged the decision in court. Eventually, the Supreme Court issued a unanimous decision in *Esquire*'s favor in 1946. According to one legal scholar, the public outcry in favor of *Esquire* and the subsequent Supreme Court decision spoke to changing mores in the American public:

The outcry ... attested not only to the popularity of Esquire, but an emergent free speech sensibility in the culture of the time. Over the previous fifteen years, the American public had moved toward greater tolerance of a variety of expression, and intolerance of heavy-handed government attempts to quash speech on moral and political grounds. This stance marked the reversal of decades of conservatism, in which much of the public had approved government restraints on expression, restrictions that were routinely upheld by the courts under prevailing free speech doctrines. (Barbas 2018, 287)

The decision also marked a change in the meaning of the First Amendment and what it protected. Previously, the Supreme Court had protected only political and religious speech. For the first time, the court protected pin-ups, purely entertainment and titillation. It would not, however, be the last time that a prominent men's magazine would appear before the Supreme Court.

The slightly more permissive obscenity rules allowed for an evolution in pin-up magazines after the war. While *Esquire* continued to peddle class—both in the sense of "refinement" and social class—a new breed of pin-up magazines ditched the Vargas-style painted girls for varying degrees of erotic photography and leaned hard on sex to sell copies. With titles such as *Rogue*, *Bachelor*, *Gent*, *Monsieur*, and *Casanova*, the genre openly pushed boundaries of sexual content and nudity that was increasingly less coy as the 1950s became the 1960s. There was a spectrum of content in these magazines, of course. Some picked up on the *Esquire* formula of recruiting highbrow authors (one issue of a magazine called *Scene* included work by Evelyn Waugh, Ogden Nash, William K. Zinsser, and photographer Weegee). But others went straight for the prurient, including *Scamp* magazine, which in one issue promised not only an exposé on "Sin Centers of Suburbia," but also a "Special Survey" on the state of "The Bosom in America" (Betrock 1993).

These magazines enjoyed varying amounts of success, with some lasting only a few issues and others continuing for years, but the sheer number of titles (one compilation of covers produced by a fan of the genre includes forty-eight titles, and his collection is almost certainly not exhaustive) speaks to their popularity. They also continued to fight the U.S. Postal Service and various other prosecutors who often put them on trial for peddling smut (Betrock 1993). The success of these slightly déclassé magazines, both on the newsstand and in the courtroom, set the stage for the next golden age of American men's magazines, in the swinging, misogynist 1960s.

BOOKS, BEBOP, BOURBON, AND BUNNIES

During the 1950s and 1960s, the high-end men's lifestyle title *Esquire* and its sibling-cum-competitor *GQ* developed a stable formula of editorial content that lasted until the contemporary reevaluation of masculinity of *GQ*'s "New Masculinity" issue in 2019. It was a formula that *The New York Times* described as "a whiff of dad's old cedar chest full of pocketknives and Mickey Mantle baseball cards" (Williams 2019). Women were often objectified and seen as less essential than men, but that view was often presented with a veneer of admiration (as in *Esquire*'s recurring "Women We Love" feature). Of course, while the editorial formula may have been established, the construction of masculinity was constantly in flux. Scholars have theorized masculinity in many ways, though the last twenty years have seen a "discursive turn"—the idea that gender identities are built through dialogue, a theory that scholars of magazines have used to define the idea of masculinity, based on the work of Judith Butler:

> Butler's basic premise is that gender is neither something we have, nor is it something we are, rather, it is something that we, with variable degrees of volition, do. Gender is a discourse we both inhabit and employ, and also a performance with all the connotations of non-essentialism, transience, versatility and masquerade that this implies. (Benwell 2003)

The 1950s and 1960s construction of masculinity in these magazines is instantly identifiable through its dominance of popular culture. This is the masculinity of the Rat Pack: Frank Sinatra and Dean Martin. It is the masculinity of James Bond. These magazines included spies and adventure, cool jazz, baseball and boxing, slick mid-century design, and cocktails made with brown liquor. It was a masculinity of fathers passing on traditions of masculinity to their sons, teaching them how to shave, how to hunt, and how to tie a necktie (Rutherford 2003; Osgerby 2005, 2003; Stevenson, Jackson, and Brooks 2003; Ward, Vandenbosch, and Eggermont 2015; Edwards 2003).

But even as *GQ* and *Esquire* perfected their formula of hegemonic mid-century manhood, a new kind of magazine debuted, combining the aspirational lifestyle coverage of those prestige titles with the sex appeal of the newer breed of pin-up magazines, including nude photo pictorials. That was Hugh Hefner's *Playboy*. Coincidentally, like *Esquire* and *GQ* before it, *Playboy* emerged from Chicago, not New York. Hefner, a former copywriter for *Esquire*, started his magazine by purchasing and publishing nude photos of Marilyn Monroe without her consent (Young 2017; Wick 2017). As Chelsea Reynolds, a scholar of magazines and sexuality has written, Hefner "started to envision a cultural awakening in which (hetero)sexual liberation and autonomy guided men's aspirations, rather than memories of war or dreams of white picket fences and corporate promotions" (2017, 2). In other words, *Playboy* reclaimed a sort of masculinity of bachelorhood from a masculinity of fatherhood—of family man—that Hefner saw as being endemic in the postwar American suburbs.

The nudity in *Playboy* was tame by comparison to much of what would come after it, and even in the context of some of its contemporaries in the photographic pin-up category. But it was very real, and it earned *Playboy* a reputation for being both a symbol of suave masculinity and a publication that its readers were supposed to be slightly embarrassed to be caught reading, giving rise to the running joke that men would only "read it for the articles." Even artist Alberto Vargas, who began painting his Varga Girls for *Playboy* (eventually producing 152 paintings over a decade and a half) was bashful about having to paint the more explicitly sexual depictions of women that *Playboy* demanded, particularly the pubic hair (Holstead 2000).

But through its famous *Playboy* "bunnies"—models dressed in skimpy outfits with ears clipped to their heads and puffy tails above their behinds—as well as the *Playboy* clubs and other brand extensions, *Playboy* became an empire, and Hugh Hefner, in a satin smoking jacket, bunnies on his arm, became one of the few magazine editors a typical American might recognize. The magazine both created and benefited from cultural cachet. Spy novelist Ian Fleming serialized his James Bond novel *On Her Majesty's Secret Service* in the magazine in 1963. And in the film of that book, James Bond was seen reading a copy of *Playboy*—the kind of man who, if he really existed, would have read it (Hines 2018).

READ THEM FOR THE ARTICLES

Nude pictorials and girl-of-the-month centerfolds aside, *Playboy*, like its men's lifestyle predecessors, legitimately did have articles that were worth reading. The magazine devoted space to fiction from authors with more of a literary reputation than Ian Fleming, including Gabriel Garcia Marquez, Roald Dahl, Margaret Atwood, and Vladimir Nabokov (Youngs 2017). While some of these authors, such as Norman Mailer, perpetuated masculine, misogynistic stereotypes, others pushed boundaries, and some, such as Atwood, truly wrote as feminists (Weiss 2015). And *Playboy* ran a series of serious interviews, most infamously with then-presidential candidate Jimmy Carter, only a few weeks before his election. In the interview, Carter admitted to looking "on a lot of women with lust. I've committed adultery in my heart many times" (Scheer 1976). Other notable interviews included Malcolm X, Steve Jobs, Miles Davis, and Martin Luther King, Jr. (Dalton 2017).

Much of the journalism strove for similar quality too. *Playboy* published the piece that would become the basis for the movie *Boys Don't Cry*, about a transgender man murdered in Nebraska. It published a piece about the mental breakdown of chess master Bobby Fischer. It also ran the profile of a bomb disposal expert in Iraq by journalist Mark Boal, which he later turned into the screenplay for the movie *The Hurt Locker*.

Esquire, too, broke new ground with its journalism, particularly in the late 1960s under editor Harold Hayes. When Hayes took over, he hired graphic designer George Lois to create a series of iconic covers for the magazine, based on photographs, but works of art in their own right. Boxer Muhammad Ali was depicted as a martyred saint, arrows embedded in his chest, a symbol of the attacks that the outspoken and controversial athlete had endured. Artist Andy Warhol appeared inside a Campbell's soup can, about to be drowned in a whirlpool of tomato soup, in reference to one of his most famous images. Richard Nixon, on the eve of his election to the presidency, was depicted, in a composite photo, having his hair and makeup done, in reference to his refusal to do so in his debates against John F. Kennedy (Guide 2010).

In addition to bringing accomplished graphic design to the covers, Hayes also made *Esquire* one of the epicenters of the so-called New Journalism, a movement that overthrew traditional modes of journalistic objectivity. Gay Talese wrote a profile of Frank Sinatra in which the author was never able to interview the subject of the profile, turning the piece into one about the concentric circles of people who protected the singer from publicity (Talese 2016). He profiled retired New York Yankees centerfielder Joe DiMaggio after the slugger returned to his hometown San Francisco. Talese made it a meditation on loss—the loss of an unparalleled athletic career and also the loss of his ex-wife Marilyn Monroe (Talese 1966). *Esquire* also published work by Michael Herr, John Sack, and Tom Wolfe (Daly 2018). It even published the essay by Wolfe (2018) that gave New Journalism its name and first self-critical (and self-aggrandizing) analysis.

As these magazines progressed through the second half of the twentieth century and into the twenty-first, they continued their tradition of publishing award-winning journalism, regularly being nominated for National Magazine Awards in reporting and writing categories. Longtime *Esquire* editor David Granger was even inducted into the Magazine Editors' Hall of Fame (Holt and Russ 2019). For the past half century at least, men's lifestyle magazines have been a part of the mainstream cultural conversation, in a way that the journalism in women's lifestyle magazines has not. Whether that speaks to the quality of the work or to the continued hegemony of men could be debated. But there is less doubt that the original idea that writing for men was mainstream, and writing for women was niche, remains current in the culture.

HARD-CORE AND LAD MAGS

The teasing nudity of *Playboy* opened the door for another, cruder form of men's magazine that would follow. *Penthouse* and *Hustler* magazines were the best-known proponents of this approach, but there was also an explosion of skin magazines that depicted explicit sex acts, an apotheosis of the pin-up magazines that were always quite a bit more coy. By the 1970s, *Playboy*'s circulation approached five million copies. *Penthouse*, started by Bob Guccione, took its predecessor's formula and pushed the sexual content even more to the forefront:

> For example, Hefner's models might strike erotic poses, but Guccione's were frequently seen simulating masturbation, and in time there were layouts of lesbians and others entwined in simulated intercourse, as well as further variations on conventional heterosexual sex. Articles and fiction, as well, were unabashedly erotic, although with some sophistication. (Tebbel and Zuckerman 1991, 283)

The magazine also ran letters, purportedly from readers, though likely at least supplemented by staff-written content, detailing their sexual adventures. The letters feature eventually spun off into a standalone magazine called *Forum*.

Hustler, which was the creation of Larry Flynt, didn't aim for even the veneer of sophistication that *Penthouse* tried for. It featured explicit sex, and none of the highbrow literary or journalistic content of *Playboy*. Flynt frequently found himself in court, most famously in *Hustler Magazine v. Falwell*, a case that determined publishers could not be sued for inflicting emotional distress on the people they wrote about. The case stemmed from the television evangelist Jerry Falwell's lawsuit against the magazine over a satirical ad that suggested that he "had a drunken incestuous relationship with his mother in an outhouse" ("Hustler Magazine, Inc. v. Falwell" 1988). It was one of a series of Supreme Court cases in which heroes of the First Amendment were people on the fringes of culture.

Most of the new skin magazines that followed in the wake of *Playboy*, *Penthouse*, and *Hustler* followed *Hustler*'s lead and went for all-out pornography, at the same time as the women's movement began to criticize them for demeaning women. The old pulp magazines continued, too, offering an alternative form of masculinity that did not include nudity—and sometimes even excluded women altogether, bringing the macho, "he-man" fantasy of male domination into the late twentieth century. Some scholars "have seen the he-man magazine as an effort to retrieve the old-fashioned hero from the past and so escape changing concepts of masculinity" (Tebbel and Zuckerman 1991, 292).

And, of course, there were always other types of magazines that appealed to men with some of the content that these men's lifestyle magazines pioneered. Sports magazines, for example, often excluded women as subjects and as audience. *Sports Illustrated* famously published an annual swimsuit issue that had little if anything to do with sports and was not marketed as a fashion photo shoot for women. But not all of these magazines exploited sex; *Popular Mechanics*, for instance, would occasionally show up in a list of men's magazines. And not all of them exploited heterosexuality, either. *Out* magazine, a lifestyle magazine for gay men, began publishing in 1992. Health and exercise magazines such as *Men's Health* also drew from the men's lifestyle category, though the pictorials were almost always of men's bodies—which also inadvertently made them appeal to gay men.

In the 1980s, Hugh Hefner turned over control of the magazine to his daughter, Christie, who moved the content back in the direction of *Esquire* or *GQ*, downplaying the nudity and repositioning the magazine as a slightly more daring version of those lifestyle magazines (Tebbel and Zuckerman 1991, 285). Under Christie Hefner, the magazine briefly banned nudity as it underwent crises of identity and circulation (Somaiya 2015). This was a direct reaction to changing social mores, but it also caused circulation to fall, creating some uncertainty for advertisers. Meanwhile, *Playboy* negotiated the divide between pornography and a respectable lifestyle magazine for men.

A seemingly inevitable backlash to this softening came in the 1990s, as a breed of magazine generally called the "lad mag" invaded the United States from Britain, where it first gained currency. *Loaded* and *FHM* (For Him Magazine) both launched in the United Kingdom in 1994, and *Maxim* followed a year later (Jackson, Stevenson, and Brooks 2001, 28). These magazines were "resolutely downmarket" compared to *Esquire* or *GQ*, which also published British editions, and they were meant to appeal to men who saw other, more middle-class or aspirational titles as denying the real desires of real men. The lad mags sought to liberate this male libido from their "crisis of masculinity" with more frank talk of sex and crude irreverence (32). *FHM* and *Maxim* each created U.S. editions, which were briefly successful, and Condé Nast relaunched its men's fashion magazine *Details* as a kind of American clone of the lad mag as well, though all of them faded from cultural relevance by the 2010s.

THE DEATH OF HEF, #METOO, AND THE LEGACY OF THE TWENTIETH-CENTURY MEN'S MAGAZINE

Hugh Hefner, the founding publisher and avatar of *Playboy*, died in 2017, and his "death triggered a tsunami of think pieces," wrote Chelsea Reynolds, who sees Hef as a complicated and contradictory figure who "simultaneously oppressed women and liberated sexual expression" (2017, 1).

In 2019, a *New York Times* style reporter published an analysis of the state of the American men's magazine in what he called "the gender tornado of 2019" (Williams 2019). That metaphorical meteorological phenomenon has most commonly been called the #MeToo movement, after a social media hashtag, but it represents a cultural moment for the women whose voices had long been marginalized, silenced, disbelieved, or otherwise minimized by men. The hashtag, which had been in circulation since 2006, gained new currency after accusations of rape and sexual harassment by movie producer Harvey Weinstein in 2017 (Chuck 2017). The *Times* story detailed changes that some venerable men's magazines were making in the face of this cultural moment, when the modifier that most often seems to be put in front of the word "masculinity" was "toxic."

As *GQ* grappled with what masculinity meant to a men's lifestyle magazine in 2019, *Playboy* went further, with a gay man as editor and women as creative director and photography editor, and a new focus on women's agency, art, and activism (Bennett 2019). The legacy of men's lifestyle and culture magazines of the twentieth century was largely one of promulgating an idea of masculine superiority over women. But within two decades after the end of that period, the public and magazine editors were beginning to be more self-aware of the potentially destructive power of their discourse.

Previous revolutions in men's magazine content framed themselves as reactions to panics about the impending loss of masculinity, or of a specific refuge for men and manhood. Smart and Gingrich wrote that *Esquire* was an escape from the feminization of general-interest magazines. Hugh Hefner started *Playboy* to counter a creeping loss of masculinity to suburban family life. The invading lad mags of Britain brought with them a renewed validation of leering male desire for female bodies. But this latest turn in *GQ*, *Esquire*, and *Playboy* may prove to be something different—an acknowledgment that the hegemony of the heterosexual male may be receding, replaced not just by a discursive negotiation of masculinity that varies over time, but by a more complex, layered understanding of masculinity in which the tensions can be perceived at once. Then again, there may always be yet another crisis of masculinity.

REFERENCES

Barbas, Samantha. 2018. "The Esquire Case: A Lost Free Speech Landmark." *William & Mary Bill of Rights Journal* 27 (2): 76.

Bennett, Jessica. 2019. "Will the Millennials Save Playboy?" *The New York Times*, August 2, sec. Business. https://www.nytimes.com/2019/08/02/business/woke-playboy-millennials.html.

Benwell, Bethan. 2003. "Introduction: Masculinity and Men's Lifestyle Magazines." *The Sociological Review* 51 (1_suppl): 6–29. https://doi.org/10.1111/j.1467-954X.2003.tb03600.x.

Betrock, Alan. 1993. *Pin-Up Mania: The Golden Age of Men's Magazines, 1950–1967*. 1st edition. Brooklyn, NY: Shake Books.

Christian, Scott. 2013. "GQ Throwback: 1957 and The Birth Announcement for GQ Magazine." *GQ*. March 28. https://www.gq.com/story/gq-throwback-1957-and-the-birth-of-gq.

Chuck, Elizabeth. 2017. "#MeToo: Alyssa Milano Promotes Hashtag That Becomes Anti-Harassment Rallying Cry." NBC News. October 16. https://www.nbcnews.com/storyline/sexual-misconduct/metoo-hashtag-becomes-anti-sexual-harassment-assault-rallying-cry-n810986.

Dalton, Meg. 2017. "Hugh Hefner's *Playboy* Did a Lot of Great Journalism. Here Are a Few Highlights." *Columbia Journalism Review*. September 28. https://www.cjr.org/b-roll/hugh-hefner-playboy-journalism.php.

Daly, Christopher B. 2018. *Covering America: A Narrative History of a Nation's Journalism*. Revised and Expanded edition. Amherst: University of Massachusetts Press.

Edwards, Tim. 2003. "Sex, Booze and Fags: Masculinity, Style and Men's Magazines." *The Sociological Review* 51 (1_suppl): 132–46. https://doi.org/10.1111/j.1467-954X.2003.tb03607.x.

Esquire #1. 1933. Vol. 1. Chicago.

Guide, The. 2010. "George Lois's Incredible Esquire Covers." *The Guardian*, February 26, sec. Art and design. https://www.theguardian.com/artanddesign/gallery/2010/feb/27/george-lois-esquire-covers.

Hines, Claire. 2018. *The Playboy and James Bond: 007, Ian Fleming and Playboy Magazine*. 1 edition. Manchester: Manchester University Press.

Holstead, Carol. 2000. "Vargas, Alberto (1896–1982), Painter and Illustrator." American National Biography. February. https://www.anb.org/view/10.1093/anb/9780198606697.001.0001/anb-9780198606697-e-1701424.

Holt, Sidney, and Susan Russ. 2019. "David Granger Elected to Magazine Editors' Hall of Fame | ASME." October 22. https://webcache.googleusercontent.com/search?q=cache:zzB_qOCy6rwJ:https://asme.magazine.org/david-granger-elected-magazine-editors%25E2%2580%2599-hall-fame+&cd=1&hl=en&ct=clnk&gl=us.

"Hustler Magazine, Inc. v. Falwell." 1988. Oyez. https://www.oyez.org/cases/1987/86-1278.

Jackson, Peter, Nick Stevenson, and Kate Brooks. 2001. *Making Sense of Men's Magazines*. Cambridge: Polity Press.

Osgerby, Bill. 2003. "A Pedigree of the Consuming Male: Masculinity, Consumption and the American 'Leisure Class.'" *The Sociological Review* 51 (1_suppl): 57–85. https://doi.org/10.1111/j.1467-954X.2003.tb03603.x.

Osgerby, Bill. 2005. "The Bachelor Pad as Cultural Icon: Masculinity, Consumption and Interior Design in American Men's Magazines, 1930–65." *Journal of Design History* 18 (1): 99–113.

Polsgrove, Carol. 1995. *It Wasn't Pretty, Folks, But Didn't We Have Fun?: Esquire in the Sixties*. New York: W. W. Norton.

Reynolds, Chelsea. 2017. "Hanging Up the Smoking Jacket: Productive Oppression and Playboy's Impacts on Mediated Sexualization." *Journal of Magazine Media* 18 (1). https://doi.org/10.1353/jmm.2017.0002.

Rutherford, Jonathan. 2003. "Preface." *The Sociological Review* 51 (1_suppl): 1–5. https://doi.org/10.1111/j.1467-954X.2003.tb03599.x.

Scheer, Robert. 1976. "The 1976 Playboy Interview with Jimmy Carter." November 1. https://www.playboy.com/read/playboy-interview-jimmy-carter.

Somaiya, Ravi. 2015. "Nudes Are Old News at Playboy." *The New York Times*, October 12, sec. Business. https://www.nytimes.com/2015/10/13/business/media/nudes-are-old-news-at-playboy.html.

Sterlacci, Francesca, and Joanne Arbuckle. 2009. *The A to Z of the Fashion Industry*. Lanham, MD: Scarecrow Press.

Stevenson, Nick, Peter Jackson, and Kate Brooks. 2003. "Reading Men's Lifestyle Magazines: Cultural Power and the Information Society." *The Sociological Review* 51 (1_suppl): 112–31. https://doi.org/10.1111/j.1467-954X.2003.tb03606.x.

Talese, Gay. 1966. "The Silent Season of a Hero | Esquire | JULY 1966." Esquire | The Complete Archive. July 1. https://classic.esquire.com/article/1966/7/1/silent-season-of-a-hero.

———. 2016. "Frank Sinatra Has a Cold." *Esquire*. May 14. https://www.esquire.com/features/ESQ1003-OCT_SINATRA_rev_.

Tebbel, John William, and Mary Ellen Zuckerman. 1991. *The Magazine in America, 1741–1990*. New York: Oxford University Press.

Ward, L. Monique, Laura Vandenbosch, and Steven Eggermont. 2015. "The Impact of Men's Magazines on Adolescent Boys' Objectification and Courtship Beliefs." *Journal of Adolescence* 39 (February): 49–58. https://doi.org/10.1016/j.adolescence.2014.12.004.

Weiss, Suzannah. 2015. "10 Iconic 'Playboy' Articles Everyone Should Know, Because You Actually CAN Read It Just for the Articles." *Bustle*. October 13. https://www.bustle.com/articles/116648-10-iconic-playboy-articles-everyone-should-know-because-you-actually-can-read-it-just-for-the.

Welch, Will. 2019. "Introducing GQ's New Masculinity Issue, Starring Pharrell." *GQ*. October 15. https://www.gq.com/story/masculinity-is-changing-editors-letter-november-2019.

Wick, Julia. 2017. "Hugh Hefner to Be Buried Next to Marilyn Monroe, Whose Photos Were Used to Launch Playboy without Her Consent." *LAist*. September 28. https://laist.com/2017/09/28/hugh_hefner_marilyn_monroe.php.

Williams, Alex. 2017. "The 'Esquire Man' Is Dead. Long Live the 'Esquire Man.'" *The New York Times*, February 4, sec. Fashion. https://www.nytimes.com/2017/02/04/fashion/esquire-magazine-jay-fielden.html.

———. 2019. "As Men Are Canceled, So Too Their Magazine Subscriptions." *The New York Times*, November 2, sec. Style. https://www.nytimes.com/2019/11/02/style/mens-magazines.html.

Wolfe, Tom. 2018. "Why They Aren't Writing the Great American Novel Anymore." *Esquire*. May 15. https://www.esquire.com/lifestyle/money/a20703846/tom-wolfe-new-jounalism-american-novel-essay/.

Young, Sarah. 2017. "The 'Devastating' Betrayal That Turned Hugh Hefner into a Playboy." *The Independent*. September 28. http://www.independent.co.uk/life-style/hugh-hefner-dead-playboy-founder-marriage-betrayal-ladies-man-mildred-williams-millie-affair-a7971711.html.

Youngs, Ian. 2017. "11 Great Authors Who Wrote for Playboy." *BBC News*, September 28, sec. Entertainment & Arts. https://www.bbc.com/news/entertainment-arts-41426419.

Section 3

THE FAMILIAR AND THE FUTURE

Chapter 10

Getting the Last Laugh
Domestic Chaos Writers Outlasted Their Critics
Betsy Edgerton

In the 2000s, when writer Heather B. Armstrong had risen to the top of the mommy blogger-verse (Lieber 2019), she likely didn't know that her snarky posts about her hectic life could trace their lineage to a group of similarly droll women writing seven decades earlier.

What these domestic chaos writers share across the decades is a self-deprecating sense of humor and a rueful acceptance that they'd never be the perfect parent or partner. They persevered through the withering criticism of media critics and authors by creating communities of supportive readers and inspiring other women to express themselves in writing, too. They gifted their loyal readers with a sense of camaraderie: we're all in this messy situation together.

Seventy years after their reign, the domestic chaos genre writers still have their charms, as well as their fans: the latest edition of Shirley Jackson's *Life Among the Savages*, a collection of essays by the prolific domestic chaos writer of the 1940s and 1950s, was published in 2015 by Penguin Books, sixty-two years after the original was released. Collectively, these authors had an influence familiar to anyone who reads contemporary women's writing about the unglamourous work of child-rearing and the tension between working moms and stay-at-home moms. Theirs is the voice of a weary and witty writer.

THE EMERGENCE OF THE HOUSEWIFE WRITER

During the 1950s and 1960s, a wave of "housewife writers" dotted the pages of popular women's magazines with their humorous and self-deprecating tales of failed efforts to be perfect wives and mothers. In an ironic twist, their first-person essays ran alongside the magazine ads and stories that promoted the flawless housewife stereotype they poked fun at. Meanwhile, several of these women were criticized for betraying their successful careers as novelists, poets, and playwrights with their lightweight magazine writing (Friedan 2013, 52, 53).

In her book *Something From the Oven: Reinventing Dinner in 1950s America*, Laura Shapiro places these writers in the genre of "domestic chaos." She could have been writing about contemporary mommy bloggers:

> The typical narrator made for an admirable heroine, bushwhacking a trail across the murky landscape of [sic] woman's world. Often she worked—she was, after all, a writer—but there was no doubt about her commitment to housekeeping and mothering. Career woman or not, her identity was inextricably attached to the emotional web of family life. . . . [Her] ability to remain ever so slightly above the fray, thanks to a sharp sense of humor, gave her a great deal of charm and more charisma than just about any other housewife in literature. (Shapiro, 150–51)

Scholar Jennifer Diamond takes the label one step further, calling this style of humor writing "domestic gothic," with its ability to cross genres, from the "female gothic" of fiction to the domestic chaos of magazine essays. In the work of three housewife writers, Diamond spots "the markers of female gothic—entropy, loss, fears of female appetite and embodiment, boundary violation" (2005, 6).

The best-known housewife writers were Jean Kerr and Shirley Jackson, who collectively wrote for magazines including *Charm, Collier's, Good Housekeeping, Harper's, Ladies' Home Journal, Mademoiselle, McCall's, Saturday Evening Post, Vogue, Woman's Day*, and *Woman's Home Companion*. This pair of writers turned their first-person magazine writing into popular books and more. Although they didn't have entire magazines to call their own, they were published in a diverse array of women's magazines, carving out a niche within a niche for the weary wife and mother.

Jackson built a career writing gothic fiction. Her short story "The Lottery," that staple of high school reading lists, was published in the *New Yorker* in 1948, and her novel *The Haunting of Hill House* was published in 1959.

In *Raising Demons*, a collection of columns Jackson wrote for *McCall's* and the *New Yorker* in the 1950s, her tone was that of a cheerful but lackadaisical young mother living in genteel chaos. Here she is describing the perils of living in a too small, ramshackle house, as she tries in vain to find a spot to stash the baby's clothes—as well as the baby:

We had three more attics, but one of them was full of old lumber and bricks left over from the various additions that had been built onto the house, and one of them was full of bats, and the last could only be reached by climbing through a trapdoor in the ceiling of the next-to-last attic and even if I could get past the bats and through the lumber and bricks I did not think I could keep taking the baby up and down through a trapdoor. (Jackson 1981, 157–58)

Her essays regularly chronicled such failures as her poor track record in hiring household help, including her latest disaster, Phoebe:

That is why I always end up with people like Phoebe. If she could make chowder or raised doughnuts she would, in our town, have a home of her own. If she had a natural gift for getting things clean, or an instinctive ability at getting three rebellious children into bed, she would be gainfully employed in our nearest big town. If she knew how to do anything right at all, she would not be working for me. (Jackson 2015, 91)

Of course it bears mentioning that some of the writing doesn't hold up—the topics are a little creaky, the jokes are a little too broad—but the writing is sharp. For instance, Jackson's comic telling of the birth of her third child includes the familiar hospital-room scene of the bewildered father and the avuncular, dismissive doctor.

The door slammed open and the doctor came in. "Heard you were here," he said jovially, shaking my husband's hand. "Look a little pale." My husband smiled weakly. "Never lost a father yet," the doctor said, and slapped him on the back. He turned to me. "How do we feel?" he said. "Terrible," I said, and the doctor laughed again. "Just on my way downstairs," he said to my husband. "Come along?" (Jackson 2015, 68)

Both of Jackson's humor-writing books were well-reviewed at the time, writes Shapiro, particularly *Life Among the Savages*. She quotes a *New York Times* critic who praised the book as perfectly illuminating the state of domestic chaos.

Jackson's cultural reach extends into the twenty-first century, and recently she's had something of a moment. In 2020, the film *Shirley* was released, based on Susan Scarf Merrell's novel of the same name that fictionalized Jackson's life. And in 2018, Netflix produced *The Haunting of Hill House*, a horror drama series loosely based on Jackson's novel. In reviewing *Shirley* in the *New Yorker*, film critic Anthony Lane (2020) mourns that the film's dark vision of Jackson's life would have been richer if it gave a nod to her other persona: a writer adept at mining "the comedy of parental mishaps."

Fans filled Jackson's mailbox with requests for advice on how they, too, could combine professional writing with housekeeping. Scholar Jessamyn Neuhaus writes that Jackson was an inspirational figure for women who read domestic humor. "When they wrote to Jackson, they felt they had joined a community of women (or, at least, found one other woman) who failed to fulfill the feminine mystique—and made a career based on writing about their failure" (Neuhaus 2009, 121).

In a letter from 1956, a housewife wrote to Jackson, poking fun at herself while also making clear her goal to be a serious writer:

> I've made one big sale ("We Had Our Baby at Home") to *McCall's*—but how often do I have a baby at home? This one sale I am beginning to regard as a fluke ... I am eating my heart out trying to repeat. I am hoping you may have some advice. (Neuhaus 2009, 122)

Another fan wrote a letter to Jackson in 1960 that held this plea:

> Is it ridiculous for me to say that I want to write; have wanted to write as long as I can remember; feel a need to write that is so strong that it is figuratively "killing me"? ... I realize it's an imposition, but I would so appreciate any advice or encouragement you could give me. (Neuhaus 2009, 121)

Neuhaus comments that the letter "suggests that when women read domestic humor, and when they wrote to Jackson, they felt they had joined a community of women (or, at least, found one other woman who failed to fulfill the feminine mystique) and made a career based on writing about that failure" (2009, 121).

THE MEDIA SENSATION

Jackson's closest peer, Jean Kerr, was a successful playwright married to theater critic and playwright Walter Kerr. She *should* have had a more glamorous home life, but, alas her domestic chaos stories echoed Jackson's.

In "Our Gingerbread Dream House," an essay published in *Ladies' Home Journal* in 1955, Kerr dreams of a large house with a slew of appliances "and a couch where I could lie on sunny days and listen to them all vibrate." Meanwhile, her husband yearns for a kitchen so small that he can fry his eggs while also answering "the thirty-eight phone calls he always gets during breakfast," including one from a young man "who wants Walter's advice about making a musical based on the first three books of the Old Testament" (Kerr 1957, 73).

Jean Kerr's national best-selling *Please Don't Eat the Daisies*, a 1957 collection of essays, became a popular movie of the same name starring Doris Day and David Niven, and subsequently spawned a TV show. Kerr and her husband, Walter, had such a cultural footprint in the arts that their lives inspired the Broadway comedy *Critic's Choice*, written by Ira Levin (Vallance 2003).

Kerr wrote numerous plays, including *The Song of Bernadette* and *Mary, Mary*. Howard Taubman, a *New York Times* theater critic, gave *Mary, Mary* a mixed review, calling it a "confection," though he did acknowledge Kerr's snappy writing. In his review he took a swipe at women's magazines, Kerr's other avocation. The "syrupy plot" of the play, he groused, "would fit neatly into the glossy pages of a women's magazine" (Taubman 1961). Perhaps Kerr had the last laugh. The play ran on Broadway for three and a half years. "Audiences packed the theater nightly and *Mary, Mary* became one of the longest-running productions of the decade," read her *New York Times* obituary (Berkvist 2003).

In a 1957 column in the *Saturday Evening Post*, Kerr shares her disdain for the trend among psychiatrists of insisting that children are "really *people*, little adults—just like the rest of us, only smaller. Really, the impression you get in some quarters is that the only difference between children and grownups is that children don't drink, smoke, or play bridge" (Kerr 1957, 157).

Children, she noted, "having linear minds and no grasp of the great intangibles, spend most of their energy yapping about trifles: 'Can I have a Coke?' 'Can I have an apple?'" Adults, by contrast, reveal "maturity and breadth of vision" in their higher-order demands: "Tell them we won't come, tell them I'm sick, tell them I'm dead, tell them anything you want!" "Who the hell took my fountain pen?" Based on which, she concludes, "Let's have no more of this nonsense about children being little adults" (Kerr 1957, 164–65).

THE TRADITIONALISTS

Phyllis McGinley, a housewife writer of a different stripe, was a Pulitzer Prize–winning poet as well as a prolific magazine writer and book author. *Sixpence in Her Shoe*, a best-selling collection of her 1960s-era columns published in *Ladies' Home Journal* and *Glamour*, is an "autobiographical ode to housewifery," write Penelope Fritzer and Bartholomew Bland in *Merry Wives and Others: A History of Domestic Humor Writing* (2002, 35–37). A prospective reader of *Sixpence in Her Shoe* would learn very quickly, were they to read the book jacket, that McGinley "is indeed a feminine woman, but she is definitely not a feminist."

McGinley's writing is not as funny as the other housewife writers, but she is more political, fashioning herself "as a judicious moderator in the early culture wars," according to Fritzer and Bland. In one of her magazine columns, she comments wryly on the cultural role of housewives.

> These days we are News. Radio panels debate our position in the world . . . Psychologists analyze our motives . . . [Anthropologist] Ashley Montagu admires us (at least as women), while Margaret Mead accuses us of escaping from our civic responsibilities in the warm nest of "fecundity." We are praised, abused, consulted, quoted, advised. We are seldom ignored. (Fritzer and Bland 2002, 15)

A prolific magazine writer, McGinley contributed to magazines ranging from *The Commonweal*, to *Good Housekeeping* and *Woman's Day*, to *The Saturday Review*, and developed a loyal following. The extensive assortment of her fan mail held at the Syracuse University archives includes letters from "the hundreds of housewives whose lives she championed from the earliest beginnings of the women's movement in the 1960s through the mid-1970s" (Anon. n.d.).

McGinley was joined in her more traditional messaging by Lenora Mattingly Weber, who wrote a monthly column in *Extension: The National Catholic Monthly*, a mission magazine with the design and feel of the *Saturday Evening Post*.

What they had in common could be neatly summed up by a line in McGinley's *New York Times* (1978) obituary that reads like a description of Weber:

> [McGinley] seldom departed from the image that her mode of life and her verse had given to her—that of a wife, mother, hard-working professional writer and observant Roman Catholic.

From 1946 to 1967, Weber, a widowed mother of six, wrote about religion in her column ("Mid Pleasures and Problems"), but she was mostly devoted to commenting on culture and society, and chronicling the hive of activity at her house:

> With six children, and five of them boys, there was often a carp or a turtle in our bathtub. Our back yard was pocked with caves. Makeshift tents were built over the clothes line. Dogs cluttered the yard with bones, and dug around the lilac bushes. (I wonder why stray dogs and waifs of cats always gravitate to us. And why all the cats turn out to be prolific mothers.) (Weber 1958, 32)

Weber wrote twenty-three novels and many short stories, and was best known for her successful girls' series novels, which are still in print. However, as the single mother of a brood of children, as well as a perpetually cash-strapped Westerner, it's no wonder that her humor was less daffy than that of her housewife writer peers on the East Coast.

Regardless, she was well-read and thoughtful about social issues—and she got plenty riled up when the topic merited it. As she aged, she carried her readers along with her as her worldview shifted. In a column she wrote when she was nearing seventy, she gave the back of her hand to the suburban ideal of like-minded people carving out a little world for themselves:

> Suburbia, too, is a form of segregation. Block after block of young couples with small children, and all in the same comparative age and income bracket. No doubt they, cut off from the 'main body' of life, do become ingrown. (Weber 1964, 46)

THE HUMORIST FROM OHIO

In her twenty-one years at *Extension* magazine, Weber churned out nearly 300 columns—the only steady paycheck she ever had, wrote her son (Weber and Weber 2002). But her audience was small and targeted. By contrast, writer Erma Bombeck was a household name. Bombeck was the queen of newspaper columnists, authoring 4,000 syndicated newspaper columns between 1965 and 1996 and casting a huge shadow over the media world; she also wrote books and all manner of articles, had a regular morning TV gig, and nurtured budding humor writers.

Bombeck mined the same topics as the mid-century domestic humor writers, but her tone was of the funny lady at the end of the cul-de-sac rather than the cultured wit from the East Coast. (Also, she had to be funny on a tight schedule; she owed her editors three columns a week.) (Braden 2009, 41)

In a 1967 column titled "The American Clothesline," she mused about the disappearance of a suburban icon:

> Never do I feel the sun on my face and the wind gently billowing my skirt that I do not hold my right hand over my heart and mourn the passing of the housewife's answer to Radio Free Europe: the American clothesline. Like the American buffalo, Irish tenors and the nickel cup of coffee, the clothesline has virtually become extinct. And with it goes the greatest communications medium the world has ever known.
>
> When I was a kid, the neighbors stretched a clothesline the day they moved in. And we watched and learned. "How many of them are there? Boys or girls? Ages? Do they have nice underwear?" (Mama always said you could judge a

woman by the underwear she hung and her character by the way she acted when her clothesline broke.) (Bombeck 1996, 100)

As a newspaper columnist, she could breezily criticize the impossible standards set by women's magazines:

> The slick magazines are forever trying to build the feminine image by pointing out that the modern-day mother is a taskmaster of a hundred skills—"She must be chauffeur, dietitian, doctor"—and a list of 20 specialized tasks, ad nauseam. Rubbish! (Bombeck 1996, 57)

MOTHERING WHILE WRITING

Throughout the mid-century years, a vigorous discussion existed about whether mothers should work. In 1960, *Cosmopolitan* magazine gathered the experiences of a slew of successful writers to explore whether housewife writers could—or should—juggle both roles. While some of the women truly needed the money a writing career would give, some clearly did not.

"You have to decide which you are—a writer who keeps house or a housewife who writes," said one author, the difference being how much household help was on hand (G. Walker 1960, 41). Another counseled that housewife writers must let go of the notion of being perfect housekeepers. And one—who, not surprisingly, refused to give her name—declared that housewife writers were "sitting in the catbird seat," bolstered by their husbands' income and freed from housekeeping by "labor-saving devices and domestic help." But many managed to make it work, the magazine concluded:

> Those women whose desire to write is an intense one will find—and are finding—their own way. From the looks of things, the day may not be far off when typewriters will be among the built-in features of the ultra-modern, fully-equipped kitchen. (G. Walker 1960, 41)

One fiction writer and mother of five interviewed in the article captured the bind of writing while mothering with the title of an essay: "Hemingway Wasn't a Mother."

Women's magazines fed the unhappiness of wives and mothers by pumping out a constant stream of articles that fixated on the difficulties of their readers' lives, writes Eva Moskowitz (1996, 67).

> Drawing upon the work of pollsters and social scientists, the magazines provided statistical as well as qualitative pictures of the precarious psychological

situation of the American housewife. As one magazine announced, it had made "a scientific study of the problem within recent years" and was in the process of "uncovering the hard, cold facts of what causes happiness and unhappiness." (Moskowitz 1996, 68)

The magazines concluded that women were more unhappy than men, apparently stemming from their dissatisfaction as wives and mothers (Moskowitz 1996, 68). Indeed, Betty Friedan made a name for herself exploring mid-century women's miserable state of being in her seminal book *The Feminine Mystique*, published in 1963.

Friedan was a fierce critic of the housewife writing genre, zeroing in on a new group of women writers who wrote about themselves disingenuously, "as if they were 'just housewives,' reveling in a comic world of children's pranks and eccentric washing machines" (2013, 52).

> When Shirley Jackson, who all her adult life has been an extremely capable writer, pursuing a craft far more demanding than bedmaking, and Jean Kerr, who is a playwright, and Phyllis McGinley, who is a poet, picture themselves as housewives, they may or may not overlook the housekeeper or maid who really makes the beds. But they implicitly deny the vision, and the satisfying hard work involved in their stories, poems, and plays. They deny the lives they lead, not as housewives, but as individuals. (Friedan 2013, 52–53)

The housewife writers' message to real housewives is that the daily slog of running a household is a hoot, that the whole lot of them are merrily paddling in the same sinking boat. That message, Friedan writes, is dangerous.

> Do real housewives then dissipate in laughter their dreams and their own sense of desperation? Do they think their frustrated abilities and their limited lives are a joke? Shirley Jackson makes the beds, loves and laughs at her sons—and writes another book. Jean Kerr's plays are produced on Broadway. The joke is not on *them*. (Friedan 2013, 52–53)

Friedan's disdain extended to women's magazines as a whole, according to Eric Savoy. She "offered a pungent critique of the entire cultural economy of women's magazines and of the women who wrote for them: 'coupled with the women editors who sold themselves their own bill of goods'" (Savoy 2017, 56–57).

McGinley, never an apologist for housewifery, was also a target of Friedan's scorn. In one essay in *Sixpence in Her Shoe*, McGinley comments on the cultural changes afoot, responding to whether married women should work outside of the home.

The new question, the one which agitates sociologists and feminists these latter days, seems to be the opposite [of whether married women should work]: do housewives have a right *not* to work after marriage? The same people who berate us for keeping our education in the pocket of a kitchen apron also scold us for clinging to the hearth as our sole profession. (McGinley 1964, 40–41)

AN INHERENT IRONY

In every tale of domestic chaos published in a glossy women's magazine lay an inherent irony: the housewife writers "satirized the very standards of perfection promulgated by magazine articles and advertisements; heroines were beset by falling souffles, naughty children, malfunctioning appliances, and a husband who had never heard of 'togetherness'" (N. Walker 2001, 186–88).

Walker argues that a close reading of *Please Don't Eat the Daisies* and *Life Among the Savages* makes clear that Kerr's and Jackson's failures shouldn't be attributed to their ineptitude but instead to the "impossibility of the standards for performance" they were expected to live up to.

As an example, Walker points to a 1956 issue of *Ladies' Home Journal*, which ran an excerpt from *The Complete Book of Absolutely Perfect Housekeeping*, a satirical book by Elinor Goulding Smith. Walker describes the disconnect between the message and the medium:

> Yet even as such satiric pieces tacitly acknowledged that the magazines' advice was susceptible to mockery, the messages that readers received remained complex and contradictory: the *Ladies' Home Journal* pages on which Smith's satire appeared also carried advertisements for hosiery, perfume, china, floor coverings, floor cleaner, sewing machines, and children's clothes, all with illustrations promising domestic harmony and bliss. (N. Walker 2001, 187–88)

And the jokes were easy to make, as long as the publications kept serving up such obvious paradoxes in their pages. As Diamond writes, "self-deprecation locates its most powerful source material in women's publications."

> Magazine and newspaper advertising, psychological advice/self-tests, and epistolary exchanges ranged from tips on how to eradicate hubby's ring-around-the-collar to treatises on women's rights, presenting diverse and often contradictory discourses next to one another. . . . Advertising, especially, consistently urged women to "be themselves" while promoting the counter-narrative that being oneself was actually not good enough. (Diamond 2005, 106–7)

Indeed, in advertisements in 1950s women's magazines, images abound of a joyful woman in a tidy home, decked out in a dress and heels promoting everything from appliances to lightbulbs. In another ad, a wasp-waisted mother instructs her identically dressed young daughter that eating Grape-Nuts will help her stay trim. Men appear in the ads less, sometimes in a scenario similar to one for Edwards Coffee: a husband happily drinks a cup of coffee, as his wife stands in the near distance, beaming.

Feminist scholars (as well as Friedan) have criticized 1950s magazine advertising as perpetuating the denigration of women. However, an analysis of the ads of that era by scholar Christina Catalano finds images of strong and self-determined women working outside of the domestic sphere, too. Not surprisingly, this type of advertising appeared more in general-interest magazines than in women's magazines. Still, Catalano pushes back against a common refrain:

> According to [feminist scholars], ads during this time period portrayed women as stupid, submissive, purely domestic creatures; they claim this is historical truth. However, through re-examining original advertisements in a variety of magazines from the 1950s while keeping in mind the culture of the time, it becomes increasingly evident that often these ads were neither belittling to women nor antifeminist. In fact, the historical truth is that they were sometimes just the opposite, picturing women in varied roles and positions of power. (Catalano 2002, 50–51)

DOMESTIC CHAOS WRITING MOVES ONLINE

When Sally Koslow, former editor-in-chief of *McCall's* magazine, wrote about the death of *Ladies' Home Journal* in 2014, she pointed out a crucial difference in community-building between now and then, referring to the powerful "Seven Sisters" of twentieth-century women's magazines.

Now, the bonding among women who are mulling over parenting and partnering occurs in an unending stream of social media, which provides "the connection once found in the town square of women's magazines" (Koslow 2014).

> I speak of the sense of community women now find in social media that they used to discover through traditional magazines. Regardless of whether the voice was preachy (cue *LHJ* or *Good Housekeeping*), friendly (*McCall's*, *Redbook*, or *Family Circle*), spiritual (*Woman's Day*, known for its Bible quotes), or grounded in earthier concerns (*Better Homes & Gardens*—always the practical Sister), women bonded in these pages in a way they had few opportunities to replicate elsewhere. (Koslow 2014)

As the housewife writers did for mid-century homemakers in books and magazines, their sister-writers now share their predicaments with humor as well as empathy on social media and blogs (Calfas 2018; Lenz 2019; Rosen 2019). Sometimes their common predicament is just getting through the day. In our age, mothers who write share the sentiment of Jean Kerr, when she describes the challenges of child-rearing:

> The Everest of my ambition is to teach my children the simple precepts of existence—"Keep your fingers out of the plate," "Don't wear your underwear to bed," "Keep out of Federal institutions"—and somehow arrive at golden middle age with my larynx intact. (Kerr 1957, 147–48)

The tension between stay-at-home moms and working mothers persists, but the gap between the two groups has widened. In 1968, 51 percent of mothers with children under 18 worked either full-time or part-time; in 2018 that number had risen to 71 percent, according to a 2019 Pew Research Center analysis of Census Bureau Current Population Survey data (J. Horowitz 2019). And those working moms feel the pressure, with 60 percent reporting that they struggle to balance work with family.

In the years since Kerr, Jackson, and their contemporaries wisecracked about the challenges of motherhood, the genre of domestic chaos writing was updated and reoriented by feminism and economic pressures, and morphed into parenting magazines, books about the "good-enough mother," and, eventually, the boom of mommy bloggers (Rosen 2019; Jezer-Morton 2019). The housewife writing genre never really went away—it evolved.

REFERENCES

Anon. n.d. "Phyllis McGinley Papers: An Inventory of Her Papers at Syracuse University." Syracuse University Libraries, Special Collections Research Center. Accessed July 8, 2020. https://library.syr.edu/digital/guides/m/mcginley_p.htm#d2e89.

Berkvist, Robert. 2003. "Jean Kerr, Playwright and Author, Dies at 80." *New York Times*. https://www.nytimes.com/2003/01/07/theater/jean-kerr-playwright-and-author-dies-at-80.html?pagewanted=1. Retrieved August 14, 2020.

Bombeck, Erma. 1996. *Forever, Erma*. Kansas City, MO: Andrews McMeel.

Braden, Maria. 2009. *She Said What?: Interviews with Women Newspaper Columnists*. Lexington: University Press of Kentucky.

Calfas, Jennifer. 2018. "The New Mommy Blogger: Instagram Famous, Highly Paid, and Sponsored by Minute Maid." *Money*. May 11. https://money.com/mommy-bloggers-success/. Retrieved July 3, 2020.

Catalano, Christina. 2002. "Shaping the American Woman: Feminism and Advertising in the 1950s." *Constructing the Past* 3 (1), Article 6. Available at: http://digitalc ommons.iwu.edu/constructing/vol3/iss1/6.

Chen, Gina Masullo. 2013. "Don't Call Me That: A Techno-Feminist Critique of the Term Mommy Blogger." *Mass Communication & Society* 16 (4): 15205436.

Damon-Moore, Helen. 1994. *Magazines for the Millions: Gender and Commerce in the Ladies' Home Journal and the Saturday Evening Post, 1880–1910.* Albany, NY: State University of New York Press.

Diamond, Jennifer. 2005. "Ivory Towers and Ivory Soap: Composition, Housewife Humor and Domestic Gothic, 1940–1970." Ph.D. Retrieve ProQuest: https://se arch.proquest.com/openview/6d2efeb7d958b8659a1eee7d5f50899f/1?pq-origsite =gscholar&cbl=18750&diss=y.

Eberhardt, Auleen B. 1944. "Women and the Catholic Press." America, February 4.

Friedan, Betty. 2013. *The Feminine Mystique.* New York: W. W. Norton & Company.

Fritzer, Penelope Joan, and Bland, Bartholomew. 2002. *Merry Wives and Others: A History of Domestic Humor Writing.* Jefferson, NC: McFarland & Co.

Gill, Jo. 2013. "'Quite the Opposite of a Feminist': Phyllis McGinley, Betty Friedan and Discourses of Gender in Mid-Century American Culture." *Women's History Review* 22 (3): 422–39. https://doi.org/10.1080/09612025.2012.726127.

Haveman, Heather A., and Marissa D. King. 2005. "Hellfire and Brimstone: Religious Politics in the Rise of American Magazines." In American Sociological Association; 2005 Annual Meeting.

Horowitz, Lisa. 2010. "In Defense of Mommy Bloggers." *The Wrap.* https://www.the wrap.com/defense-mommy-bloggers-15633/. Retrieved July 3, 2020.

Horowitz, Juliana Menasce. 2019. "Despite Challenges at Home and Work, Most Working Moms and Dads Say Being Employed Is What's Best for Them." Pew Research Center. September 12. https://www.pewresearch.org/fact-tank/2019/09 /12/despite-challenges-at-home-and-work-most-working-moms-and-dads-say-bein g-employed-is-whats-best-for-them/. Accessed July 3, 2020.

Isaacs, Rebecca Frances. 2010. "The Feminine Mystake: Betty Friedan and the Dogma of Domesticity in 1950s America." Thesis, University of Birmingham.

Jackson, Shirley. 1981. *Life among the Savages and Raising Demons: A 2-in-1 Volume.* New York: Farrar Straus Giroux.

———. 2015. *Life among the Savages.* New York: Penguin Books.

Jezer-Morton, Kathryn. 2019. "Online Momming in the 'Perfectly Imperfect' Age." *The Cut.* April 10. https://www.thecut.com/2019/04/online-moms-mommyblogs-i nstagram.html. Accessed January 24, 2020.

Kerr, Jean, 1957. *Please Don't Eat the Daisies.* New York: Doubleday & Company Inc.

Koslow, Sally. 2014. "What We Lose in Losing Ladies' Home Journal." *The Atlantic.* May 1. https://www.theatlantic.com/business/archive/2014/05/what-we-lose-in-l osing-ladies-home-journal/361520/. Accessed July 3, 2020.

Lane, Anthony. 2020. "'Shirley' Takes a One-Sided View of Its Subject." *The New Yorker.* May 29. https://www.newyorker.com/magazine/2020/06/08/shirley-takes- a-one-sided-view-of-its-subject. Accessed June 11, 2020.

Lenz, Lyz. 2019. "The Mommy Blog Is Dead. Long Live the Mommy Blog." *Topic*. May. https://www.topic.com/the-mommy-blog-is-dead-long-live-the-mommy-blog.

Lieber, Chavie. 2019. "She Was the 'Queen of the Mommy Bloggers.' Then Her Life Fell Apart." *Vox*. April 25, 2019. https://www.vox.com/the-highlight/2019/4/25/18512620/dooce-heather-armstrong-depression-valedictorian-of-being-dead. Accessed July 3, 2020.

McGinley, Phyllis. 1949. "Suburbia: Of Thee I Sing." *Harper's*, December.

———. 1964. *Sixpence in Her Shoe*. New York: Macmillan.

Morrison, Aimée. 2011. "'Suffused by Feeling and Affect': The Intimate Public of Personal Mommy Blogging." *Biography* 34 (1): 37–55. https://doi.org/10.1353/bio.2011.0002.

Moskowitz, Eva. 1996. "'It's Good to Blow Your Top': Women's Magazines and a Discourse of Discontent, 1945–1965." *Journal of Women's History* 8 (3): 66–98. https://doi.org/10.1353/jowh.2010.0458.

Neuhaus, Jessamyn. 2009. "'Is It Ridiculous for Me to Say I Want to Write?': Domestic Humor and Redefining the 1950s Housewife Writer in Fan Mail to Shirley Jackson." *Journal of Women's History* 21 (2): 115–37. https://doi.org/10.1353/jowh.0.0071.

The New York Times. 1978. "Phyllis McGinley, Essayist and Poet Who Won Pulitzer in '61, Dies at 72," February 23, sec. Archives. https://www.nytimes.com/1978/02/23/archives/phyllis-mcginley-essayist-and-poet-who-won-pulitzer-in-61-dies-at.html. Accessed July 8, 2020.

Powell, Rebecca. 2010. "Good Mothers, Bad Mothers and Mommy Bloggers: Rhetorical Resistance and Fluid Subjectivities." *MP: An Online Feminist Journal*, February.

Rosen, Christine. 2019. "Requiem for the Mommy Blogger." *Commentary Magazine*. November 13. https://www.commentarymagazine.com/articles/requiem-for-the-mommy-blogger. Retrieved July 3, 2020.

Savoy, Eric. 2017. "Between as If and Is: On Shirley Jackson." *Women's Studies* 46 (8): 827–44. https://doi.org/10.1080/00497878.2017.1392797.

Shapiro, Laura. 2005. *Something from The Oven*. New York: Penguin Books.

Taubman, Howard. 1961. "Theatre: A Bit of Summer Reading; Jean Kerr's 'Mary, Mary' in Premiere Barbara Bel Geddes Stars at Helen Hayes." *The New York Times*, March 9. https://www.nytimes.com/1961/03/09/archives/theatre-a-bit-of-summer-reading-jean-kerrs-mary-mary-in-premiere.html. Retrieved August 14, 2020.

Time. 1964. "The Home: A Woman's Place." October 9.

Vallance, Tom. 2003 "Jean Kerr: Author of 'Please Don't Eat the Daisies'." *The Independent*, January 10. www.independent.co.uk/news/obituaries/jean-kerr-123603.html. Retrieved August 13, 2020.

Walker, Gerald. 1960. "Typewriters in the Kitchen." *Cosmopolitan*, August.

Walker, Nancy A. 1998. *Women's Magazines, 1940–1960: Gender Roles and the Popular Press*. Boston: Bedford/St. Martin's.

———. 2001. *Shaping Our Mothers' World: American Women's Magazines*. Jackson: University Press of Mississippi.

Weber, Lenora Mattingly. 1950. "Women, Gainfully Employed." *Extension: The National Catholic Monthly*, September.

———. 1958. "Same Old Track." *Extension: The National Catholic Monthly*, January.

———. 1964. "I'm Against It." *Extension: The National Catholic Monthly*, January.

Weber, Lenora Mattingly, and David E. Weber. 2002. *Nonie: An Autobiography and Biography of the Life of Lenora Mattingly Weber*. United States: Image Cascade.

Zuckerman, Mary Ellen. 1998. *A History of Popular Women's Magazines in the United States: 1792–1995*. Westport, CT; London: Greenwood Press.

Chapter 11

Craving to Connect

Zines and the Celebration of Creativity and Control

Peggy Dillon

Fanzines, also known as "zines," reached their zenith in the 1990s, with publications such as *Temp Slave!*, *FAT!SO?*, and *Thrift SCORE*, about the pitfalls of temp work, the refusal to apologize for one's size, and the thrills of thrift-shopping, respectively. Irreverent, digressive, alternately cynical and enthusiastic, and often with slipshod photocopied layout and design, zines were opinionated and idiosyncratic in a way that mainstream magazines were not.

And that, it turns out, is the point of zines (pronounced "zeens"). Zines are "individualized booklets filled with diatribes, reworkings of pop culture iconography, and all varieties of personal and political narratives. They are self-produced and anti-corporate. Their production, philosophy and aesthetic are anti-professional" (Piepmeier 2009, 2). Zines are basically noncommercial, usually intentionally, and most lose money. They are mostly small-circulation publications with widely varying aesthetics, from barely legible images to all-caps-handwritten text to slick four-color production values. In tone, their content could resemble a personal letter, diary entry, rant, or magazine editorial. During their heyday—pre-internet—zines were often photocopied and stapled together, and circulated via mail or in person at zine conventions or other locations.

In sharp contrast to the circulation of magazines and newspapers, the very act of distributing and sharing zines strengthens community ties. People who create and read zines trade them in person and via mail, and also attend zine fests and events that include picnics, potlucks, readings, tours, release parties, workshops, and tabling events.

Zines are also found in independent bookstores and record stores, and available via "zine distros" (short for distributors), which are usually modest mail orders, online shops, or sometimes zine collections brought somewhere to show or sell. Zine reviews are located in *Maximum Rock'n'Roll*, *Broken Pencil*, and *Razorcake*, among other places. Online zine resources include StolenSharpieRevolution.org, and community resources such as WeMakeZines.com, Facebook, and Tumblr zine groups (Wrekk 2006, 11–12, 87).

DIVERSE BY DESIGN

While they are most certainly niche vehicles, zines are not aimed at mainstream audiences the way even the most highly targeted consumer magazines are. Traditional consumer magazines seek to reach a finely tuned audience for the purpose of exposing readers to the marketing messages of advertisers who buy space in those pages. By contrast, zinesters' intentions are as creator-centric as they are topic-specific:

> This hyperspecialization of zines—science fiction, punk rock, eight-track tapes, defunct Missouri garage bands—is a bit misleading, for unlike mainstream "niche market" periodicals, zines don't follow well-laid plans for market penetration or move purposefully in a defined direction courting profitable demographics. The majority of zines are specialized, but only to the point that they communicate the range, however wide or narrow, that makes up the personal interests of the publisher. Zines meander and change direction, switching back, then back again, flowing wherever the publisher's interest takes them. (Duncombe 1997, 9–10)

Part of what makes zines unique and drives people to keep making them is a craving to connect, wrote Seth Friedman, former editor of Factsheet Five, the seminal publication about thousands of zines. "[W]hat unites all zine publishers is their passion for communication. Zine makers are driven to publish their ideas purely for the sake of communicating, generally with complete disregard for money, let alone profit" (Friedman 1997, 8). That craving for connection has forged significant connection among zine makers and readers, leading to sprawling communities. "People who make zines often build and participate in communities that celebrate the tangible written word," according to author Alex Wrekk. "They support each other's efforts to do so by trading zines with other zine contributors or attending zine events" (2006, 10).

As a result, "zine writers form networks and forge communities around diverse identities and interests.... [T]he zine community is busy creating a culture whose value isn't calculated as profit and loss on ruled ledger pages, but is assembled in the margins, using criteria like control, connection, and authenticity" (Duncombe 1997, 2). Every zine, author Stephen Duncombe writes, "is a community institution in itself, as each draws links between itself and others." Zines typically have "letters" either in a column or spread throughout the publication, and often don't draw a distinction between letters and other editorial content. Most publish reviews of other zines, and even tell how to subscribe to them (48).

In these ways, zines have also played the important cultural role of politics by example. "Zines, in their content, form, and organization, constitute an alternative ideal of how human relations, creation, and consumption could be organized. Critically, their strength lies not in what they say they will do, but in what they actually are" (Duncombe 1997, 196).

Fanzines have covered pretty much every topic available. Among the tens of thousands of zines published over the years are science fiction zines, music zines, girl zines, queer zines, punk zines, and literary zines. A random selection of titles includes *Big Pain*, about childhood trauma; *I Hate You*, composed of love stories from hell; *Don't Say Uh-Oh!* with lists about topics such as Foods to Eat on a Dare; *Teenage Gang Debs*, about *The Brady Bunch* television show; and *Mac and Me*, for people with a Macaulay Culkin obsession (Block and Carlip 1998, 2; Rowe 1997, 12).

Over the years, zines also played a crucial role as an outlet for marginalized groups, especially those experiencing sexism, racism, and/or homophobia, thus making zine audiences culturally and politically diverse. "People of every age, race, gender, economic standing, sexual preference, and belief system are writing, designing, printing, and selling their own zines" (Block and Carlip 1998, 1).

This is because their message is genuine.

> Many people write zines featuring journal entries, poems, essays, and letters on abuse, rape, eating disorders, racism, sexism, misogyny, and suicide. What makes these so powerful is that they're the real thing, not like magazines where you flip the page to a glossy image of a skinny model after reading about the rise in cases of anorexia. (16)

Zines by such groups have included *Character Comics*, drawn by a seven-year-old boy; *Red Geraniums and Banana Peels*, which included writings by three generations of women, the oldest of them 85; *Coocooloco*, Casandra Melee Stark's zine written with mentally disabled adults; and *The Duplex Planet*, David Greenburger's zine that features pieces by senior citizens (19).

THE ROOTS OF ZINES

The ancestral spirit of zines' feisty, unconstrained eclecticism harkens back to Thomas Paine's 1776 pro-independence pamphlet *Common Sense*, Benjamin Franklin's 1773 *Poor Richard's Almanack*, and the early twentieth-century writings of Dadaists and surrealists. However, zines' cultural niche as a distinct medium originated with early fans of science fiction magazines. Originally published in 1926, *Amazing Stories* was the first magazine that exclusively published original science fiction stories. Its founder, Hugo Gernsback, printed addresses of letter writers so they could contact each other, and within a few years, readers had formed associations and discussion groups (Friedman 1997, 9–11).

The first-ever fanzine was started by one of Gernsback's science fiction groups; it was an amateur publication in 1930 that allowed members to easily keep in touch with one another. Titled *The Comet*, it was later renamed *Cosmology*. In 1949, *The New Republic* referred to magazines published by science fiction fans as "fanzines," an abbreviation of "fan magazines." The 1930s through the 1950s became a vibrant era for the publication of fanzines about science fiction and fantasy literature, mysteries, and comic books—aided by the availability of mimeograph duplicating machines (Friedman 1997, 9–11).

This fertile zine environment continued into the 1960s, with the birth of alternative newspapers and other publications covering political unrest, literary experimentation, and rock 'n' roll critiques—showing that the line between zines and other kinds of "alt" publications could be blurred in an era of social upheaval.

This environment was also aided by the availability of cheap offset printing. In the mid-1970s, "the other defining influence on modern-day zines [after science fiction] began as fans of punk rock music, ignored by and critical of the mainstream music press, started printing fanzines about their music and cultural scene" (Duncombe 1997, 7). Zines again took off with the likes of *Punk* and *Sniffin' Glue*. *The Whole Fanzine Catalogue*, first published in the mid-1970s and focused on science fiction fanzines, by 1981 "was listing over 150 zines from nine countries" (157).

The ubiquity of office photocopy machines and self-service copy shops in the 1980s, followed by desktop publishing technology that allowed people to make zines on computers, brought zines to a peak in the 1990s. This critical mass was both reflected and reinforced by Mike Gunderloy's inaugural 1982 publication of *Factsheet Five*, a zine that reviewed hundreds of zines per issue on any subject and became known as *F5* and the "zine bible" (Friedman 1997, 12–13). During the 1990s, publications from *Details* to the *New York*

Times sought to "document the zine phenomenon, spurring interest in a whole new wave of both zine readers and zine makers" (8–9).

Sometimes a subculture still felt that it was not depicted in zines, leading to the creation of even more specifically focused zines. When queer punk rockers felt unrepresented in predominantly straight punk zines, they found connection in zines like *Homocore* and *J.D.s*, "virtual meeting places, spaces to define and communicate who they are, and remind themselves (and others) that they are not alone" (Duncombe 1997, 71).

THE EMERGENCE OF GIRL ZINES

Another reason for the proliferation of zines in the 1990s was the emergence of "grrrl zines"—zines made by girls and women. These zines grew out of that decade's "Riot Grrrl" feminist and musical movement as well as the punk movement and third-wave feminism. Popular grrrl zines included *Jigsaw* and *Snarla*; two others, *Bust* and *Bitch*, evolved from zines to become magazines that still exist today (Arnold 2016). These zines, wrote Alison Piepmeier in *Girl Zines*,

> are sites where girls and women construct identities, communities, and explanatory narratives from the materials that comprise their cultural moment: discourses, media representations, ideologies, stereotypes, and even physical detritus. . . . Grrrl zines offer idiosyncratic, surprising, yet savvy and complex responses to the late-twentieth-century incarnations of sexism, racism, and homophobia. (Piepmeier 2009, 2, 4)

For girls and women in particular, zines have provided an outlet to express hope, frustration, and a sense of connection. Common topics included "struggles with body image, with sexuality, with anger, with feeling important in the lives of other girls, with wanting to be free in a way that wasn't tidily summed up" (Zeisler 2009, xiv). Girl zines also covered politics, feminism, relationships, taboo subjects such as rape and incest, being in high school, and worshiping female personalities such as Joan Jett. "What threads these zines together is that they are all very real and very much from the heart" (Green and Taormino 1997, xiii).

The intersection of zines and feminism made for a powerful convergence. Zine writing by girls and women "tends to integrate information in a way we're not used to seeing. . . . This is a personal approach, one that integrates static categories like race, class, and sexuality" (Green and Taormino 1997, xiv). Andi Zeisler echoed that idea, noting that the book *Girl Zines* is a crucial way to understand—and to appreciate—the many different ways girl zines have been and continue to effect the ongoing work of feminist thought and activism. For both readers and creators, they are education and revelation, empowerment and healing, giddy secret and proud f-you, and with this book they are given a well-deserved place of prominence in the history, and the future, of feminism. (Zeisler 2009, xiv)

However, even as print zines reached their apogee in the 1990s, their peak of popularity during that decade bumped up against the coincidental and unrelated availability of the internet to the general public in the form of dial-up online services, email services, bulletin board systems, and server networks (Lisa's Nostalgia Café). Indeed, some zines were already migrating to the internet, a phenomenon reflected in the summer 1995 issue of *Factsheet Five*. That issue focused on electronic zines, "with six pages of e-zine reviews, articles on how to put zines online, and an essay arguing for a 'new definition for zines'" (Duncombe 1997, 197). In 1992, the "alt .zines" Usenet newsgroup was created as an online forum for zinesters, and today it remains an influential site for zine publishers (http://zinewiki.com /alt.zines).

Today, anyone seeking self-expression can do so via Twitter, Facebook, blogging, or other social or online media. With these digital forms of communication, there is a sense of immediate or short-term gratification, whereas zines have always required time and focus to create; the slowed-down communication that zines represent makes them especially relevant and appealing in this fast-paced digital age. "No matter how sloppy a zine is—and they really can be a mess—someone has taken responsibility for the thing as a whole. Blogs are in danger of only being as strong as their most recent post" (Freedman 2005, 3–4).

In the pre-digital era, zines provided the same do-it-yourself expression of participatory media, only in analog fashion. It was a concept that zinesters, aka zine makers, found to be exuberantly liberating and a way to influence broader cultural conversations. Wrekk wrote:

> We all have stories to tell and no one is going to tell them for us. We can be our own media and share our experiences with the world on our own terms. Zines can be a powerful tool and they are a very versatile medium. With zines, you can incorporate many different skills from writing, art, production and even research. Zines are what you make of them and they also offer a chance to be part of a community that also enjoys sharing their experiences on paper. (2006, 13)

MOTIVATIONS OF ZINE CREATORS AND CONSUMERS

Many zinesters were attracted to the subversive, anti-capitalist nature of zines. In the words of Alphonse Coleman, who published the zine *Bubba's Live Bait*, "Creating something that transcends capitalism (i.e., losing money hand-over-fist) is a revolutionary act. That's why I don't care too much for zines trying to get bigger and bigger. If they succeed, all they've achieved is creating another consumer good."

Nancy Bonnell-Kangas, publisher of the zine *Nancy's Magazine*, described publishing a zine as "part of my plan to change the world. I'm starting with the magazine industry." And Aaron Cometbus, who published the all-caps, hand-lettered punk zine *Cometbus* in 1981 at age thirteen, said: "I publish because I don't know anything else. I grew up with it, and I don't know how you stay sane without some kind of creative outlet and connection with other people" (Rowe 2006, xii, 161, 120, 56).

The creative outlet that zines provide is also a draw to zinesters. Digital outlets are intangible in contrast to zines' tactile nature. "People like the tangible physicality of zines: they are portable, accessible, physical art objects, meant to be handled" (Wrekk 2006, 140). Wrekk also noted: "You can write however you want in your zine. What are the stories that you and your friends tell that always make you laugh? Why not commit them to print? Why not make your own history?" (2006, 16).

One upside of zines is that they speak to so many slices of the population. But Duncombe warned in 1997 of a potential downside, one that has manifested itself in mainstream media today, that having so many microcommunities in the zine world could lead to the Balkanization of readers:

> Ideally the individuals who make up the network of micro-communities of the zine world communicate to one another, sharing their differences, and speaking across voids. . . . But there is also a tendency to move in the opposite direction: hunkering down in your micro-community, surrounded by only your own reality. . . . In the virtual world of zines, creators and readers can pick and choose who to call on and who to entertain. This means you can visit and be visited by people who have interests and experiences far outside your own. But it can also mean that you can limit interaction to people *just like you*. (195)

Duncombe raised a legitimate concern. However, members of the zine community overwhelmingly spoke of the positive aspects of the connections forged through the world of zine makers and readers:

Tania Rudy has made friends all over the world through STOOL PIGEON. Ceci received a letter from the actress Heather Mattarrazo after raving about her film *Welcome to the Dollhouse* in SUBURBIA. Al Hoff had a book published based on her zine THRIFT SCORE. Stephanie Kuhnert heard from girls who had been sexually abused and were helped by reading HOSPITAL GOWN. (117)

ZINES IN THE INTERNET AGE

Today, zines and zine culture continue to thrive. In July 2019, the Portland Zine Symposium in Oregon held its nineteenth annual event, "a yearly free conference and zine social exploring facets of independent publishing and DIY culture." (The fest was virtual in 2020 because of the pandemic.) July is also International Zine Month, a status conferred in 2009 by Wrekk, who, besides writing *Stolen Sharpie Revolution*, created *Brainscan Zine* (Rosales 2019). Olympia, Washington, hosts an annual Zine Fest (canceled in 2020 but scheduled for May 2021) to promote zines and do-it-yourself culture. Chicago's annual zine fest will be held that month, too. At least once a year, librarians gather at the Zine Librarians unConference somewhere in the United States to discuss zines and their preservation.

At Salem State University in Massachusetts, biology professor Lisa Delissio has incorporated group zines into one of her courses, and Salem State librarian Dawn Stahura created a LibGuide to Making Zines. The public library in Salem, Massachusetts, hosted a monthly Zine Club until 2020 at which students in grades four through twelve could create zines and donate them to the library's young authors' collection. The zine resurgence has become mainstream. Zines can be bought on Etsy or read at the Barnard College library. They are also accessible to marginalized communities; the Queer Zine Archive Project is dedicated to preserving queer zine culture, and the POC Zine Project is designed to make zines by people of color easy to find and share.

Sure, the internet has changed zines, said Wrekk, "but that doesn't mean that zines are dead or that change is bad. The truth is that zines will continue to be published as long as people enjoy making and reading them." If anything, said Wrekk, the internet and blogs have helped to further connect zinesters. "In a way, it's helped create better and stronger communities and networks. I mean, anyone can type up a rant and post it to a blog instantly. If you want to create a zine, it takes time and craft to make it, and a lot of work and energy goes into the process of production and distribution" (Wrekk, 2006, 140–41).

Although zines aren't "a utopian alternative to the internet," Piepmeier wrote, they "do provide a kind of intimacy, and demand a kind of effort, that seems to block some of the more opportunistic aggression that is prevalent online." The zine creators she spoke to "reported receiving a great deal fewer hostile responses from their zines than from their blogs." Digital media also strikes "zine creators as both atemporal and ephemeral in ways that zines are not," Piepmeier said. "Although zines and blogs have relevant similarities, the blog has not replaced the zine. Zines are a living medium with both historical and contemporary relevance for the lives of girls and women and for feminism's third wave" (Piepmeier, 2009, 15–17).

Why do zines still matter? Piepmeier said that

> Zines instigate intimate, affectionate connections between their creators and readers, not just communities but what I am calling *embodied* communities, made possible by the materiality of the zine medium. My students have become inspired to become part of the zine community because of physical encounter with actual zines, not by reading anthologized zines. In a world where more and more of us spend all day at our computers, zines reconnect us to our bodies and to other human beings. (2009, 58)

Zines remain a thriving medium in the digital twenty-first century, despite a false perception by some that they lost cultural currency and then made a "comeback." Wrekk wrote:

> In fact, not only are zines alive, but I would say that zines have become an even more valid form of art and media where our mainstream media has become more and more centralized. Examples of zines' legitimacy can be seen all over. Public and academic libraries have started archiving zines. There are serious academic studies involving zines as a focus of study. Zines being used in a variety of educational contexts. And the number of zine fests around the world continues to grow. (2006, 140)

Perhaps Duncombe was prophetic when he noted in 1997 that computers would not entirely supplant print zines. "After all, the telegraph, telephone, radio, and television never did away with the underground presses," he wrote. "There is something about the materiality of a zine—you can feel it, stick it in your pocket, read it in the park, give it away at a show—that I myself would be reluctant to give up" (Duncombe 1997, 198).

REFERENCES

Arnold, Chloe. 2016. "A Brief History of Zines." *Mental Floss*, November 16. http://mentalfloss.com/article/88911/brief-history-zines.

Barnard Zine Library. Barnard College. Accessed September 19, 2019. https://zines.barnard.edu/.

Block, Francesca Lia, and Hilary Carlip. 1998. *Zine Scene: The Do it Yourself Guide to Zines*. Los Angeles: Girl Press.

Chicago Zine Fest. 2019. Accessed September 19, 2019. http://chicagozinefest.org/.

Duncombe, Stephen. 1997. *Notes from the Underground: Zines and the Politics of Alternative Culture*. London: Verso.

Fales Library and Special Collections. "Biographical/Historical Note." Outpunk Archive. New York University. Accessed September 14, 2019. http://dlib.nyu.edu/findingaids/html/fales/outpunk/index.html.

Fateman, Johanna. 2013. *The Riot Grrrl Collection*. New York: The Feminist Press.

Freedman, Jenna. 2005. "Zines Are Not Blogs: A Unbiased Analysis." *Columbia Academic Commons*, Columbia University Libraries. https://academiccommons.columbia.edu/doi/10.7916/D81N89N5.

Friedman, R. Seth. 1997. *The Factsheet Five Zine Reader: The Best Writing from the Underground World of Zines*. New York: Three Rivers Press.

Green, Karen, and Tristan Taormino. 1997. *A Girl's Guide to Taking Over the World: Writings from the Girl Zine Revolution*. New York: St. Martin's Press.

Lisa's Nostalgia Café. "1990s Internet & World Wide Web." Accessed September 19, 2019. http://nostalgiacafe.proboards.com/thread/133/1990s-internet-world-wide-web.

Olympia Zine Fest. 2019. *Facebook*. Accessed September 14, 2019. https://www.facebook.com/olympiazinefest.

Piepmeier, Alison. 2009. *Girl Zines: Making Media, Doing Feminism*. New York: New York University Press.

POC Zine Project. Tumblr. Accessed September 19, 2019. https://poczineproject.tumblr.com/.

Portland Zine Symposium. "About Portland Zine Symposium." Accessed September 14, 2019. http://www.portlandzinesymposium.org/about-us-simply/.

Queer Zine Archive Project. Accessed September 19, 2019. http://archive.qzap.org/.

Rosales, Romeo. 2019. "July Is International Zine Month: What Zines Are & How to Celebrate." *Book Riot*, July 12. https://bookriot.com/2019/07/12/international-zine-month/.

Rowe, Chip, ed. 1997. *The Book of Zines: Readings from the Fringe*. New York: Henry Holt and Company.

Stahura, Dawn. 2019. "Making Zines." Zines LibGuide. Accessed September 14, 2019. https://libguides.salemstate.edu/zines.

Wrekk, Alex. 2006. *Stolen Sharpie Revolution: A DIY Resource for Zines and Zine Culture*. 5th edition. Portland, OR: Lunchroom Publishing.

Zeisler, Andi. 2009. "Foreword." In *Girl Zines: Making Media, Doing Feminism*, by Alison Piepmeier, xi–xiv. New York: New York University Press.

Zine Librarians unConferences. *Zinelibraries.info*. Accessed September 19, 2019. http://zinelibraries.info/events/zine-librarian-unconferences/.

Chapter 12

Branding the Local Lifestyle
City, State, and Regional Magazines
Norma Green*

Pride-of-place periodicals, those mostly monthly publications that cover a particular geographic area, proliferated in the last quarter of the twentieth century, featuring a steady stream of "best of" issues that celebrated the locales' top offerings in everything from food and music to attorneys and doctors. These publications reached their zenith as white flight altered the demographic composition of the nation's major urban centers, making city and regional periodicals the perfect guides for affluent suburbanites seeking the trendiest restaurants, boutiques, and nightspots in the metro areas they had abandoned.

In addition to their bread-and-butter service pieces and celebrations of society soirees, city and regional magazines served up profiles of leading local and national personalities, as well as long-form narrative and investigative articles that probed a wide range of sociopolitical issues. They also offered local angles on national matters, including civil rights, the environment, and the women's movement. City magazines also have been credited with creating and refining a form of literary nonfiction that came to be known as "the new journalism." In both their form and function, city and regional magazines have influenced the storytelling and architecture of magazines across all categories (Tebbel and Zuckerman 1991).

Even as other legacy media succumbed to the disruption of the digital revolution, city and regional magazines proved to be relatively resilient. Of the nearly 200 such magazines begun since the 1950s, about half were still in existence in the last decade of the twentieth century. A few of the largest-circulation magazines went on to celebrate multi-decade anniversaries and maintain loyal followings thanks, in part, to the adoption of digital

---

*with contributions from Charles Whitaker

newsletters and topic-specific offshoots, as well as the creation of events that help promote the publications' brands beyond the printed page.

A FOUNDATION OF BOOSTERISM

Many of the early city and regional magazines started as booster publications endorsed, if not actually produced, by local businesses, chambers of commerce, or government agencies at both the city and state levels. *Atlanta* (1961), *Baltimore* (1907), *Boston* (1910), *Louisville* (1950), *Philadelphia* (1908), and *Phoenix* (1966) all were launched and supported by local chambers of commerce to promote city events and urban development to both residents and tourists. Most of those publications eventually severed their civic ties and became editorially independent, enabling them to pursue more hard-hitting content.

For example, in 1908, the *Philadelphia Chamber of Commerce Journal* was launched to promote the city's business interests. In 1946, the chamber sold the publication to newspaper publisher Arthur Lipson, who rechristened it simply as *Philadelphia* magazine. Lipson's son, Herbert, revamped the magazine in 1967, "separating the editorial and advertising departments . . . allowing the magazine to operate free of direct influence from Philadelphia business" (Selnow 1991, 258). *Philadelphia* magazine went on to become known for its award-winning investigations. It dared to take on Philadelphia's entrenched political establishment and faced libel suits from several prominent politicians.

State agencies around the country also launched periodicals to promote tourism and highlight natural resources and cultural heritage. The oldest magazine in the category is a prime example. *Honolulu* magazine was launched in 1888 with the title *Paradise of the Pacific*. It was chartered by Hawaiian King David Kalakaua, who intended it to attract tourists to the islands. In 1966, a few years after statehood, the magazine shifted its focus inward to the local lifestyle needs and interests of state residents, including special heritage features and cultural guides focusing on favorite foods and arts. Other titles started with government backing include *Arizona Highways*, launched in 1925 by the Arizona Highway Department (now the Arizona Department of Transportation); *Maryland* magazine, launched in 1968 by the Maryland Department of Economic and Employment Development; and *Nevada* magazine, launched in 1936 as *Nevada Highways and Parks*. It originally was published by the State of Nevada and continues as an offshoot of the Nevada Commission on Tourism. Over the years, these magazines have come not only to promote their attractions to outsiders, but also to evaluate and celebrate them for locals.

CHANGING DEMOGRAPHICS NECESSITATE NEW GUIDES

After World War II, as metropolitan daily newspapers grappled with competition from radio and then television, they ceased printing broadcast schedules. Some of the niche publications of the nation's biggest cities homed in on their community's better-educated and most moneyed listeners and viewers to fill that service void. Both *Chicago* magazine and *Los Angeles* magazine trace their roots to printing guides listing local FM classical radio and public television programming, respectively. *Chicago* magazine began as *WFMT Guide* in 1952 and *Los Angeles* magazine started in 1960 as the *Southern California Prompter*, taking its name from a small arts and entertainment publication listing FM station logs. In 1984, *Louisville* magazine started including the local PBS program guide, which helped boost readership for its other content. All these publications eventually evolved into the familiar city magazine formula mix of features about local people and places along with service departments that highlighted particular shopping, dining, and entertainment districts each month (Sternadori and Sivek 2020). Over time, as arts and entertainment coverage diminished with staff cuts in daily newspapers around the country, these metropolitan magazines increased their coverage of local theater, dance, music, art, architecture, museums, fashion, films, and books (Svachula 2019).

In addition, the mid-twentieth century brought rapid change to central cities across America. As the civil rights movement broke down barriers in employment and housing, African-Americans began moving in droves from the cramped, segregated pockets in which they were confined by law and intimidation since the Great Migration into white ethnic enclaves throughout the country's major cities (Historyplex). In response, white residents—spurred by unscrupulous real estate agents who played upon racial animus and fears—fled for the suburbs, rapidly changing the demographic composition of many American cities (Historyplex).

During this time, city and regional magazines proliferated, taking on the editorial personas that would distinguish them for the next fifty years. Many, like *Memphis* magazine, begun in 1976, addressed the changing nature of the cities head-on. Early on, *Memphis* caused a local uproar when it took on the subject of interracial marriages—at the time still taboo in many parts of the country, particularly the South. In 1984, *Memphis* became the smallest-circulation magazine ever to win the national Society of Professional Journalists' award for a thirty-two-page special report on local race relations. The following year it hired a black editor, believed to be the first for a city magazine anywhere (Hoskins 1991, 150).

Utah Holiday, started in 1971 by a former trade magazine journalist in his Salt Lake City basement, was known to its affluent audience for its in-depth reporting of state issues, including modern polygamy, murders, and financial fiascos, as well as arts and entertainment criticism not found in other media outlets in the state. The magazine garnered numerous journalism awards for its investigative reporting, especially about the finances and influence of the Church of Jesus Christ of Latter-Day Saints.

Despite their sometimes-progressive coverage, the audiences of these burgeoning city and regional magazines became increasingly more affluent and suburban. While city and regional newspapers continued to see themselves as publications of record, designed to appeal to the broadest cross section of the population, city and regional magazines, by necessity, cultivated a "sophisticated, class-conscious audience that buys new cars, stereo equipment, and fine clothes and is highly attractive to advertisers" (Shaw cited in Hynds, 1995, 176).

Like their urban counterparts, state-wide magazines also strove to distinguish themselves in their particular regions. *Texas Monthly*, which today claims one out of every ten adult Texans as a reader, has catered to its audience's seemingly insatiable taste for lengthy narrative nonfiction. Along with in-depth political coverage, it has been winning national magazine awards for its reporting, graphic design and artwork since its founding in 1973. In its first year alone, it won the National Magazine Award for Outstanding Editorial Achievement in Specialized Journalism and later earned more than a dozen other NMA awards (known as the Ellies).

A PAIR OF METROPOLITAN MAGAZINES RAISE THE BAR

In the media capital of the United States, two outsiders—veteran journalists a generation apart but both insatiably curious about the nation's largest metropolis—made their mark by creating weekly magazines celebrating the New York City lifestyle they imagined and later lived. Colorado-born Harold Ross, son of a Kansas schoolteacher and immigrant miner, founded *The New Yorker* as a Manhattan-centric literary weekly in 1925, the year the future *New York* editor Clay Felker, from suburban St. Louis, was born to journalist parents.

In the prospectus for *The New Yorker*, Ross famously noted the magazine is "not edited for the old lady in Dubuque" (a swipe at Henry Luce's *Time* magazine, which was launched two years earlier and was designed to make world news accessible to readers in America's heartland). Of his new vehicle, Ross went on to state: "It will not be concerned in what she is thinking about. This is not meant in disrespect, but *The New Yorker* is a magazine avowedly published for a metropolitan audience and thereby will escape an influence which hampers most national publications. It expects a considerable national circulation but this will come from persons who have a metropolitan interest" (Kunkel 1995, 440). *The New Yorker* was to become the city magazine for a virtual, national city of New York.

Still, the advertising was local. Ross "realized that it made little sense for a New York retailer to try to appeal to readers far outside the metropolitan area. Thus, the *New Yorker* . . . would draw on the commerce, as well as the creative talent and raw material of the immediate vicinity" (Vinciguerra 2016, 16–17). Local upscale advertisers helped *The New Yorker* survive the Depression. "It became a totem for the educated American middle and upper-middle class. It became the repository for increasingly high standards of English prose, taste conscience and civility." But over time, "all that weight proved to be too much for a weekly magazine to bear" (Yagoda 2000, 24).

New Yorker editors came and went during the rest of the century after Ross's death in 1951. It faced near extinction until 1992 when, in a last-gasp effort to restore the magazine to its former glory, S. I. Newhouse, chairman of the venerable Condé Nast publishing empire (which had purchased *The New Yorker* in 1985), tapped Tina Brown, a British import who made Condé Nast's *Vanity Fair* the must-read publication of the Reagan era, to breathe new life into *The New Yorker*. With an uncanny eye for writing talent and a keen intuition for trending cultural topics, Brown turned *The New Yorker* into a literary force, read by the cognoscenti and those who aspired to be of that ilk. She laid the foundation for the winning formula that her successor, David Remnick, would preside over and build upon for more than twenty years.

New York magazine founder Clay Felker built that magazine from the remnants of the former *New York Herald Tribune*'s Sunday supplement, which folded in 1967. The bold new weekly debuted in April 1968 with an all-star team of writers, including Tom Wolfe, Gail Sheehy (whom Felker later married), Jimmy Breslin, and Gloria Steinem. Felker also revived a way of writing dating from the nineteenth century that became known as New Journalism. Sheehy said "Clay stumbled upon it [the writing style] . . . when he came upon bound volumes of the Civil War era (New York) Tribune. He began reading gripping accounts from the Virginia battlefield, not from a disinterested correspondent, but vivid stories with narrative structure written by soldiers in the trenches" (Sheehy 2014, 87). He encouraged his staff, many of whom came from the defunct *Herald Tribune*, to write as long as a story warranted, which sometimes meant 50,000 words, and "began borrowing the dramatic techniques used by novelists, scene-by-scene construction, dialogue, and use of status details to denote social class. We treated protagonists of nonfiction stories like characters in a novel. What was their motivation? What were they thinking? What was it like living inside their reality?" (Sheehy 2014, 86–87).

As Gloria Steinem, who later went on to found *Ms.* magazine, explained:

> This was the home of the New Journalism as practiced by Tom Wolfe and also of Jimmy Breslin, an in-the-streets chronicle of New York life. Since Wolfe wrote satirically from outside about subjects he probably disliked, and Breslin wrote from inside about the lives of people he probably loved, they established the right of nonfiction writers to be both personal and political—as long as we got our facts straight. (2015, 132)

Felker unsuccessfully tried to branch out to California in 1976 with *New West* magazine, which was shuttered in 1981. Nonetheless, Felker's magazines had an outsize influence on city magazines, offering a formula that combined service-oriented "best of" pieces for the affluent lifestyle along with a fresh style of narrative nonfiction. In *The Gang that Wouldn't Write Straight*, journalism historian Marc Weingarten deems *New York*'s initial expression "an unprecedented outpouring of creative nonfiction, the greatest literary movement since the American fiction renaissance of the 1920s." Even though "new Journalism . . . died a long time ago," Weingarten maintains that "its influence is everywhere. Once a rear guard rebellion, its tenets are so accepted now that they've become virtually invisible. The art of narrative storytelling is alive and well; it's just more diffuse now spread out" (2006, 293).

STAYING AFLOAT IN THE DIGITAL MAELSTROM

City and regional magazines have proven remarkably durable. Many survived the death of dynamic founders, multiple ownership changes, and the disruption of the digital revolution. Some managed to reinvent themselves in the twenty-first century through new designs, brand extensions, advertising supplements, and mergers.

The "mass to class" editorial and advertising shift, begun in the 1970s, that directed these publications away from true city dwellers toward a more moneyed, suburban readership continued into the twenty-first century. Still, many of these publications did suffer from the circulation and advertising declines that hastened the demise of their newspaper counterparts (Project for Excellence in Journalism 2012). And while city and regional magazines serve a different function than newspapers (the content is less "newsy" and subsequently more evergreen), they nevertheless have faced competition for time, eyeballs, and revenue from social media platforms like Facebook and Twitter.

Resourceful editors in the city and regional magazine space have supplemented their print editions with digital versions and offered a variety of ways to access their information, from videos to podcasts. They have cut frequency and provided free subscriptions to residents in affluent zip codes. Many of these efforts have paid off. In the early 2000s, *New York* developed a cache of popular online offshoots, such as *Vulture* (entertainment), *The Cut* (style and culture), *Grub Street* (food), and *Intelligencer* (politics), each of which has cultivated its own loyal following, almost divorced from the print mothership (Tracy and Lee, 2019). Still, the print magazine suffered. *New York* magazine went to every-other-week frequency in 2014, before it was acquired by Vox Media in 2019.

Texas Monthly's multimedia extensions started with publishing a line of books in the 1970s. It was among the first of the regional periodicals to launch a website in 1995, and as of 2019 was experimenting with an "online-first" strategy of featuring stories different than those that would appear in its print editions. Knowing the strong Texas pride about particular foods, it also boasted the first dedicated barbecue editor and, as of 2019, the first taco editor of any regional magazine.

A former editorial content director for *Midwest Living* magazine discussed the fracturing of reading communities for city and regional magazines in a blog interview with mrmagazine.com's Samir Husni (2019a):

> The digital world has done a lot to segregate us off into intellectual feed fills where we can set things up to only feed us the information that we already either know about or agree with. And when you purchase a magazine, I talk to our editors about the fact that it's really a contract with the reader. Giving a contract to a trusted team of curators to present content that you know you're going to like even if you're not sure you know anything about it yet. You're trusting that these people have the taste and that they understand this audience, that they're going to give me information that I am going to find interesting and it's going to be reliable.

But in a media ecosystem where so much content is atomized, disconnected from its editorial home, and largely consumed via mobile devices through social media gateways, the terms of the contract between audience and content curators is fractured. The loyalty that publications rely on for repeat viewing of both editorial and advertising is mediated and obscured by third-party platforms. Many city and regional magazines, with their older, more affluent audiences, have done better than other legacy outlets at retaining their core audience, but even that base is eroding.

In the twentieth century, city, state, and regional magazines were heirs to both nineteenth-century booster journalism of the frontier press, enticing travelers and would-be settlers, as well as the service journalism of the immigrant press orienting newcomers to help them navigate where to live, work, shop, what to eat and wear as well as how local government functions. In the twentieth century, they found new audiences, invented new journalistic forms and championed causes, while continuing to promote their locales' best offerings. In the digital age, they are attempting to hold on to their base with new extensions that connect readers with even more specialized content provided on both old and new platforms. But the longevity of these publications will depend on their leaders' ability to continue adapting to the changing media landscape. It will take vision, stable management, and financial backing to remain relevant to their audiences.

REFERENCES

American Society of Magazine Editors. 2019. www.magazineorg/asme/national-magazine-awards.

Andereck, Kathleen L., and Evelyn Ng. 2005. "Arizona Highways Magazine's Impact on Tourism, 2005 Final Report 568." AZmemory.azlibrary.gov/digital collection/statepubs/id/1258.

Baker, Nora 1991. "The New Yorker." In *Regional Interest Magazines of the United States*, edited by S. Riley and G. Selnow, 229–35. Westport, CT: Greenwood Press.

Bennett, David. 1991. "Chicago." In *Regional Interest Magazines of the United States*, edited by S. Riley and G. Selnow, 48–54. Westport, CT: Greenwood Press.

Black, Jonathan. 2015. "Examining Social Media and Digital Practice among Southeastern Magazines." *Elon Journal of Undergraduate Research in Communications* 6:2 (Fall 2015), 91–98.

Boynton, Robert S. 2005. *The New New Journalism: Conversations with America's Best Nonfiction Writers on Their Craft*. New York: Vintage Books, 2005.

Bramlett-Solomon, Sharon. 1991. "Phoenix Magazine." In *Regional Interest Magazines of the United States*, edited by S. Riley and G. Selnow, 265. Westport, CT: Greenwood Press.

City and Regional Magazine Association. 2019. https://citymag.org/member-directory (2019).

Derousseau, Ryan. 2018. "City Magazines Fill the Newspaper Gap." *Folio*, January 25. www.foliomag.com.

Dresser, Michael. 1994. "Baltimore Magazine Gets Change of Ownership." *Baltimore Sun*, November 24. www.baltimoresun.com/news.

English, John, 1991. "Atlanta Magazine." In *Regional Interest Magazines of the United States*, edited by S. Riley and G. Selnow, 26–30. Westport, CT: Greenwood Press.

Fuller, Melynda. 2019. "Midwest Living Launches Live 'Cabin Living' Issue." *Mediapost*, April 18. mediapost.com/publications/articles/334698.

Gotliffe, Harvey. 1991. "Sunset Magazine." In *Regional Interest Magazines of the United States*, edited by S. Riley and G. Selnow, 305–10. Westport, CT: Greenwood Press.

Greenberg, Miriam. 2000. "Branding Cities: A Social History of the Urban Magazine." *Urban Affairs Review* 36:2 (November 2000), 228–63.

Heilburn, Carolyn. 1995. *The Life of Gloria Steinem*. New York: Dial Press.

Historyplex. "A Quick Look Into the History of the White Flight in America." https://historyplex.com/look-at-history-of-white-flight-in-america.

Hogan, Donna. 2007. "Arizona Highways Good for Business." *East Valley Tribune*, September 11. http://www.eastvalleytribune.com/money/arizona-highways-good-for.

Hoskins, Robert L. 1991. "Memphis." In *Regional Interest Magazines of the United States*, edited by S. Riley and G. Selnow, 147–52. Westport, CT: Greenwood Press.

Husni, Samir. 2017. "The New Yorker's Editor, David Remnick to Samir 'Mr. Magazine' Husni: I Have Great Alarm About This War Against Fact; This Profusion of Lying in High Places. But I Also Stake My Claim with a Journalism That Tries to Do the Best It Can. And Do an Honest Job. Whether It's Traditional Media or New Media. That Doesn't Matter. It's a True Media." The Mr. Magazine Interview. December 17. mrmagazine.com.

———.2019a. "Midwest Living: Defining Life in the Midwest with the Brand That Knows It Best—The Mr. Magazine Interview with Trevor Meers, Editorial Content Director, Midwest Living/Meredith Travel Marketing Content Studio." January 28. mrmagazine.com.

———. 2019b. "Texas Monthly Magazine: Keeping Texas Stores Alive and Kicking—The Mr. Magazine Interview with Dan Goodgame, Editor in Chief." *Texas Monthly Magazine*, April 8. mrmagazine.com.

Hynds, E. C. 1995. "Research Review: City and Regional Magazines." In *The American Magazine: Research Perspectives and Prospects*, edited by D. Abrahamson, 172–185. Ames, IA: Iowa State University Press.

Ibsen, Katy. 2018. "City and Regional Magazines Capitalize on Custom Publishing." *Folio*, June 26. www.foliomag.com.

Jenkins, Joy. 2014. "Characteristics of Online Editors at City and Regional Magazines." *Journal of Magazine and New Media Research* 15:1 (2014): 1–12.

Johnson, Sammye. 1991. *Regional Interest Magazines of the United States*, edited by S. Riley and G. Selnow, 68–75. Westport, CT: Greenwood Press.

Knudson, Max B. 1993. "Utah Holiday Will Stop the Presses After 22 Years of Publication." *Deseret News*, May 7.

Kunkel, Thomas. 1995. *Genius in Disguise: Harold Ross of the New Yorker*. New York: Random House.

Limpert, Jack. 2017. "Herb Lipson RIP: He Loved Journalism but Not His Editors." December 26. About Editing and Writing blog. https://jacklimpert.com.

Marmarelli, Ronald S. "New York Magazine." In *Regional Interest Magazines of the United States*, edited by S. Riley and G. Selnow, 208–23. Westport, CT: Greenwood Press.

McCormick, Andrew. 2019. "Q&A: New York's Adam Moss Talks of Moving on from His 15-Year Home." *Columbia Journalism Review*, January 16. www.cjr.org.

Meyer, Larry L. 1991. "Los Angeles Magazine." In *Regional Interest Magazines of the United States*, edited by S. Riley and G. Selnow, 125–26. Westport, CT: Greenwood Press.

Murray, Michael. 1991. "San Diego." In *Regional Interest Magazines of the United States*, edited by S. Riley and G. Selnow, 273–78. Westport, CT: Greenwood Press.

Nuwer, Hank, and Robert Waite. 1991. "Boston." In *Regional Interest Magazines of the United States*, edited by S. Riley and G. Selnow, 31–34. Westport, CT: Greenwood Press.

Philadelphia Magazine. 1970. *The Improper Philadelphians: A Dossier of Investigative Reporting from Philadelphia Magazine*. New York: Weybright & Talley.

Pratte, Alf. 1991. "Utah Holiday." In *Regional Interest Magazines of the United States*, edited by S. Riley and G. Selnow, 346–50. Westport, CT: Greenwood Press.

Quate, Shirley B. 1991. "Louisville." In *Regional Interest Magazines of the United States*, edited by S. Riley and G. Selnow, 136–39. Westport, CT: Greenwood Press.

Redhagen, Tony. 2017. "City Magazines, Dependent on Print, Face Uncertain Future Amid Wave of Deals." *Columbia Journalism Review*, April 18. www.cjr.org.

Riley, Sam, and George Frangoulis. 1991. "Southern Living." In *Regional Interest Magazines of the United States*, edited by S. Riley and G. Selnow, 289–94. Westport, CT: Greenwood Press.

Riley, Sam, and Gary Selnow, Editors. 1991. *Regional Interest Magazines of the United States*. Westport, CT: Greenwood Press.

Rosman, Katherine. 2019. "Events Are the New Magazine." *New York Times*, February 2.

Royer, David. 2019. "Memphis Magazine Pulls Issue, Apologizes after Cover Art Controversy." September 2. www.wreg.com.

Selnow, Gary. 1991. "Philadelphia." In *Regional Interest Magazines of the United States*, edited by S. Riley and G. Selnow, 258. Westport, CT: Greenwood Press.

Sewell, Edward H. 1991. "Texas Monthly." In *Regional Interest Magazines of the United States*, edited by S. Riley and G. Selnow, 317–22. Westport, CT: Greenwood Press.

Shapiro, Ali. 2019. "An Exit Interview with New York Magazine Editor in Chief Adam Moss." *All Things Considered*, National Public Radio, March 13. https://www.nrpr.org.

Sheehy, Gail. 2014. *Daring: My Passages*. New York: William Morrow.

Sivek, Susan Currie. 2013. City Magazines and Social Media: Moving Beyond the Monthly." *Journal of Magazine and New Media Research* 14:2 (2013).

———. 2015. "The Contribution of City Magazines to the Urban Information Environment." *Journal of Magazine and New Media Research* 16:1, Fall 2015.

———. 2018. "City Magazines Expand Audience and Revenues with Web Apps." November 15. www.mediashift.org.

Steinem, Gloria. 2015. *My Life on the Road*. New York: Random House.

Sternadori, M. and Sivek, S.C. 2020. "City and Regional Magazines." In *The Handbook of Magazine Studies,* edited by M. Sternadori and T. Holmes. https://doi.org/10.1002/9781119168102.ch23

Svachula, Amanda. 2019. "The City Magazine, Reimagined." *Medium*, March 12.

Tawa, Steve. 2017. "Herb Lipson, Outspoken Owner of Philadelphia Magazine, Passes Away at 88." CBSPhilly, December 26. https://kywnewsradio.com.

Tebbel, John, and Zuckerman, Mary Ellen. 1991. *The Magazine in America, 1741–1990*. New York: Oxford University Press.

The State of the News Media 2012. *Pew Research Center's Project for Excellence in Journalism*. https://www.pewresearch.org/2012/03/19/state-of-the-news-media-2012/.

Tracy, Marc, and Edmund Lee. 2019. "Vox Media Acquires New York Magazine, Chronicler of the Highbrow and Lowbrow." *New York Times*, September 24.

Van Doren, Adam. 2001. "Top Hat and Tales: Harold Ross and the Making of the New Yorker." FirstRunFeatures.com. DVD.

Vinciguerra, Thomas. 2016. *Cast of Characters: Wolcott Gibbs, E. B. White, James Thurber and the Golden Age of the New Yorker*. New York: W. W. Norton and Co.

Volk, Steve. 2013. *Gosnells' Babies: Inside the Mind of America's Most Notorious Abortion Doctors*. Amazon Kindle Books.

Weingarten, Marc. 2006. *The Gang That Wouldn't Write Straight: Wolfe, Thompson, Didion, and the New Journalism Revolution*. New York: Crown Publishers.

Wolfe, Tom. 1973. *The New Journalism*. New York: Harper & Row.

Yagoda, Ben. 2000. *About Town: The New Yorker and the World It Made*. New York: Scribner.

Chapter 13

A Style Guide for the Digital World

Aileen Gallagher

The American Society of Magazine Editors (2019) has a broad definition of what a magazine is: "a print or digital publication issued or updated regularly in a consistent format, shaped by a distinctive editorial perspective and trusted by readers to provide timely information relevant to their interests." From YouTube makeup tutorials to true-crime podcasts, today's digital media mirror the great magazines of the twentieth century in tone, style, and story format. Successful outlets have adopted magazines' commitment to niche audiences, specialized coverage, intimate voice, and a clear point of view.

Blogs, service journalism, longform reported narratives, podcasts, and social media are all digital extensions of magazine media, whether they are part of existing magazine brands or independent online publications. The voice of the internet is the voice of twentieth-century magazines, unbound.

BLOGS

The internet's de facto adoption of a magazine approach to content began almost at once, with blogs. Early publishing platforms such as Blogger, which launched in 1999, enabled writers to publish without having to learn HTML or host their own websites (C. Thompson 2006). They also had no editorial gatekeepers.

Bloggers wrote about their passions and interests with delightful specificity, developing a like-minded audience by linking out into the digital void. Though early blog champions considered the form native to the web because of its reliance on hyperlinks, some blog characteristics sound similar to what audiences have long treasured about magazines and the editors who lead them: "A good weblog on any subject provides a combination of relevance, intelligent juxtaposition, and serendipity. . . . When a weblogger and his readers share a POV, a weblog constantly points its readers to items they didn't know they wanted to see" (Blood 2002, 12).

By the early 2000s, the most popular types of blogs were of the "personal journal" or "filter" variety (Herring et al. 2004). The personal journal published the inner thoughts and feelings of the writer, while the blogger behind a filter site served an editorial function by identifying and directing the audience to specific content. The personal blog has been declared dead several times in the past decade, but it really just transmuted. The LiveJournals, Blogspots, and Tumblrs of Internet 1.0 made way for other, better platforms that allowed people to post about their lives (Facebook, Instagram) or their ideas (Medium, Twitter) with less upkeep than individual blogs and a greater range of publishing options (Kottke 2013; Drum 2015).

The confessional style of personal journal blogs recalls both zines and the magazine staple, the personal essay. Zines—"hardcopy, photocopied and hand collated collections of texts and images" (Knobel and Lankshear 2002)—could be about a particular subject, but by the late 1990s, they were increasingly about the "everyday life of the publisher" (Chu 1997, 75). This trend transposed to the digital setting beginning as early as 1999. LiveJournal, one of the first widely used blog platforms, embraced this personalized approach to content and allowed users to customize their own pages and follow and comment on others' (Perez 2014).

Even after personal journal blog contents migrated to social media, the personal essay remained popular online. Long a fixture of women's magazines, the personal essay was uniquely suited to both the confessional spirit of the internet and the most judgmental tendencies of social media. Digital publications that relied on a traffic-based business model were happy to publish "a specific sort of ultra-confessional essay, written by a person you've never heard of and published online" (Tolentino 2017, para. 3) that generated viral reaction and commensurate clicks.

But this success was not without its critics. Editors were blamed for exploiting the stories of marginalized writers and leaving them vulnerable to criticism and humiliation in exchange for a byline and a nominal fee (Bennett 2015). Though many of the sites that used to publish these kinds of essays, such as XOJane, have shuttered or pivoted, audiences still thirst for the voyeur-like pleasure of learning someone else's secrets. Today, they read them on Slate or on HuffPost Personal, a vertical specifically designed for personal essays. Sites like Refinery 29 and Vice have repurposed the form by publishing week-in-the-life diaries about an anonymous individual's spending, sex, or eating habits (Tepper 2019). While bloggers continue to share their stories on their own sites, these professional publications offer a larger audience and the imprimatur of editorial oversight—more personal essay than blog post.

The filter blog, which typically focuses on news and politics with the goal of sharing a perspective and influencing an audience, is the form journalists quickly latched onto (Blood 2002). Blogs offered limitless space and no editor between the journalist and the audience. The form also played to journalists' strengths, such as finding new angles for talked-about stories and synthesizing complex issues in a memorable way. The lack of formal editorial structure meant that journalists could put more of themselves and their voice into online writing: "Weblogs allow complete editorial freedom and enable the journalist to adopt a much more interpretative or even opinionated position in comparison to the standards of mainstream media" (Domingo and Heinonen 2008, 9). Writers like Andrew Sullivan and Ta-Nehisi Coates built their own audiences on these types of blogs, which remain popular today as the digital equivalent of the traditional opinion column.

But this voice-forward writing style was not simply the purview of opinion columnists online. The filter blog can also be seen as kin to the special-interest magazine, which creates a community to which readers feel they belong (Abrahamson 2008). In the early 2000s, these niche online publications covered everything from New York celebrities and media (Gawker) to technology (Engadget). In Brian Abrams's *Gawker: An Oral History*, nascent blogger Lockhart Steele recalls publisher Nick Denton saying in 2002, "'My plan is to launch a series of blogs, each with a very specific content area. Every category that could be a magazine could be a blog'" (2015, 10).

Gawker, which would rise to become one of the most popular and successful digital media sites before collapsing under the weight of a privacy lawsuit filed by former pro-wrestler Hulk Hogan and bankrolled by Gawker target Peter Thiel (D. Thompson 2018), was influenced by magazines, particularly the British magazine *Private Eye* and the American magazine *Spy* (Abrams 2015). *Spy* co-founder and former *Vanity Fair* editor Graydon Carter denied, with some distaste, the proposition that his satirical magazine was a "tonal progenitor of a lot of Internet writing" (Marchese 2019, para. 20). "The Internet is filled with bile and snark and accusation. *Spy* was much subtler," he said. But his co-founder, Kurt Anderson, readily admitted the connection (Kafka 2016). Gawker spawned many imitators, asserted *New Yorker* writer Jia Tolentino (2016, para. 4): "It had done a great deal to shape the prickly, punchy, intimate sensibility of the Internet that gleefully watched it go."

SERVICE JOURNALISM

Beyond blogs, the earnest enthusiasm of magazine service journalism—"responding to and offering commentary and advice on the everyday concerns of their audiences" (Eide and Knight 1999, 526)—has translated seamlessly to the internet. This content is beloved by magazine readers and honored by the American Society of Magazine Editors with two standalone categories in the industry's coveted National Magazine Awards: "personal service" and "leisure interests."

In the twentieth century, service journalism was essential to the appeal of women's magazines, especially the magazines known as the Seven Sisters: *Better Homes & Gardens*, *Family Circle*, *Good Housekeeping*, *Ladies' Home Journal*, *McCall's*, *Redbook*, and *Woman's Day*. These magazines dispensed advice and expertise that helped readers do everything from choose a wedding venue to unclog a drain. This content was useful and offered "immediate applications to readers' lives" (McCracken 1992, 195). Cover lines touting service content were a selling point for magazines beginning in the 1940s and began to dominate covers by the 1970s (Grow 2002). This service content was often evergreen; recipes and how-to stories could be kept far past the publication date, or clipped and shared with friends and family.

That service content had both staying power and sharing potential made it a natural fit for an internet navigated primarily by search engines and social media. The value of service content for professional media organizations is threefold. First, much of the content is evergreen, at least in the near term. Publishers can post the content without fear that it will quickly appear outdated. Second, service content lends itself to search-engine optimization strategies that drive audiences querying Google and other search engines with a simple "How to [X]" (Bakker 2012). Finally, service content is highly shareable, generating traffic and audience engagement—two valuable metrics—through social media.

News organizations have embraced this highly practical content, too. When the *New York Times* launched its "Smarter Living" section in 2017, it appointed an editor with a background in social media and growth strategy (Bloomgarden-Smoke 2017). The section began by surfacing previously published content before offering new material. Recent "Smarter Living" headlines include "How to Improve Your Outdoor Space" and "Why You Need a Password Manager. Yes, You." National Public Radio followed suit in 2018, launching a podcast series called "Life Kit" that promised "to give listeners practical information and guidance to help them navigate life's big and small challenges" (NPR 2018). Recent entries in the series include "How to Succeed at College" and "Find Money You Didn't Know You Had." In all of these instances, a form that was intrinsic to magazines seamlessly moved online, bringing with it the same niche audience appeal.

LONGFORM NARRATIVE

The magazine feature story is also experiencing a digital renaissance in the form of subject-specific digital verticals that publish feature-length, original reporting, often known as "longform journalism." "The term long-form," wrote James Bennet, then-editor of *The Atlantic*, "has come to stand for narrative and expository and deeply reported journalism. . . . You might just call it magazine writing" (2013, para. 2, 10).

While reading several thousands of words on a desktop was daunting, and indeed frowned upon by early usability experts (Morkes and Nielsen 1997), audiences grew comfortable with scrolling on handheld digital devices. Services like Instapaper and Pocket not only elevated the reading experience on digital devices but allowed readers to save and savor the story later when they had more time (DVorkin 2012). The ubiquity of smartphones and tablets (Pew Research Center 2019a), combined with the advent of social media, meant that audiences were not only reading magazine-length features but also sharing them. On Twitter, especially, a story shared and tagged #longreads suggests a certain editorial prestige, a narrative worth the audience's time and attention.

The National Magazine Awards, which for years had separate print and digital categories, allowed digital publications to compete with print in all of the major writing categories by 2008. Digital native outlets like BuzzFeed, Politico, and Eater hired features editors (sometimes from the print world) and assigned reported pieces that were thousands of words long and received print-magazine levels of editing and fact-checking. The Atavist Magazine was founded in 2011 specifically to publish longform stories online, and has been recognized several times as a National Magazine Award finalist. In 2015, The Atavist was the first digital publication to win a National Magazine Award for Feature Writing. That same year, a Slate article—"The College Rape Overcorrection"—was a finalist in the public interest category, and the online sports magazine Grantland was also a finalist for feature writing. The prestige surrounding this most traditional kind of magazine writing remains, though today's young journalists are more likely to say they want to "write longform" than "write features."

Narratively, BuzzFeed, and many other sites now publish longform stories. Aggregator Longreads says it identifies "stories that are best enjoyed away from your desk—whether it's on a daily commute, an airplane, a subway, or your couch. It's in-depth stories, perfect for the iPad, iPhone or Kindle, and apps like Read It Later, Flipboard and Instapaper." And true to longform, most of the stories surfaced by Longreads were originally published in magazines.

PODCASTS

Podcasts first emerged in the mid-aughts with the advent of digital music players like iPods, but they did not explode in popularity for another decade (Quah 2017). Early podcasts resembled talking-head radio or television panel shows more than narrative storytelling. Though they shared a magazine's strong voice, clear point of view, and niche subject matter, podcasts did not attract similar audiences. In 2006, only about 11 percent of internet users had downloaded a podcast (Pew Research Center 2019b). By 2019, nearly a third of Americans reported listening to a podcast in the past month. In a rare instance of the magazine industry being a digital innovator, the National Magazine Awards had a podcasting category in 2010 and 2011, and then reintroduced it in 2019. Now, it is rare to find a media brand, magazine or otherwise, that does not produce a podcast, and the number and range of standalone podcasts has exploded. In 2019, more than half of Americans ages 12 and over had listened to a podcast (Edison Research 2019).

What changed between the advent of podcasts and their current ubiquity can be attributed—among other things—to the format's adoption of magazine-style reporting and storytelling: a compelling, well-structured narrative; exhaustive and empathetic reporting; and a writing voice that moves audiences. Deeply reported narrative podcasts have the structural feel of a magazine story. Their rich soundscapes provide a level of detail and intimacy familiar to readers of print features.

The narrative podcast exploded in 2014 with the popularity of *Serial* (a podcast offshoot of the longtime public radio show "This American Life"), which was downloaded 175 million times (Spangler 2017). Listeners followed along with host Sarah Koenig as she explored the 2000 conviction of a Chicago high school student accused of killing his girlfriend. Koenig's presence in *Serial* as a central figure filtering the story through her own experience is recognizable to any reader of New Journalism.

Like the best magazine features, podcasts hold up on repeat listening. These audio narratives, meticulously edited and often timeless, are crafted not for an ephemeral broadcast, but for the audience that will download and listen to them again and again (Walker 2011).

FROM EDITORS TO INFLUENCERS TO INFLUENCER-EDITORS

While today's digital editorial has adopted many of the characteristics of traditional print magazine content, magazine culture has not fared so well. The once omnipotent editor in chief is diminished, and the fierce, hierarchical masthead culture has flattened. The latter part of the 2010s saw the departure (voluntary or otherwise) of editors whose tastes and sensibilities dictated much of their magazines' content, including Graydon Carter (*Vanity Fair*), Adam Moss (*New York*), Cindy Leive (*Glamour*), and David Granger (*Esquire*). Their replacements often are not household names in the magazine industry or even people with magazine experience. Leive's successor at *Glamour*, Samantha Barry, was previously the head of social media at CNN. She had never worked at a magazine.

This shift in magazine power structures prompted digital fashion editor Harling Ross to wonder if the "glory days of old-school editors-in-chief are coming to an end" (2017, para. 3). Condé Nast's Anna Wintour, who remains a cultural powerhouse, is the exception. In general, the magazine editor's influence has shifted to literal influencers. Where magazine editors previously used the pages of a magazine to highlight trends, ideas, and recommendations, social media influencers use social media platforms to shape audience attitudes (Freberg et al. 2011).

Today, celebrities bypass magazines (and their editorial standards) by promoting their personal brands on Instagram or TikTok. Previously, celebrities turned to magazines to announce their pregnancies or seek public absolution from a scandal. Social media has displaced the traditional media's role as information distributor. Magazines now cede power to the social media influencers in order to lure them to appear in their publications. The September 2018 issue of *Vogue* featured singer Beyoncé on the cover. In exchange, Beyoncé assumed editorial responsibilities and assigned the photographer, approved the cover, selected photos, and wrote captions (Ali 2018).

The audience's appetite for celebrity content, of course, was fueled by magazines throughout the twentieth century, reaching a fever pitch as the century turned and *Us Weekly*, *InTouch*, *People*, and *Star* battled for newsstand dominance. By the late 2000s, celebrity gossip blogs—just like fashion blogs—competed with the magazines, as did tabloid television shows like *Entertainment Tonight* and *Access Hollywood*, and digital celebrity powerhouse TMZ. The celebrity magazine, even with a weekly publishing schedule, was too slow to compete.

Fashion and lifestyle editors, especially, have lost much of their cultural cachet in the digital age. Fashion bloggers could also spot trends and identify fresh designers, sometimes by illegally using the same photos published by the print fashion bibles. Some of these bloggers, such as The Sartorialist or Style Bubble, ended up working in legacy fashion media. These blogs are credited with democratizing fashion or at least wrestling taste-making powers away from just a few editors around the world (Alexander 2018). Social media opened up the fashion gates even more, with influencers appearing on Instagram and other platforms wearing particular brands and styles, acting as both fashion editor and model in exchange for money or simply free clothes. Like editors, influencers have become a part of the fashion scene—spotted at parties and in the front row during Fashion Week.

The prominence of social media also means that magazines no longer have the final say when it comes to the popular celebrity profile. Traditionally, gaining access to celebrities and negotiating everything from time spent with reporters to clothing approval was the role of the bookings editor, and once the magazine shipped there was little the celebrity could do about their portrayal. Social media, of course, offers a means of recourse. In 2019, Madonna complained about her treatment at the hands of award-winning writer Vanessa Grigoriadis, who profiled "Madonna at Sixty" for the *New York Times Magazine*. Madonna told her nearly 15 million Instagram followers that Grigoriadis disparaged and degraded her and focused unnecessarily on her age (Rao 2019).

Social media celebrities, including YouTube stars and Instagram influencers, do not need a magazine for promotion, nor do they need to risk what might be an unflattering portrayal. Audiences, however, deserve the critical questions posed by journalists, asserts music critic Jon Caramanica (2018) in an essay titled "R.I.P., the Celebrity Profile." Magazines today have essentially lost editorial control of the celebrity narrative and are reduced to reposting or republishing what the star has already shared on social media (Petersen 2019).

While social media has displaced much of the function of a certain type of magazine editor, the editors themselves are also extending their titles' brand across Instagram, Twitter, and other platforms. Posting to social media is part of their job, as is engaging with the audience in real time. Editors are now brand ambassadors for both their publication and themselves.

Lifestyle editors, especially, use social media to perform traditional editorial functions, such as taking audiences behind the scenes at fashion shows or highlighting new products. Trade publication *Business of Fashion* observed in 2018 the rise of "the influencer-editor [who] now occupies a new place in the fashion media establishment, where bloggers and social media stars have fought for acceptance" (Fernandez, para. 4), and reported that editors at Hearst are compensated for shilling sponsored content in their personal social media feeds. For some editors, social media has become the bridge to working directly for lifestyle brands and other roles outside of magazines.

Even though magazine editors have lost some of their previous cachet and some publications are no longer in print, the legacy of the American magazine lives on in the editorial content itself. Magazine journalism embraced perspective and point of view, providing specialized content for specific audiences. Magazine editors innovated with story forms and design, and built communities around their audiences' shared interests and aspirations.

Magazine editorial became the basis for digital media content, from blogs to service to longform online narrative. Magazine editors were themselves social influencers, playing an outsized role in what the American public wore, ate, read, watched, and thought about. Magazines, the cultural arbiters of the twentieth century, wrote the style guide for the next editorial age.

REFERENCES

Abrams, Brian. 2015. *Gawker: An Oral History*. Amazon Digital Services LLC. Kindle.

Abrahamson, David. 2008. "Magazine Exceptionalism: The Concept, the Criteria, the Challenge." *Mapping the Magazine: Comparative Studies in Magazine Journalism* (2008): 146–48.

Alexander, Ella. 2018. "What Is the Difference between a Fashion Influencer and Blogger?" *Harper's Bazaar*. September 14. https://www.harpersbazaar.com/uk/fashion/fashion-news/news/a41898/fashion-influencer-fashion-blogger-definition/.

Ali, Yashar. 2018. "Beyoncé Given Unprecedented Control Over Vogue's September Issue Cover, Sources Say." HuffPost. August 7. https://www.huffpost.com/entry/beyonce-vogue-september-issue_n_5b5f4e19e4b0b15aba9b694c?8dn=.

American Society of Magazine Editors. 2019. "National Magazine Awards Call for Entries 2020." October 1.

Armstrong, Mark. 2020. "What Are Longreads?" Longreads. April 30. https://web.archive.org/web/20130112210704/http://blog.longreads.com/about.

Bakker, Piet. 2012. "Aggregation, Content Farms and Huffinization: The Rise of Low-Pay and No-Pay Journalism." *Journalism Practice* 6, no. 5–6: 627–37.

Bennet, James. 2013. "Against 'Long-Form Journalism'." *The Atlantic*. December 14. https://www.theatlantic.com/business/archive/2013/12/against-long-form-journalism/282256/.

Bennett, Laura. 2015. "The First-Person Industrial Complex." Slate, September 15. http://www.slate.com/articles/life/technology/2015/09/the_first_person_industrial_complex_how_the_harrowing_personal_essay_took.html.

Blood, Rebecca. 2002. *The Weblog Handbook: Practical Advice on Creating and Maintaining Your Blog*. Basic Books.

Bloomgarden-Smoke, Kara. 2017. "'The New York Times' Focuses on 'Smarter Living.'" *WWD*. January 10. https://wwd.com/business-news/media/the-new-york-times-smarter-living-tim-herrera-10743380/.

Caramanica, Jon. 2018. "R.I.P., the Celebrity Profile." *The New York Times*. September 19. https://www.nytimes.com/2018/09/19/arts/music/celebrity-profile-death.html.

Chu, Julie. 1997. "Navigating the Media Environment: How Youth Claim a Place through Zines." *Social Justice* 24, no. 3 (69): 71–85.

Domingo, David, and Ari Heinonen. 2008. "Weblogs and Journalism." *Nordicom Review* 29, no. 1: 3–15.

Drum, Kevin. 2015. "Blogging Isn't Dead. But Old-School Blogging Is Definitely Dying." *Mother Jones*. June 24. https://www.motherjones.com/kevin-drum/2015/01/blogging-isnt-dead-old-school-blogging-definitely-dying/.

DVorkin, Lewis. 2012. "Inside Forbes: How Long-Form Journalism Is Finding Its Digital Audience." *Forbes.* May 29. https://www.forbes.com/sites/lewisdvorkin/2012/02/23/inside-forbes-how-long-form-journalism-is-finding-its-digital-audience/#330679261c8d.

Edison Research. 2019. "The Infinite Dial 2019." https://www.edisonresearch.com/infinite-dial-2019/.

Eide, Martin, and Graham Knight. 1999. "Public/Private Service: Service Journalism and the Problems of Everyday Life." *European Journal of Communication* 14, no. 4: 525–47.

Fernandez, Chantal. 2018. "Fashion Editors or Influencers? Sometimes It's Hard to Tell." *The Business of Fashion.* May 31. https://www.businessoffashion.com/articles/intelligence/fashion-editors-or-influencers-sometimes-its-hard-to-tell.

Freberg, Karen, Kristin Graham, Karen McGaughey, and Laura A. Freberg. 2011. "Who Are the Social Media Influencers? A Study of Public Perceptions of Personality." *Public Relations Review* 37, no. 1: 90–92.

Godoy, Maria. *Life Kit*, podcast audio, 2018. https://www.npr.org/lifekit.

Grow, Gerald. 2002. "Magazine Covers and Cover Lines: An Illustrated History." *Journal of Magazine and New Media Research* 4, no. 2 (2002).

Herring, Susan C., Lois Ann Scheidt, Sabrina Bonus, and Elijah Wright. 2004. "Bridging the Gap: A Genre Analysis of Weblogs." In *Proceedings of the 37th Annual Hawaii International Conference on System Sciences.* IEEE.

Kafka, Peter. 2016. "Donald Trump Is Still a 'Short-Fingered Vulgarian.'" *Recode.* Podcast audio, October 13. https://www.vox.com/2016/10/13/13261610/donald-trump-kurt-andersen-spy-pro-wrestling-wwe-recode-media-podcast.

Knobel, Michele, and Colin Lankshear. 2002. "Cut, Paste, Publish: The Production and Consumption of Zines." *Adolescents and Literacies in a Digital World* (2002): 164–85.

Kottke, Jason. 2013. "The Blog Is Dead, Long Live the Blog." Nieman Lab, December 19. https://www.niemanlab.org/2013/12/the-blog-is-dead/.

Marchese, David. 2019. "Graydon Carter on Vanity Fair, Jeffrey Epstein and an Editor's Power." *New York Times Magazine*, July 19. https://www.nytimes.com/interactive/2019/07/19/magazine/graydon-carter-jeffrey-epstein-vanity-fair.html.

Matheson, Donald. 2004. "Weblogs and the Epistemology of the News: Some Trends in Online Journalism." *New Media & Society* 6, no. 4: 443–68.

McCracken, Ellen. 1992. *Decoding Women's Magazines: From Mademoiselle to Ms.* McMillan.

Morkes, John, and Jakob Nielsen. 1997. "Concise, Scannable, and Objective: How to Write for the Web." *Useit.com* 51, no. 1 (1997): 1–17.

Perez, Sarah. 2014. "Under Ex-Googler CEO, LiveJournal Gets a Revamp, Promises New Services, Apps and More in 2014." TechCrunch. May 16. https://techcrunch.com/2014/05/16/livejournal-wants-to-be-medium/.

Petersen, Anne Helen. 2019. "How the 2010s Killed the Celebrity Gossip Machine." BuzzFeed News. January 3. https://www.buzzfeednews.com/article/annehelenpetersen/decade-celebrity-gossip-tabloids-paparazzi-social-media.

Pew Research Center. 2012. "The Future of Mobile News." October 1. https://www.journalism.org/2012/10/01/indepth-news-reading-tablet/.

———. 2019a. "Smartphone Ownership Is Growing Rapidly Around the World, but Not Always Equally." February.

———. 2019b. "Audio and Podcasting Fact Sheet." July 9. https://www.journalism.org/fact-sheet/audio-and-podcasting/.

Quah, Nicholas. 2017. "The Three Fundamental Moments of Podcasts' Crazy Rise." *Wired*, October 4. https://www.wired.com/story/podcast-three-watershed-moments/.

Rao, Sonia. 2019. "Analysis | Madonna's Furious Response to Her New York Times Profile Raises Questions about What Stars Expect from Journalists." *The Washington Post*. June 7. https://www.washingtonpost.com/arts-entertainment/2019/06/07/madonnas-furious-response-her-new-york-times-profile-raises-questions-about-what-stars-expect-journalists/.

Ross, Harling. 2017. "The Glory Days of Old School Magazine Editors Are Fading." Man Repeller. September 29. https://www.manrepeller.com/2017/09/editors-leaving-magazines.html.

Spangler, Todd. 2017. "The 'Serial' Team's New Podcast, 'S-Town,' Tops 10 Million Downloads in Four Days." *Variety*. December 7. https://variety.com/2017/digital/news/s-town-podcast-10-million-downloads-serial-productions-1202020302/.

Tepper, Taylor. 2019. "The Unbearable Lightness of Money Diaries." *New York Times*. April 23. https://www.nytimes.com/2019/04/23/smarter-living/wirecutter/money-diaries-benefits-drawbacks.html.

Thompson, Clive. 2006. "The Early Years: A Timeline of How Blogging All Began." *New York Magazine*. February 20. http://nymag.com/news/media/15971/.

Thompson, Derek. 2018. "The Most Expensive Comment in Internet History?" *The Atlantic*. February 23. https://www.theatlantic.com/business/archive/2018/02/hogan-thiel-gawker-trial/554132/.

Tolentino, Jia. 2016. "Gawker's Essential Unevenness." *The New Yorker*. August 20. https://www.newyorker.com/culture/jia-tolentino/gawkers-essential-unevenness.

———. 2017. "The Personal-Essay Boom Is Over." *The New Yorker*. May 18. https://www.newyorker.com/culture/jia-tolentino/the-personal-essay-boom-is-over.

Walker, Rob. 2011. "On 'Radiolab,' the Sound of Science." *The New York Times Magazine*. April 8. https://www.nytimes.com/2011/04/10/magazine/mag-10Radiolab-t.html.

Notes

INTRODUCTION

1. The first magazine to practice methodical fact-checking was *Time*, but *The New Yorker* refined the process and created the model that set the standard and spread to other magazine media.

2. MRi-Simmons, Starch Advertising Research, January–December 2019.

CHAPTER 3

1. The phrase "things you want to keep" is part of an interview with Dave Eggers, quoted by Bollen, Craps, and Vermeulen (2013, 5).

CHAPTER 5

1. This percentage is derived from a content analysis of selected issues from March 2003 through July 2005, as well as from personal communication with founder Roy Reiman and Senior Editor Bob Ottum. The remaining 20 percent consisted of such elements as bios of "field editors" and intros to stories and sections, for example, in *Taste of Home*, monthly contests and "Our Family's Favorite Grace"; in *Country Woman*, monthly features such as "Editor in the Country," a write-up of a visit to a farm or garden by editor Ann Kaiser.

2. The magazines included cooking titles: *Taste of Home*, *Simple Delicious*, *Healthy Cooking*, *Cooking for Two*; rural-focused titles: *Farm Wife News* (renamed *Country Woman*), *Farm Ranch Living*, *Country*; gardening and birding: *Birds and Blooms*, *Backyard Living*; and nostalgia: *Reminisce*.

CHAPTER 7

1. Human immunodeficiency virus and acquired immune deficiency syndrome.
2. An inclusive term for the lesbian, gay, bisexual, transgender, and queer or questioning communities.

Index

826, 41

ABC TV *Hootenanny*, 67
Acres U.S.A., 95
activism, 25, 55, 65
activist, 31–32, 53, 59, 62, 105–6, 109–11
advertising, 21, 38–39, 88–89, 98, 160–61, 184–85
agriculture magazines, 84
AIDS, 105–16
AIDS activism, 106, 109, 111
alternative farming, 92, 94, 99
Animal Liberation, 121
Arizona Highways magazine, 180
Armstrong, Heather B., 151
Atkinson, Wilmer, 90
Atlanta magazine, 180
Atlantic, The, 3, 9, 12–13, 15, 17–20, 22, 195
auteur theory, 65

Baltimore magazine, 180
Believer, The, 37
belletristic, 9, 13
"best of" issues, 179, 184
Better Homes and Gardens, 96, 161, 194
blogs, 4, 81, 116, 162, 172, 174–75, 191–93, 197–99

Bombeck, Erma, 157–58
booster publications, 180, 185
brands, 81, 99, 180, 191, 197–98
Breslin, Jimmy, 183–84
Broadside, 55–57, 59–60, 67–68
Brown, Tina, 183
business publication, 94
business-to-business magazines, 97

Caravan, 60–63
Chicago magazine, 181
civil rights, 19, 30–31, 54–55, 59, 65, 68, 74, 108–9, 179, 181
Cohen, Rachel, 41
Cold War, 19, 30, 55
communism, 32
community/ies, 1–4, 75–78, 80–81, 111, 116, 121, 124–25, 127, 167, 171, 173–75
Condé Nast publishing, 138, 144, 183, 197
connections, 40–41, 47, 73, 77–78, 116, 125, 173–75
content marketing, 97
controlled circulation, 97
country aesthetic, 77–78
Cowles Enthusiast Media, 129
creator-centric, 168
criticism, 9–11, 15, 17, 19, 21, 65, 151, 182, 192

Croly, Herbert, 15, 26, 28–29
Cunningham, Agnes (Sis), 59–60, 65, 68
Cut, The, 185

Dane, Barbara, 57–58
Davis, Lydia, 39
Deere, Charles, 98
Deere, John, 97–98
Diet for a Small Planet, 121–22
digital revolution, 2, 179, 184
Dissent, 30–32, 34
do-it-yourself, 172, 174
domestic chaos writers, 151–54, 160–62
Dunson, Josh, 54, 57
Dylan, Bob, 58, 60, 65, 67

Eastman, Max, 28
editors, 25–27, 67–68, 75–76, 78–81, 141–42, 145, 191–92, 194–99
Eggers, Dave, 37–49
Espionage Act, 28–29
Esquire, 44, 135–40, 142, 144–45, 197
Extension: The National Catholic Monthly, 156

Factsheet Five, 170, 172
Family Circle, 161, 194
fanzine, 60–61, 63–64, 66, 167, 169–70
The Farm, 122
farmers, 83–85, 87–98
Farmer's Wife, The, 92
Farm Journal, The, 84–85, 89–94
farm magazines, 74, 76, 83–85, 88–94, 96–99
farms, 83–99
Felker, Clay, 182–84
feminism, 162, 171–72
Folklore Center, 58, 62
folk music magazines, 53–58, 65, 67–68
Foster Wallace, David, 39, 41
Freedom Singers, The, 54
Friedan, Betty, 152, 159, 161
Friesen, Gordon, 57, 59–60, 65, 68

Furrow, The, 97–98

Gardyloo, 63–64
Gaskin, Stephen, 122
Gawker, 193
gay, 31, 105–16, 144–45
Godkin, Edwin Lawrence, 10–11, 26
Goldman, Emma, 27–28, 34
Good Housekeeping, 152, 156, 161, 194
GQ, 137–40, 144–45
Great Depression, 16, 30, 91, 137
Great Migration, The, 181
Greenwich Village, 28, 58, 63
grrrl zines, 171
Grub Street, 185
Guthrie, Woody, 66

Harper's, 9, 11–13, 16, 18, 20–22, 40, 152
Hatch Act, 90
A Heartbreaking Work of Staggering Genius, 38, 45
Heti, Sheila, 41
HIV, 105–7, 111, 113–16
HIV/AIDS, 105–6, 115–16
HIV-positive, 105–7, 113
Hoffman, Lee, 60–64
Honolulu magazine, 180
Hootenanny: The National Folk Singing Magazine, 67
House Un-American Activities Committee, 67
housewife writers, 151–52, 155–60, 162
Houston, Cisco, 65
Howe, Irving, 30–32

imagined community, 75, 77
immigrants, 33
immigration, 29, 80
intellectual, 9–22, 25–27, 30–32, 34, 47, 185
intellectual history, 9
Intelligencer, 185
Internet Tendency, 38

Ivins, Molly, 20, 31

Jackson, Shirley, 152–54, 159, 162
Jones, David G., 97–98

Kerr, Jean, 152, 154–55, 159–60, 162
Kurns, Dave, 85, 93–94, 97

labor, 14, 26, 29, 31–32, 54, 57–58, 88, 96
Lacy, Steve, 96
Ladies' Home Journal, 152, 154–55, 160–61, 194
lad mags, 143–45
Lappé, Frances Moore, 121–22
lattice, 40–42
leftist, 25, 31, 33–34, 59–60, 66
LGBTQ, 106, 111
liberal, 12, 18–19, 25–31
liberalism, 15, 30, 32
Life Among the Savages, 151, 153, 160
Lipson, Arthur, 180
Lipson, Herbert, 180
Little Sandy Review, The, 65–66
longform, 191, 195, 199
Los Angeles magazine, 181
Louisville magazine, 180–81
Luce, Henry, 137, 182

magazine as object, 45
magazine century, 1
Maryland magazine, 180
masculinity, 135, 140–41, 143–45
Masses, The, 27–29
"mass to class" shift, 184
McCall's, 152, 154, 161, 194
McCarthyism, 67
McGinley, Phyllis, 155–56, 159–60
McSweeney's Quarterly Concern, 37–49
Memphis magazine, 181
men's magazines, 135, 139, 143–45
Meredith, Edwin T., 85–88, 93, 96
Meredith Corporation, 96–97
middle class, 12, 25, 32, 53

Midwest Living, 185
Might magazine, 38, 41
Moodie, David, 38
Mother Earth, 27–29, 34
Mother Earth News, 95
Mother Jones, 22, 25, 33

Nation, The, 9–13, 15, 18, 20, 22, 25–31, 34
National Magazine Awards, 142, 182, 194–96
Nelson, Paul, 65–66
Nevada Highways and Parks magazine, 180
Nevada magazine, 180
New Deal, 30
Newhouse Jr., S. I., 183
New Journalism, 142, 179, 183–84, 196
New Left, 31–33
New Republic, The, 9, 15–16, 18, 21, 25–31, 34, 170
New West magazine, 184
New Yorker, The, 3, 9–10, 16–21, 40, 112, 152–53, 182–83, 193
New York magazine, 182–85
niche, 1–4, 135–36, 152, 168, 170, 181, 191, 193–94, 196
noncommercial, 62, 73, 167
nonprofit, 31, 33–34
North American Vegetarian Society, 127

Obis, Paul, 121, 125–26, 128–29
Ochs, Phil, 55–56, 60, 67
Organic Farming and Gardening, 92, 95, 99
organic farms, 83, 94–96, 99

Palmer, Lane, 90
Pankake, Jon, 65–66
Paradise of the Pacific magazine, 180
participatory, 172
pastoral/core values, 74–78, 80–81
Paxton, Tom, 56–57, 60

Penthouse, 143
People for the Ethical Treatment of Animals, 127
People's Songs Bulletin, 57–59
Philadelphia Chamber of Commerce Journal, 180
Philadelphia magazine, 180
Phoenix magazine, 180
pin-ups, 138–41, 143
Playboy, 140–41, 143–45
Please Don't Eat the Daisies, 155–56, 159–60
podcasts, 191, 194, 196
Polk, Leonidas L., 89
POZ, 105–6, 112–16
printed object, 42
print magazines, 1, 3–4
Progressive era, 27, 29
Progressive Farmer, 89–90, 97, 99
progressive movement, 14, 25
progressivism, 33

race issues, 29
racial discrimination, 29, 33
Radical America, 32–33
radicals/radicalism, 27–29, 31–33
Raising Demons, 152
reader response, 59
Redbook, 40, 161, 194
reform, 25, 27, 29–31, 123
refusalon, 44
Reiman Publications, 73–74, 76, 78–79
Remnick, David, 20, 183
Requa, Marny, 38
Reynolds, Malvina, 59
Rodale, Inc., 95
Rodale, J. I., 3, 92, 94–95
Rodale, Maria, 95
Ross, Harold, 182–83
Rural Schools Bulletin, 87
Rural Schools Service Bureau, 87

Salon des Refusés, 39
San Francisco, 37–38, 41–42, 122, 142

Saunders, George, 39, 41
science fiction, 60, 62, 168–70
SDS. *See* Students for a Democratic Society
Seeger, Pete, 53–54, 57–60, 63, 65, 67
Serial, 196
service journalism, 185, 191, 193–94
Seventh-Day Adventist Church, 123–24
Shapiro, Laura, 152–53
Sheehy, Gail, 183
shelter magazine, 4
Shelton, Robert, 65, 67
Shuttleworth, John, 95
Silber, Irwin, 56, 58–59, 62
Singer, Peter, 121
Sing Out!, 56–59, 62, 66, 68
Sixpence in Her Shoe, 155, 159
Smith-Lever Act, 90–91
social justice, 25–26, 29, 33, 68
social media, 2, 115, 161–62, 184–85, 191–92, 194–95, 197–98
Society of Professional Journalists, 181
Solomon, Linda, 67
Southern California Prompter, 181
Southern Living, 97
Steinem, Gloria, 183–84
stigma, 105, 107–8, 122
Strub, Sean, 105–6, 112–15
Students for a Democratic Society (SDS), 31–32
submission model, 45, 47, 73–78, 80
Successful Farming, 84–89, 91–97, 99

Texas Monthly, 182, 185
Texas Observer, 31, 33
In These Times, 25, 33
thought leaders, 3, 9–10, 12, 18, 22
Time magazine, 182
topical songs, 54–56, 60, 68
trade publications, 96, 112, 137, 198
Traum, Happy, 59

urban folk revival, 53, 67
Utah Holiday magazine, 181

Van Ronk, Dave, 60, 62–63
vegan, 122, 126–27, 129
Vegetarian Journal, 127, 129, 131
Vegetarian Resource Group, 127, 129–30
Vegetarian Times, 121–22, 124–31
Vegetarian Voice, 127
Vietnam War, 31–32, 56, 74, 108
Villard, Oswald Garrison, 26, 29
Voice of Witness, 41
Vulture, 185

Walker, Nancy, 160
Washington Square Park, 62, 64
Weavers, The, 67
Weber, Lenora Mattingly, 156–57
WFMT Guide, 181
Wolfe, Tom, 142, 183–84
women's rights, 31, 33

Young, Izzy, 58, 62

zines, 62–64, 167–75

About the Editors and Contributors

ABOUT THE EDITORS

Sharon Bloyd-Peshkin is professor of journalism at Columbia College Chicago, where she is coordinator of the program's magazine concentration. She is the former head of the Magazine Media Division of the Association for Education in Journalism and Mass Communication, and one of the co-organizers of the international conferences Mapping the Magazine 5, 6 and 7.

Before joining the Columbia College faculty, Bloyd-Peshkin spent thirteen years as a consumer magazine editor, including as senior editor of *Vegetarian Times* magazine and editor of *Chicago Parent* magazine. Her work has been published in the *Columbia Journalism Review*, the *Gateway Journalism Review*, *Chicago* magazine, the *Chicago Tribune*, the *Chicago Tribune Magazine*, the *Chicago Sun-Times*, *In These Times*, *Belt* magazine, *Huffington Post*, the *Common Review*, *Realtor*, *Ocean Paddler*, *Adventure Kayak*, *Sea Kayaker*, and other publications. Bloyd-Peshkin also serves as a volunteer proofreader for *In These Times* magazine, and as a judge for the National Magazine Awards.

Bloyd-Peshkin's scholarly work has been published in *Journalism Practice* and the *Handbook of Magazine Studies*, as well as translated into a course on fact-checking for *Mediabistro*. Her contributions to solutions journalism have been published in *The Whole Story*, and she facilitates workshops for educators on teaching solutions journalism.

Charles Whitaker is dean and professor at Northwestern University Medill School of Journalism, Media, Integrated Marketing Communications. He previously served as the Helen Gurley Brown Professor and associate dean of journalism for the school. Whitaker was one of the rotating directors of Medill's graduate Magazine Publishing Project, an enterprise in which teams of students developed a new magazine or worked in collaboration with an existing publishing company to reinvigorate the editorial and business approach of an existing magazine.

Before joining the Medill faculty, Whitaker was a senior editor at *Ebony* magazine, where he covered a wide range of cultural, social, and political issues and events on four continents, including two U.S. presidential campaigns and the installation of the first black members of the British Parliament. He has received commendations for his work from a number of journalism societies, including the National Association of Black Journalists, Society of Professional Journalists, and National Education Writers Association.

Whitaker is the coauthor of *Magazine Writing* and the author of four statistical analyses of the hiring of women and minorities in the magazine industry and has served as an adviser on diversity issues for the Magazine Publishers of America. He has been published in the *Chicago Tribune*, *Chicago Sun-Times*, *Chicago* magazine, *Jet* magazine, *Essence* magazine, the *Philadelphia Inquirer*, *The Saturday Evening Post*, *Chicago Parent* magazine, and *Folio*, the magazine of the magazine industry. In addition, he is an editorial consultant to *CATALYST* magazine, a publication dedicated to coverage of the Chicago Public Schools, and served as president of the editorial board of the *Chicago Reporter*, an acclaimed investigative publication that covers issues of race and class.

Whitaker has served as a judge for the National Magazine Awards and the International Regional Magazine Awards Association. He currently serves on the board of directors for both the American Society of Magazine Editors and the Center for Public Integrity.

ABOUT THE CONTRIBUTORS

Pablo Calvi is the author of *Latin American Adventures in Literary Journalism* (2019). An associate professor at Stony Brook University School of Journalism, he is also the associate director for Latin America for the Marie Colvin Center for International Reporting. His long-form work has appeared in *The Believer*, *Guernica Magazine*, *Grey Magazine*, and *El Mercurio* among others. Calvi has been listed as notable in *Best American Essays*, *Best American Travel Writing*, and *Best American Nonrequired Reading*.

Peggy Dillon is professor of media and communication at Salem State University in Massachusetts. She is the former editor of *Sextant: The Journal* of *Salem State University* and *Windswept: The Quarterly Bulletin of the Mount Washington Observatory*. She has more than thirty years of combined experience as a newspaper reporter and photographer, magazine writer and editor, publication designer, historian, oral history interviewer, and speechwriter. Her research interests include memoir writing, oral history, travel and adventure journalism, and the preservation of local news outlets.

Betsy Edgerton is associate professor in the Communication Department of Columbia College Chicago, with a specialization in magazine writing and editing. Her research focuses on mid-twentieth-century "domestic chaos" writing. She's the editor of an upcoming collection of columns by one such writer: *One Woman's World: The Lost Columns of Lenora Mattingly Weber*. She's also the managing editor of Rate.com News & Analysis and copy editor for Ipsos' *What the Future* magazine, and has worked for several of Crain Communications' business-to-business magazines as executive editor and managing editor. She's a member of the board for the American Society of Business Publication Editors National Foundation.

Aileen Gallagher is a former senior editor at *New York* magazine, where she worked on the magazine's award-winning website. With her colleagues, she won multiple National Magazine Awards for NYMAG.com. In 2010, she joined the faculty of Syracuse University's Newhouse School, where she focuses on digital editorial, journalism education, and magazines. Her journalism has appeared in *The Washington Post*, *Slate*, *New York Magazine*, and elsewhere. She presents regularly at the Association for Education in Journalism and Mass Communication and Broadcast Education Association, and has published essays and reviews in the *Journal of Magazine Media*, *Journal of Media Education*, *JMC Educator*, and *Newspaper Research Journal*.

Norma Green is professor emerita of journalism at Columbia College Chicago. She spent twenty-five years in newspaper, magazine, and book publishing before committing to a full-time academic career, and received several grants including a fellowship to the National Endowment for the Humanities institute "City of Print: New York & The Periodical Press." Her historical scholarship has been published in four journals and eleven books, including the award-winning *Print Culture in a Diverse America* and *Women's Periodicals in the United States*.

Krystyna Henke is editor in chief of the *Canadian Journal of Netherlandic Studies*. A photographer and broadcast and print journalist with graduate degrees in journalism, ethnomusicology, and musicology, her work has appeared in museum exhibits and radio and television programs in Canada and the Netherlands. She has consulted on American folk music and early to mid-twentieth-century American popular music for *The Victory Collection: The Smithsonian Remembers When America Went to War* and the documentary audiobook *Nobel Voices for Disarmament: 1901–2001*. Her current research for a doctoral degree at Brock University in Ontario, Canada, focuses on music education in conflict zone refugee camps.

Gary R. Hicks is professor in the Department of Mass Communications at Southern Illinois University Edwardsville. After nearly a decade of work for both newspapers and as a producer for network television news, Hicks entered the academy. For the past twenty-five years his research has focused on media portrayals of marginalized communities, including the representation of LGBTQ-identified people, and media depictions of disability and mental illness. His research has appeared in many academic publications, including the *Journal of Homosexuality* and the *Oxford Encyclopedia of LGBT Politics and Policy*, and has been noted in such mainstream media outlets as *AdWeek* magazine and the National Geographic Channel.

Kevin M. Lerner is associate professor of journalism at Marist College and the editor of the *Journal of Magazine Media*. His book, *Provoking the Press: (MORE) Magazine and the Crisis of Confidence in American Journalism* was published in 2019, and examined the role of an anti-institutional journalism review in shaping the standards of the mainstream press in the 1970s. He is a historian of journalism whose research examines journalism as an intellectual activity. He has been published in *Journalism Practice*, *American Journalism*, *Journalism History*, *Columbia Journalism Review*, *The Nieman Lab*, *The Conversation*, and *The Washington Post*. He began his career as the first web editor for the magazine *Architectural Record*.

Erika J. Pribanic-Smith is associate professor of journalism at the University of Texas at Arlington. A past president of the American Journalism Historians Association and past chair of the Association for Education in Journalism and Mass Communication History Division, her research focuses on political topics in nineteenth- and early twentieth-century magazines and newspapers. She is the coauthor of *Emma Goldman's No-Conscription League and the First Amendment* (2019). She has also authored numerous articles in journals such as *American Periodicals*, *American Journalism*, and *Journalism History*.

Catherine M. Staub is the Fisher-Stelter Chair of Magazine Media and associate professor in the School of Journalism and Mass Communication at Drake University. Her research focuses on farm magazines as well as the relationship between brand media and journalism. Staub has presented her research at multiple Association for Education in Journalism and Mass Communication annual conferences, Mapping the Magazine international conferences, and has been published in the *Journal of Magazine Media* and *Teaching Journalism & Mass Communication*. Staub is a judge for the annual American Society of Magazine Editors ASME Ellie Awards—the industry's most prestigious awards. Staub's industry experience includes time at Meredith Corporation, Wells Fargo Home Mortgage, and most recently as CEO of Lexicon Content Marketing, a communications and marketing agency.

Sheila Webb is professor in the Department of Journalism at Western Washington University. Her research is devoted to the cultural role of magazines and new media in framing narratives of American life and culture, including the portrayal of a middle-class lifestyle in the pages of *Life* magazine, the role of media in the advancement of suffrage and the education of women, and counternarratives of partisans in photographs. Her work has appeared in *Journalism & Communication Monographs, American Journalism, Journalism History, Journalism & Mass Communication Quarterly, Studies in Popular Culture, American Periodicals, The Routledge Handbook of Magazine Research*, and the *Journal of Magazine Media*.

www.ingramcontent.com/pod-product-compliance
Lightning Source LLC
Chambersburg PA
CBHW052059300426
44117CB00013B/2207